"With his 30+ years of working with clients, training CFP® certificants, CPAs, and consumers, writing multiple books, and working profound roles within the financial planning profession, Jeff provides a succinct and easy-to-digest book showcasing the financial planning secrets that he has learned. These secrets will enable you and your firm to better navigate the ever-changing landscape of the financial planning profession. It is especially timely as the profession seeks to have more, and better, communication training. Jeff shares his secrets on how to better converse with clients amid complex technical aspects of financial planning. This book will become a handy resource and guide for your firm's future as we embark on this new decade of financial planning."

—**Derek R. Lawson**, Ph.D., CFP®; Assistant Professor, Personal Financial Planning, Kansas State University; Partner and Financial Planner, Priority Financial Partners

"Whether you are early in your career or a seasoned professional, this book has worthwhile advice for anyone looking to run a more vibrant and successful financial planning practice. Jeff shares wisdom gained from his 30+ years as an author, speaker, teacher, and financial planner in this how-to guide filled with best practices and practical suggestions that can be implemented immediately. As someone who worked with Jeff when he was with CFP Board many years ago on major projects that have helped influence our profession, Jeff's ability to cut to the chase and provide critical information through a wealth of valuable tools bundled into one resource is ideal for those in our profession. The ideas presented will help you grow your practice and provide a higher level of service to your clients. This is a must-read for professionals offering financial planning. If he'd written it 44 years ago, he could have saved me a lot of headaches."

—**Bill Carter**, CFP®, President, Carter Wealth

"This is the guidebook every planner should read at any stage of their career. It is like attending hundreds of conferences and retreats, not the formal sessions but the real-life stories shared between colleagues. On your own, it would take a few lifetimes to gather all the practical wisdom and real-life experiences contained in *Rattiner's Secrets*."

—**Susan Bradley**, CFP®, CeFT®, Founder, Financial Transitionist Institute

"I first met Jeff when he was a student of mine in the NYU CFP® program over 30 years ago. I was so impressed with his knowledge of the material, we had him teaching one of the sections while he was still going through the program. Jeff has gone on to teach so many CFP® Certificants nationwide in our profession. His background as an educator and practitioner makes him one of the most important people in the financial planning profession. His book provides the reader with an understanding of the critical issues inherent in our profession and provides insight and strategies for those who want to be on top of their game. Rattiner's book is a must-read for all people in the profession."

—**Scott M. Kahan**, CFP®, President and Senior Financial Planner, Financial Asset Management Corporation

"No matter your experience as a financial advisor—six months or 30 years—we all need mentors. Jeff Rattiner's *Secrets of Financial Planning* combines all the best of mentoring from the simplest "how-to's" such as putting your kids to work to the more nuanced and fraught conversations you will one day have with a client couple who is divorcing. I plan to keep this 'wisdom' manual next to my keyboard."

—**Cheryl R. Holland**, CFP®, Founder and President, Abacus

"Within the financial planning industry Jeff has the unique perspective of being a practitioner, a teacher, as well as a mentor. I've had the privilege of working with him on all three areas and can attest to the positive impact he's had on our profession as well as on my own development as a financial planner. *Rattiner's Secrets* is a must-read for those of us who continuously look to serve our clients at a higher level."

—**Marc Milic**, CFP®, RICP®, Partner and Relationship Manager, Douglas C. Lane & Associates

"For much of my nearly 40-year career in financial services and financial planning, we have experienced many waves of evolution and reinvention. In recent years, the pace has definitely picked up. Today, the financial planning profession has never been more exciting and challenging at the same time. For those who are joining our profession and beginning the journey, or for those who are deep in it, you will find many worthwhile nuggets of wisdom in Jeff's book that will be of great value to you, helping you either set your course or improve your course."

—**Vincent Rossi**, CFP®, President and Chief Investment Officer, Intelligent Capitalworks

Rattiner's Secrets of
Financial Planning

Rattiner's Secrets of Financial Planning

From Running Your Practice to Optimizing Your Client's Experience

Jeffrey H. Rattiner

WILEY

For general information on our other products and services or for technical support, please contact our Customer Care Department within the United States at (800) 762-2974, outside the United States at (317) 572-3993, or fax (317) 572-4002.

Wiley publishes in a variety of print and electronic formats and by print-on-demand. Some material included with standard print versions of this book may not be included in e-books or in print-on-demand. If this book refers to media such as a CD or DVD that is not included in the version you purchased, you may download this material at http://booksupport.wiley.com. For more information about Wiley products, visit www.wiley.com.

Library of Congress Cataloging-in-Publication Data:

Names: Rattiner, Jeffrey H., 1960– author.
Title: Rattiner's secrets of financial planning : from running your practice
    to optimizing your client's experience / Jeffrey H. Rattiner.
Description: First Edition. | Hoboken : Wiley, 2021. | Includes index. |
    Description based on print version record and CIP data provided by
    publisher; resource not viewed.
Identifiers: LCCN 2020026980 (print) | LCCN 2020026981 (ebook) | ISBN
    9781119594291 (epub) | ISBN 9781119594260 (adobe pdf) | ISBN 9781119594277
    (hardback) | ISBN 9781119594277q(hardback) | ISBN 9781119594260q(adobe
    pdf) | ISBN 9781119594291q(epub)
Subjects: LCSH: Financial planners. | Investment advisors. |
    Investments—Planning. | Finance, Personal–Planning.
Classification: LCC HG179.5 (ebook) | LCC HG179.5 .R387 2021 (print) | DDC
    332.0240068—dc23
LC record available at https://lccn.loc.gov/2020026980 LC record available at
https://lccn.loc.gov/2020026981

Cover Design: Wiley
Cover Image: © PPAMPicture/Getty Images

Printed in the United States of America.

SKY10020909_090220

To my best friend in the entire world,
Diane Elizabeth, for her constant devotion, dedication, support,
and encouragement. Her genuineness, true love, and inspiration
have been my guiding light every step of the way.

Contents

Foreword

Financial planning, like most professions, relies on the dual roles of technical proficiency and an empathy to educate. The wisdom of the profession comes in the juxtaposition of these two elements to produce competence in advice that inspires change and leads to confidence both in our teams and through to our clients.

Jeff has written numerous books that challenge and inspire financial planners toward a holistic understanding of the financial planning process. His experience as a financial planner, certified public accountant, professional speaker, and educator have given Jeff the unique vantage point of seeing not only the evolution of financial planning but also the progression of new financial planners into industry leaders. Few authors in this profession have tackled the breadth of financial planning while keeping their thumb on the pulse of immediate developments and a forward-thinking vision for positive change. As Jeff so aptly writes, "This is one of the most rewarding professions out there." The reward comes in watching the success of a financial plan lived out through financial confidence and accomplishment of our clients. Successfully developing a roadmap to financial success and navigating the obstacles of client behavior and ultimately trust in the process requires an inclusive perspective, vulnerable leadership, and a never-ending intellectual curiosity. Jeff has done a masterful job of collecting, even more than a manual or a textbook, a guided narrative through the journey of both practitioner and practice.

This seminal collection of work brings together the diverse knowledge of the author as a framework to voice the experience of a multitude of industry veterans and academic innovators. From new entrants to the profession to those managing a multitude, this book can serve as a best practice guide to understand the competitive landscape and the holistic process of developing a lasting strategy of success, while effectively "managing our clients' expectations." Take note of the policy outlines, engagement letters, and communication philosophies throughout that will bring understanding and instant leverage to your business.

As a college professor in financial planning, one of the greatest difficulties is conveying both the technical proficiencies and the practical methodologies in a way that is relatable and retainable for each generation entering into our profession. The same is true when training new employees within a firm – the process can create paralysis without a palatable message and a comprehensive policy. *Rattiner's Secrets of Financial Planning* begins with an aerial overview of the profession, practice, and planning process but quickly moves into the practical dispensing of ordered advice within each domain of financial planning. Like the culinary notes of a master chef placed within the margin of a cookbook, Jeff has placed "Rattiner's Secrets" throughout the text to add the spice of wisdom that would take seasons to perfect. If you were to read this book simply to capture these coveted secrets, you would find immense value, but that would be only the tip of the iceberg buried within the pages of this book.

Nathan Harness, Ph.D., CFP®
TD Ameritrade Director of Financial Planning
Texas A&M University

Preface

We work in the greatest profession! Where else can we personally assist other individuals in helping make their lives better? Over the years, I have worked in my Denver and Scottsdale offices with many clients who were concerned, nervous, and even scared when they started out by trying to wrap their arms around their financial situations. These lifestyle possibilities, whether realistic or not, looked very overwhelming and unsettling for many. I can remember vividly clients approaching me and asking for guidance on many different fronts while not knowing where or how they should begin. Probably the most rewarding of those were concerning their game changing objectives that I witnessed and sometimes contributed towards. Many of these clients were starting out at a young age when I met them. I was fortunate in helping them set up a game plan from the time they were married, during the stage of parenthood and starting their careers, and in continuing to expand their lifelong horizons along the way through a multitude of life changing experiences.

As the years went by, while continuing to work on those lasting relationships, I genuinely felt a part of the family, by being included as a close participant all the while enjoying and reflecting with them on their many personal achievements, such as attending their children's college graduations, commemorating family births, recognizing promotions, and celebrating other family milestones.

Having clients personally thanking me for being supportive in the background and assisting them in making their dreams come true is genuinely rewarding.

We serve a unique and high-level purpose which is not available in many professions. Many fields work from a reactive standpoint instead of a proactive one. For example, during my CPA lectures I tell the attendees who wish to offer financial planning services in addition to their existing accounting and tax practices that it's a wonderful complement but that the approach in reaching this marketplace may be different. For example, if we are working on a tax return for the client and we don't know the answer to a specific question, we can look it up in a variety of places, including the Regs, and get the clients a definitive answer. Unfortunately, we can't do that for our clients in our profession in many areas. That's partly because we don't know what the future holds. For example, we don't know what rates of return or conditions will be like going forward to help meet their objectives. We don't know how our clients will age and what their health will be. We don't know what responsibilities they will need to undertake and which will become most important at that time. We don't know when they will officially retire or how long they will live. Essentially, we don't know what curveballs life is going to throw at them along the way. Because if we did, this would be an easy profession! So we need to develop a thoughtful and thorough working approach (by incorporating the financial planning process) in devising an appropriate game plan when working with our clients. This is not easy and unfortunately not always done. Some may try to take a shortcut and develop a cookie-cutter approach when working with their clients, considering it to be more economical and efficient. But listening to our clients – I mean really listening – and understanding how they wish to live their lives, the objectives they wish to achieve, and a means for attaining them, will help provide us with greater focus and more guidance in helping our clients make those game-changing differences and for us in helping contribute towards each. In a nutshell, this approach will result in helping our clients live better lives. In my mind, there is nothing more rewarding from a work standpoint.

My past three books for Wiley have focused on the initial stages of practice, taking the next level of steps in moving your existing practice in the right direction, and the intricacies of working through the personal financial planning issues surrounding divorce. Other books I have written for Bloomberg Press, Harcourt Brace, Commerce Clearing House, Aspen Publishing, American Management Association, and others helped pinpoint specifics from within our profession. All my books provide important messages and help readers digest the information in an easier-to-understand and humorous manner. The same holds true here. Please do not take offense at any humor as it is included purposely to provide a more realistic outlook and lighten the load on a particular topic.

This book does take a different approach, however, by reflecting on experiences I have encountered in my 30-plus years working in all aspects of the profession and in listening to and understanding clients' issues and concerns in my tax and financial planning practices, and in hearing, conversing, and debating issues that have arisen through the teaching and lecturing I provide in my live and webinar venues. This book is a handbook of readily available and valuable knowledge to help create opportunities to take your practice in the appropriate direction for this next decade. Each chapter offers practical and technical information that you can apply and use for dissecting planning concerns, and in initiating client resolve, thereby creating unique planning privileges. Throughout the book I have added "Rattiner's Secrets," my practical thoughts on situations that I have experienced in this profession over the years, written with a direct and sarcastic New York humor. I have been fortunate to be able to take those ideas, strategies, thoughts, learned observations, and commentaries discussed in my Financial Planning Fast Track® classes, lectures, webinars, and other venues over the years and incorporate them into this book. I am confident that we can challenge the norm and take it up several notches and truly make a difference. I hope this book provides you with the knowledge you need to prepare for this upcoming decade, better understand the marketplace, recognize opportunities available to us, incorporate new, untested ideas, challenge the way things may be currently done, grow and market your practice, employ an appropriate infrastructure, approach the technical disciplines to identify issues, recognize exposures, and provide well-thought-out, appropriate recommendations in the areas of cash flow management and budgeting, insurance, investing, income tax, retirement, and estate, and in niche areas such as divorce, closely-held business owners, and education to truly make a difference in your clients' lives.

In all walks of life, the secret to creating a successful working environment centers around managing those expectations surrounding you. Everybody needs to be on the same page at the beginning, throughout, and at the end of the process. In our business, it is all about managing our clients' expectations. You will see that thought process emphasized heavily throughout this book.

A special heartfelt "thank you" to my good friend and confidante, Lisa Riehl Zimmerman, who has helped me manage my professional life and has been there for me always by offering her kindness and support.

We do make a difference and it is very rewarding. It doesn't get any better than this!

It has been an honor and a privilege serving the financial planning profession for the past 36 years.

Acknowledgments

I have been very fortunate over my career. I have met, shared ideas, challenged the status quo, and formed lasting friendships with many of the most competent, passionate, dedicated, and devoted game changers in our profession.

I wish to thank the following individuals, all noted experts on their respective subject matter, who have volunteered their time and shown energy and enthusiasm in providing me with great insight for this book – their thoughts, feelings, and direction about where our wonderful profession is going during the 2020s.

Mitch Anthony
Evan Beach
David Blanchett
Susan Bradley
Lawrence Brody
Caleb Brown
Dan Candura
Bill Carter
Ron Carson
Kurt Czarnowski
Vicki Fillet
Sheryl Garrett
Nathan Harness
Cheryl Holland
Scott Kahan
Michael Kitces
Tim Kochis
Rick Konrad
Annalee Kruger

Derek Lawson
Ross Levin
Cam Marston
Mark Milic
Robert Mauterstock
Carolyn McClanahan
Adam Minsky
Alan Moore
Wade Pfau
Tom Potts
Vince Rossi
Dan Rubin
Larry Swedroe
Jeff Tomerang
Tom Wauschauer

I would like to thank Susan Cerra, Senior Managing Editor at Wiley, and Kevin Harreld, Senior Acquisitions Editor at Wiley, for their continued support.

About the Author

Jeffrey H. Rattiner, CPA, CFP®, MBA, is a well-known professional speaker, educator, and author of ten major financial planning books, including the bestsellers *Personal Financial Planning for Divorce*, *Rattiner's Review for the CFP Certification Examination – Fast Track Study Guide*, *Rattiner's Financial Planner's Bible*, for Wiley, and *Getting Started as a Financial Planner*, for Bloomberg Press (which is now part of Wiley), *Financial Planning Answer Book*, for CCH/Wolter Kluwers, *Adding Personal Financial Planning to Your Practice*, for the American Management Association, *Personal Financial Planning Library*, for Harcourt Brace, and the co-authored *Practicing Financial Planning* textbook. He has been an editor for *Personal Financial Planning* and *Financial Advisory Practice* for Warren Gorham and LaMont, *Financial Planning Digest* for Harcourt Brace, *Audio Financial Planning Report* for Totaltape (Bisk) Publishing Company, *Financial Planning Monthly Journal* for Aspen Publications, *The Planner* for the AICPA, and was a columnist for *Financial Planning* and *Financial Advisor* magazines.

Rattiner is a leading innovator on financial planning educational programs, and his nationally acclaimed program, *Rattiner's Financial Planning Fast Track*®, continues to raise the industry bar by training financial services professionals to obtain their Certified Financial Planner® (CFP®) certification in an accelerated format nationwide. Rattiner won critical acclaim as the cover story in the December 2001 issue of *Financial Planning magazine*. His lively and entertaining teaching style has served professionals well for more than 31 years. He has provided extensive employee training programs to many large financial services and consumer firms. He offers live and webinar training for CPAs, CFP® certificants, and other financial services professionals.

Rattiner has worked for the CFP Board, the Institute of CFP®, the Financial Planning Association (FPA), the AICPA PFP Division, was named one of the 2003 CPA All-Stars in Personal Financial Planning by *CPA magazine*, has been quoted in many trade and consumer publications, and has been a columnist for many of the industry trade journals.

CHAPTER 1

Today's Financial Planning Profession

OVERVIEW

Today's financial planning profession is very different from the profession of the past. To put it into perspective from a TV commercial, "This is not your father's Oldsmobile!" The main reason for this is the world is changing rapidly. Probably too rapidly for most. Just look at the past year and notice the added stress, concern, and uncertainty many of our clients, friends, and family members have had with their financial portfolios, as well as other critical aspects that need to be addressed and thought out well, and ultimately put into motion so our clients have a legitimate chance of making their financial lives better going forward. In fact, probably one of the best things that is happening in these uncertain times is that many people who have not put in the time to manage their financial affairs are finally realizing the significance of being well prepared going forward.

So, the question becomes, how can you effectively plan to maintain your edge in this unique profession while managing your clients' expectations from the get-go? It's not a straight shot for your clients. Planners have to be forthright in their discussions with clients, which is no easy task. We will cover all aspects of making these objectives happen.

You will need to make changes to your practices to cover the new norm. The 2020s will certainly take our practices to the next level. The uncertainty that will exist going forward as well as the technological advances will tend to affect how we go about planning. Guidance will be provided for those planners looking to advance their practices to the next level, and for those individuals looking to becoming involved for the first time, through the development of a practical work program for entering a rich and rewarding profession in a no-nonsense manner.

This profession is all about "give-backs" and truly making a difference. If your practice is properly positioned to take advantage of helping others in a wonderful and rewarding manner, and you have the mantra necessary to better enlighten your clients' financial lives, then this book is for you.

As with any business, it is essential to build your infrastructure properly. Defining who you are, what business you are in, working in a large or niche firm, becoming a generalist or a specialist are all important pieces of the infrastructure. Establishing a solid approach to gaining the overall critical knowledge and how to relate that information to clients in a win-win manner are the keys. At any age or at any stage in your practice, arming yourself with the proper background and training is essential. The designation of choice for most advisors is attaining the CERTIFIED FINANCIAL PLANNER™ (CFP®) certification. Whether or not you are currently employed in this field, you need to carefully think through what's essential for you to pursue going forward.

For those of you already in the field, it is important to look at your existing practice to decide which way to take it during this decade. For those advisors who want to specialize in their field(s) of choice, or for those individuals looking to enter the profession, it is important to be specific as to what you are looking to accomplish. With the changes surrounding our profession, this re-evaluation is key to helping our clients become better financially prepared and in continuing to expand our practices going forward.

For those of you looking to enter the profession or those who have recently done so, working at some of the larger firms in various functions – such as in generalist, specialist, back office assistant, or sales capacities, in niche practices, with advisory or ancillary responsibilities, or other realms of the profession – is a good starting point to gain an understanding of what is necessary. I am an advocate of learning on someone else's nickel. Acquiring a strong foundation and proper infrastructure to set up your practice is necessary to shorten the learning curve and to be productive from the get-go. Internships and mentorships are excellent ways of learning some valuable habits and insights from true professionals, especially when starting out. It's now time to take your valuable experience to an even higher level.

FINANCIAL PLANNER VS. FINANCIAL ADVISOR

Let's start by making a key distinction between individuals working as a financial planner and as a financial advisor. Many times, these terms are used interchangeably. While there may be similarities between these jobs, there are some key differences. A financial planner is a professional who helps companies and individuals create a program to meet long-term financial goals and objectives, whereas *financial advisor* is generally a broader term for those individuals who help manage client money, including investments and other financial accounts.

A financial planner generally looks at the entire client picture as it relates to the various stages in life to help in the development and monitoring of a personalized financial plan. The plan incorporates many important general aspects for the client's well-being, including understanding client issues, dissecting the critical exposures, and recommending solutions and guidelines when dealing with many core subject areas, such as risk management and insurance planning, investment planning, income tax planning, education planning, retirement and employee benefits planning, estate planning, and many niche topics specific to certain client issues. While many financial planners do manage money for clients, as well as sell appropriate products and services for clients, they tend to integrate the above issues from both a monetary and behavioral platform to incorporate the necessities in each.

There are many services to which financial planners can subscribe to help them acquire the appropriate information for servicing their clients. They are all categorized by specialty. Many of the leading industrywide publications do annual comparisons to see what the differences are in the marketplace. But more on this later.

I have taught the education courses for eligibility to take the CFP® Certification Examination nationally for over 30 years, mainly through my Financial Planning Fast Track®, Inc. program. Constant feedback I receive is that the students are taught to gather information from the client and either transfer that data to another area of the company or enter it themselves into a software program, essentially acting as data gatherers. The thrust of this action is being pinpointed mainly for investment results and decisions when in fact the entire gamut of planning issues needs to come under focus first. Investment results are important, but they represent part of the overall picture and landscape.

This book will take you through the proper way to approach this profession. In addition to guidance from the author, many industry movers and shakers were interviewed for this book and their interpretations of what is needed to prepare and be successful during this next decade are incorporated throughout. Supplemental materials have also been included.

WHAT ARE THE "EXPECTATIONS FOR CHANGE" IN OUR PROFESSION?

Change is inevitable. Throughout life, things change. Progress represents change. We need to embrace it and learn from the past. Know where you are coming from and where you are going. The model for how we dispense advice has been rapidly changing.

"In today's world, you need to show clients value beyond a doubt. With complexity of needs, people want a singular experience that is powerful," says Ron Carson, Founder and CEO, Co-Chief Investment Strategist, Carson Wealth, Omaha, NE.

"Planners who will succeed in our profession have the genuine desire to give back to it. Part of the reason is that we need to expand the cadre of high-quality financial planners. Demand is enormous while supply is constrained. We need to greatly expand the size of supply," says Tim Kochis, Chief Executive Officer of Kochis Global, San Francisco. We are sitting on a goldmine, both in terms of what we can help our clients accomplish and in the overall good we can bring to society.

Rattiner's Baker's Dozen: "Expectations for Change" in Our Profession

1. Financial Planning as a "Profession"
2. Landscape
3. Developing Human Capital: Training and Recruiting Techniques for Entering the Profession
4. Specific Ideas for Growing Your Skill Set in Our Profession
5. Compensation
6. Technology
7. Growth and Entry into Our Profession: Buy vs. build
8. Change in Regulation
9. Holistic Financial Planning

FINANCIAL PLANNING AS A "PROFESSION"

In our landscape, financial markets struggle with how we pay for the advice we are getting and are looking to continue revamping, as stated earlier. Based on that scenario, we can make the argument that perhaps we are not a profession, says Nathan Harness, Ph.D., CFP® TD Ameritrade Director of Financial Planning, Texas A&M University, College Station, TX. There should be a sense of unity in our profession that forms the future, perhaps, rather than a loose band of individuals. As a profession, we need to consider revenue generation around our consultative service, not just the products our advice entails. This more closely aligns with other professions, such as medical, legal, and accounting. Based on where things stand today, being subject to additional regulation down the road may occur on a state level.

"Firms will continue to shift from brokerage firms to RIAs [registered investment advisors] and even mega RIAs, with extreme aggregation and core revenue from products and services being the driving forces," says Michael E. Kitces, MSFS, MTAX, CFP®, CLU, ChFC, RHU, REBC, CASL, Publisher, Nerd's Eye View blog. Kitces asserts that the legitimate distinctive purpose of broker/dealers who were in the business of capital formation was synonymous with broker/dealers who were in the business of providing investment advice. He says, "Years ago for the typical advisor, the adage was that I represented a company with better products than your company."

"History has shown us that many clients were burned from stockbrokers in the 1980s. It was cool to be a broker at that time," says Carson. He goes on to say that too many scandals plagued the industry, and many of us know someone who was ultimately burned by a financial person back then. The profession has shifted a lot since.

Tom L. Potts, Professor of Finance, Department of Finance, Insurance and Real Estate, Hankamer School of Business, Baylor University, Waco, TX, sums it up as we all have over the years. "When we all start out, you eat what you kill!" Historically, if we broke down the past into two stages, stage 1 translated to our value for the client as our product that we provided, while stage 2 transformed historically into the value/knowledge approach for our clients.

Derek R. Lawson, Ph.D., CFP®, is Assistant Professor, Personal Financial Planning at Kansas State University, and Partner and Financial Planner at Priority Financial Partners, Manhattan, KS. He has seen his students wanting to climb the corporate ladder. Many found out after joining a firm that it was too small, with little room to grow. Lawson says, "The industry has traditionally been set up for maximum efficiency and used a 'plug and play' model for firmwide advisors."

We need to know where we came from in order to know which direction to take going forward. In order to understand today's financial planning profession, let's take a quick look at how the industry originated, up to where we are today. Tom Wauschauer, long-time chair of the Finance Department for San Diego State University, divided the past into three categories: Maverick era, Marketing era, and Professional era.

Planners were discontent during the initial Maverick era. Securities and insurance firms, which originated mainly for the sale of limited investment and insurance products and advice, participated in these arenas by acting as company agents.

The Marketing era showcased big financial firms, which were based on prospect lists provided to the companies for the purpose of selling products and services to advisors' friends and family, with the promise of teaching financial planning to the advisor along the way. Meetings would be held annually or sometimes more frequently to help the client stay on track. Other undue influencers, such as family, friends, and surroundings, quite often kept the planner off track.

"The financial planning profession needs to continue to evolve into a true profession, like other high-profile professions have done historically over time, moving from a product orientation and customer mentality into a disciplined wealth management approach with a client mentality," says Potts. The different disciplines need to be coordinated and worked on together.

"Our business will stay a relationship business, it's not going to change," says Bill Carter, CFP®, ChFC, CLU, Chief Executive Officer, Carter Financial Management, Dallas, TX.

"Many firms in the financial planning profession follow the accounting profession model using a planning-centric firm model with a differential in price," says Harness. Advisors can enter these firms and progress along the traditional channel just as in the accounting firms. The setup includes partners, managers, senior staff, junior staff, and support staff. Many advisors have begun copying this model to parallel the accounting profession model. As the industry embraces greater planning sophistication and technical proficiency, it would be worthwhile to copy the accounting model of five years of college and 150 hours to graduate, says Harness.

The future of the profession will center around teaching appropriate skill sets designed to enable students to become engaged in thinking critically and analytically, and in applying those skill sets for all types of clients. Having a mentor work with you is the quickest and most efficient way of learning what you need to become a successful financial planner. The ideal move for someone entering the profession may be to take a position to get your foot in the door to learn those skills. Essentially, learning and demonstrating the appropriate skill sets now could ultimately lead to working through succession issues later on (more about that later). It's a great sure-fire path for getting into and benefiting from a strong system.

Another example is to have NexGen planners work with their peers and with all generations. "Don't limit yourselves in working only with NexGen clients. This type of cookie-cutter training does not enable the NexGen planner to feel comfortable working with clients perhaps twice the planner's age. There are many others who desperately need your help," says Potts.

LANDSCAPE

The Professional era, where the profession is today, is built around the fiduciary standard, which encompassed doing the type of work exclusively and primarily that is in the client's best interests. Where it could go may depend on legislation that could be brought on board by the federal government or the states. There seems to be a potential conflict of interest between what the financial services industry wants and what the government wants.

"Going forward, we will see a change and influx from the old guard to the new guard and that will create tension," says Alan Moore, CEO and Co-Founder, www.xyplanningnetwork.com. Moore states that we will see a shift to younger and more diverse business models designed to work with younger clients. A monthly subscription model will gain prominence. Younger planners will prefer to work with their peers vs. an older clientele. Moore had a great quote: "Thirty years ago in our business a phenomenal salesperson could sell water to a drowning person. The goal is to help people by building relationships vs. transactional sales."

Grow big and systematize! Big firms will continue to do that and set the standards for the industry, says Moore. Big firms are desperate to develop young talent. We need acceptable models for ways of practice that will help us develop proper career paths for the industry. An algorithm cannot replace what we do. However, we need to use technology appropriate for scale. This area will continue to grow.

Many of the situations today are causing a change in cash flow alignment. "What you'll see when we start shifting away from being retirement centric is becoming focused and aligning with cash flow and spending advice that is aligned to personal life goals. It will emphasize the will to live until we can't," says Kitces. It will be much more powerful and impactful. We won't be able to help the client who doesn't know where their money is going. We won't need product knowledge but rather advice knowledge. Our competencies have been built around products we used to sell.

"Jobs will continue to be had through the big firms because that's where the jobs are. But there is no annihilation of mom-and-pop shops because the bar to entry is low, which could make it hard to find someone to trust," says Sheryl Garrett, of Garrett Planning Network, Inc., Eureka Springs, AR. The shift into holistic planning (discussed below) will enable you to be surrounded by a team of financial advisors which supports the jobs and infrastructure needed to train well. This shift away from the sales mentality and toward advice jobs has been long overdue.

"Probably the biggest shift we will see is the changing focus for planners going forward to financial planning from investment management," says Carolyn McClanahan, M.D., CFP® of Life Planning Partners, Inc., Jacksonville, FL.

If advisors do not align with a broker/dealer, they will still need a support structure. There are companies that provide advisors with a shared infrastructure, essentially replicating broker/dealers without products from an advice standpoint. This trend could drive a shift from brokers to RIAs.

A valuable advisor helps people fight the system, says McClanahan. Big organizations, custodians, and insurance companies are designed primarily to make money while not necessarily helping the client. The financial planner needs to act as the go-between. It's important to talk directly with the client to understand their problems as opposed to helping clients do things online and perhaps not fully understanding the client's problem. The issue could be hampered for some since our industry is built on how we get paid for the services we provide.

"The future of our industry will look like this, a collection of fewer large national and international firms, and most will operate as smaller firms which are independent entrepreneurs, where they can do things their own way," says Kochis. Custodians will continue to support small operations. Middle-size firms will grow in both directions where they merge and take equity in the merged firm. Firms will be reorganizing, where competition will be a driver for developing strong client relationships.

Harness adds, "This will help differentiate large wirehouses and mega-RIAs, which still control the majority of assets, from looking similar to each other going forward, based on the services provided and their revenue sources."

Evan T. Beach, CFP®, AWMA®, of Campbell Wealth Management, Alexandria, VA, believes a massive consolidation has already started in our industry and will continue. As Harness stated earlier, he views the industry as looking and growing more like the CPA (certified public accountant) industry.

While many advisors are moving into the fee space, Beach has the majority of his revenue coming from this segment, but he does a small broker/dealer line where he provides insurance products and services as more of a convenience for clients.

"Internal succession will develop and sell to the next generation of people within the firm," says Kochis. He goes on to say that the regulatory side will embrace quality and consumer reliability, which could drive out some people. Where there's a problem, usually a solution arises. Firms will also hire out a service to comply with these requirements. As firms get larger, we can provide a quality level of service because there will be more talent in the firm and this will protect the firm from the risk of having clients leave the firm with the advisor.

"We still need to meet with our clients in person or virtually to ensure the human connectivity," says Garrett. She believes the tools and technologies we uncover will help us connect at a deeper level. "We need to see the client's body language and their ability to interact with family and other advisors. A special significance needs to be present, especially in the short term, with our clients. They will fare well over the long term if they provide input and adhere to a plan we have developed together with the client."

Garrett warns about the possibility of the marketplace becoming more commoditized or transactional whereby advisors are instructing clients what to buy without perhaps getting into the entire client experience. "As advisors, our mission is help clients become more integrated in their approach, then we can provide many possible solutions for clients," says Garrett. She sees the profession becoming more virtual because of the health-care crises and other issues that have arisen as well as keeping costs down.

Clients are feeling more comfortable buying "paychecks" going forward, through annuities and similar products, because of the issues going on in the marketplace today as well as remembering what happened in 2008.

DEVELOPING HUMAN CAPITAL: TRAINING AND RECRUITING TECHNIQUES FOR ENTERING THE PROFESSION

Education training is continuously getting better, says Kochis. In speaking with university professors, many see their students taking their first positions at some of the larger companies in order to get exposure to the overall background of financial planning, as well as at smaller niche firms where advisors who have an idea of how they would like to practice are being drawn to a particular firm's specialty.

For those students and others entering the profession, historically employees paid for all of their own licenses and lived off commissions earned, essentially showcasing that the company did not have anything invested in that individual. The hiring process focused on what kinds of clients and how many you could bring into the firm. In these traditional situations, the company was not going to support that individual. It was commonplace to see companies in the industry get together with academics from the universities and ask them what their students were being taught so they could be productive as soon as they joined a particular firm.

Instead, in today's world, what you want is the company stating: we believe in you and we are here to invest in and support you. We will help you prepare and will pay for your securities and insurance licenses, for your CFP® certification, and for you to become a better overall planner. What is happening with the better firms is that the name on the letterhead will be the driving force for bringing in new clients to the firm. The advisors will grow through the traditional channels and ultimately grow into those individuals whose name could appear on future letterheads.

Potts encourages his students to develop their most important asset when starting out: human capital. This turns to financial capital as the student gets older. Potts tells his students to invest in themselves. Take a job to make sure you'll be better off and learn on the job. Be a sponge and soak it all in. Deciphering the many possibilities and selecting whom you will be working for, who will be investing in you and making you better, will help answer the fundamental question when starting out: "Will I be able to add to my human capital?"

"Regarding planners entering our profession, we look for planners that come through a CFP® educational program," says Caleb Brown, MBA, CFP®, CEO and Co-Founder, New Planner Recruiting. "Their success is your success." Brown states that there are many good ones out there. Once the firm begins hiring planners, a good way to develop them is to create a "farm system" in-house. "Know the talent inventory before doing a custom search and have each planner play more than one position," says Brown.

In the foreseeable future, Brown sees mega-RIAs continuing to develop based on economies of scale. Newly minted CFP® certificants will go into retail positions since there are no traditional wirehouses. "I see younger planners going to the monthly retainer fee model, essentially a subscription model. Clients want more services for a lot less. Demonstrate a value proposition. The value of that approach will be demonstrated when meeting with clients."

Wauschauer sees half of his undergraduates going to work as interns at larger companies, unsure of their clear career path, and more graduate students obtaining the top standards in the industry, working at professional firms and not firm centric, whereby they are taking positions at some of the top companies across the nation. Many advisors have told me that they employ internship-type programs to try out candidates. When Carson hires advisors, he has them attend Carson University, where they go through rotational internships.

Harness emphasizes placing greater emphasis on including practice management in core education. "Whenever you are teaching someone, re-share the story. From the old last random phone call of the day, your desire is to want to be known. When people make that leap, many of those firms have surged in financial growth." Hiring the right people through a mentoring program makes a lot of sense. Invest in people who can come behind you to represent core values in your firm. The difference is moving forward to produce the talent to meet the needs of internal growth.

Many of my students work at the larger firms and most of them work at niche planning firms. They understand the importance of learning the process through which they can manage a client's overall wealth and financial success. Many of them have the goal of rising to the top of their respective companies, pay scales, influence, and centers of responsibility. A fair number of mid-career change students are also in these classes, who have retired from their first careers and have developed an interest in helping individuals through the planning process. They recognize the maturity they possess in helping people from all stages of life. Still others have received large inheritances and are looking for an appropriate skill set to help them manage their newfound wealth on their own.

Taking this in another direction, there should be a condensed CFP®-type educational program for professionals in other fields to give them a skill set to understand the financial exposures and potential solutions in addressing these concerns as well as to land a way to work with financial planners. In my tax practice, many of my doctor and lawyer clients tell me repeatedly that with all the education they have had in their respective fields, there was never any type of financial course to help them when they started earning a great livelihood. Many times they made misinformed decisions and then found out it was too late to make corrective changes. I have seen such professionals lose it all in the midst of their careers.

"It's very important for the university faculty to work with the profession and help set professional mentor standards. This give-back by professionals can lead to job offers for graduates because now they are being sought after," says Lawson.

Lawson uses a "peer mentoring" approach in his firm whereby seniors and juniors mentor the freshmen and sophomores. Often the mentors attend the instructor's class and seek out students for the mentoring and/or internship process. Many of Lawson's graduates prefer to learn their trade through smaller firms during internships because of the ability to learn better in those types of environments, but ultimately they end up in the larger firms. Lawson says two-thirds of his students are entrepreneurial and one-third are not. They simply do not want to buy in and do not want to take on the risk factor.

Carson uses a "Depth for Financial Planners Checklist" for a practice to be successful in the future. The goal for getting your practice set up the right way is to establish a consistent experience now in developing an ensemble practice.

1. Associate yourself with a large RIA.
2. Become a CFP® certificant.
3. Rotate around and learn every part of this business.
4. Specialize once you have explored everything.
5. Employ human capital.

SPECIFIC IDEAS FOR GROWING YOUR SKILL SET IN OUR PROFESSION

My thoughts on this parallel those of students first entering my financial planning program. Those students initially do not truly understand what they have gotten themselves into and what it is all about. Only by attending our many classes and learning the many aspects of financial planning do they officially get it. I use this analogy for advisors who join the profession, begin working with their first company, and then find out the way things really are.

Many of the larger firms have niches in most financial categories for helping clients. These firms serve the benefit of disclosing to employees the many ways they can direct their careers. Many of those individuals decide to specialize in an area once they become familiar with the potential client issues, exposures, and recommendations in that chosen field. Sometimes they are attracted into an area where they believe they can truly make a difference. I often advise these new career entrants to trail their mentors and other people at the firm so they can learn the process for their specialty of interest. Once they experience that, they can essentially write their own game plan to approach their niche in a particular manner. This bona fide approach in helping clients transition to managing their wealth at a higher level is truly a rewarding experience.

Moore says, "There are riches in the niches." Niche practices remove some of the competitiveness in our industry. "One and done financial won't cut it. You need to differentiate in value," says Moore.

Some firms are set up by dividing the functionality of their practices into separate divisions, such as the interpersonal and analytical divisions. The interpersonal advisors are the ones who meet with the client, get to know them, solicit information necessary for the development of the plan, understand where the client wants to go and what they would like to ultimately accomplish, and then hand it over to the analytical staff for development. The analytical people are the ones behind the scenes, the tacticians who receive the data, work on incorporating it into the software, and develop the financial plan. They generally stay out of the client's sight for plan delivery but are there to adjust the plan when necessary.

Another practical way of setting up shop that I have seen from advisors and my students is the specialty approach. For example, there may be six advisors in the shop. Each advisor has their own specialty. The generalist, or lead planner, is the one who meets initially with the client, gathers the quantitative and qualitative data, and helps set and prioritize objectives, talks through issues with the client, is the face for general follow-up with the firm, and keeps the clients at ease. Once the information is gathered and the client has been assessed, the client is turned over to specialists at the firm who guide them in a particular area. For example, the client meets with the insurance advisor, then the investment advisor, then the CPA for income tax planning, the retirement specialist, the attorney to work with estate planning, perhaps a business advisor for their business, and other potential specialists if applicable. The "specialists" work in their specialty only, so the knowledge base of the firm that is immersed with the client is pretty special and rewarding since this is all the specialists do at the firm. The practice owns the clients outright, so if an advisor leaves, that individual does not have any ownership interest in the client and that client generally stays with the firm.

Where potential problems exist is when a new planner learns a particular technique and is taught to work only in that type of setting. That could make it troublesome to learn a second technique, which perhaps could end up preventing the planner from being trainable in adjusting to new situations.

What needs to happen in the industry is for role players to be developed, in essence by backing up existing staff, so they can be included in the human resource pipeline of the firm so that when a vacancy occurs, or perhaps when one advisor progresses into a different area of the firm, or even leaves because of the skill set developed at the firm, another one can immediately follow directly behind and replace that individual. As Brown mentioned earlier, it's the "farm system" adage of baseball.

What firms should do is pair up advisors to make them more knowledgeable in a variety of client situations. For example, Potts says, "Take a 55-year-old planner and pair that person with a 25-year-old, new-entry planner, and have that individual work with the children of your 55-year-old client." It's pretty common knowledge that many times the children of clients will leave their parents' planner down the road and work with someone they feel they have more connectivity with, thus creating a huge potential gap which could further erode the firm's business.

Get away from the big binders and project into multiple decades. In the old days we'd call it "planning by the pound." The client cares about me having their backside. They want to be reassured that I am part of their team. Checking the client's financial health at a minimum of once per year is essential.

Beach points out a new practical reality for this decade and in moving forward. With the effects of COVID-19, and people staying at home and learning to conduct business and essentially live life in a new reality, your competition is now the entire country or perhaps beyond, and not just your local geographical area. With this increased landscape and marketing base, firms can move away from core and expensive business areas, thereby paying less in office space since many clients will continue to work with their advisors virtually as the new norm. For example, Beach, who is based in Alexandria, VA, a high-cost area, can now find labor at lower cost throughout the country. Beach makes more cost-effective decisions, employing virtual techniques and hiring planners, para-planners, and other office specialists. In his virtual capacity, Beach can increase traffic and expand his practice by providing three webinars per week to a base in every conceivable point of the United States.

He says there are two client scenarios: you can outlive your money, or your money can outlive you. The client essentially checks the box to say whether they are better off with the firm or without the firm.

A good analogy Beach gives for growing his practice and attracting clients is that he sits in the passenger seat of the client's automobile while the client is driving and using his experience helps the client navigate through a lifelong relationship. The basic question is whether the client will follow the map Beach builds for them. The client is the final decision maker in whether they wish to pursue the course. If the client wants Beach out, they can make a U-turn, push him out of the car, and regroup.

COMPENSATION

Commission-based financial advisors are seeing a decline in their traditional business model. That is because of the shift away from a one-time sale of product to a wealth management model focusing on fee-based financial advice. Many are moving in the direction of a monthly subscription-based model, similar to the model doctors have developed. For an annual or monthly fee, you have unlimited access to that professional.

Advisors still receive compensation based on a model of what is being brought into the firm and then managed on an ongoing basis in order to be retained. The model also reflects what firms are getting in return from their employees rather than rewarding them for longevity. The idea is to motivate employees and pay them to strive for financial rewards.

"The broadest change we are in the midst of facing in our profession is from products to advice. Essentially the evolution of commissions to fees and subscription models, which is a value proposition of the financial advisor," says Kitces.

History has shown that years ago planners represented a particular company that had better products than those of its competitors. Kitces states that there is a fundamental shift in domain selling over knowledge and expertise. "Pay me for the knowledge between my two ears!"

"The profession needs to target away from the assets under management (AUM) model. The fixed-rate model seems to be where many advisors are headed. Clients appreciate it," says Scott Kahan, CFP®, President and Senior Financial Planner, Financial Asset Management Corporation of Chappaqua, NY and New York City. Kitces adds that fees are not going down for advisors. Our regulators are reacting since this is not where profits are being driven from. Product expenses have moved because most advisors are no longer paid through selling products. Fees are collapsing only if you look at product true cost. To defend our fees, we look at the cheaper stuff. These costs will not be moving in the foreseeable future.

Carter sees retainer fees as real hot but starting to phase out, inevitably stating that fees will continue to come down.

Beach adds a good point. "For years we have depended on the technical person to be the salesperson, like Bill Gates is viewed as the lead salesperson for Microsoft. It is essential for the roles of business development (technical sales) and technician to be kept separate."

TECHNOLOGY

Not all technology is created equal. Software is getting better all the time, but there are programs and platforms out there that do not tie the needs of the client together well. The reliance on software and other technology programs is at an all-time high, which could prove dangerous if the planner does not have a strong understanding of the behind-the-scenes aspects of what makes the software's output what it is. A strong initial sampling of software programs can help buy into appropriate client packages. I encourage advisors, students, and others to review the different products in the marketplace for the key items like initial price, ongoing annual price or fees, system requirements, functionality, support system by telephone or online, and whether there is a charge for that service, ease of use, and many other things that are necessary for the program to be used properly in the office.

I encourage office advisors and other staff to try out comprehensive and modular programs for themselves, such as doing their own financial plan, budgeting and cash flow management, asset allocation, income tax planning, retirement and education needs analysis, and legacy, to name a few. Become familiar with each program's capabilities and ease of use. This is a better indicator of how the program will operate when working on these software programs in the office with clients, or even if the clients work on them themselves. The staff will soon find out how realistic it is to their actual scenario. If each of the programs works well, then the staff will see which ones are most likely to line up and assist with their clients' situation. In addition, from a staff morale standpoint, they are each receiving the benefit of working with a financial planning firm, in this case their own, because, as stated earlier, everyone is affected by financial planning at their own level.

Artificial intelligence (AI) is getting better and it is not going away. "Depending on the type of practice created, it will either represent a complete resource for parts of the market or for others it will be a starter part of the market. The planner–client relationship will dictate how AI is used as their proprietary tool that produces more reliable results," says Kochis. Carson concurs as he does not see AI replacing the human element.

"Technology, including artificial intelligence, replaces what took long periods of time to do and automates those functions in an easy-to-digest format, whereby the planner of the future can focus on an upper-level skill set," says McClanahan. What took vast computing power to send someone to the moon years ago is in my pocket. That phone helps us do the job better. It will take out the bottom rung because of tech automation. If you don't use technology to improve, it will take you out. It doesn't eliminate all advisors. Saying technology will replace what we do as planners is just not accurate. It will be from a different perspective and we can build on where the technology leaves off. Kitces' best quote was "abundances create new scarcities." Google succeeded since it was one of the first to find that out.

For some clients, there can be a backlash against too much technology. Performing mundane and routine tasks, as with Social Security tools, could be a good use of technology, but using AI is only as good as the inputs, and you don't want too much bias to show from the people building it.

The flipside of firmwide protection is definitely true these days. "Cybersecurity issues have become a big concern at our firm," says Carter. He adds, "We had something get pfished to 1,000 people. We have seen other breaches of contracts. We have our information technology (IT) guy solely deal with these issues."

Don't substitute software for knowledge. Software is a technical tool, it's not a problem solver. For me, technology is only as good as the manual understanding of what is transpiring. For example, in my classes I use an excessive number of whiteboards to showcase flowcharts, equations, pictures, macro/micro infrastructure, and other diagrams that truly signify the meaning of important elements for clients, and which can be more easily identified and explained to them rather than relying overly on technology. Using this information, the advisor should be able to explain to their clients in a meaningful and clear-cut way which they can truly follow. They should be able to explain the "what" and why things are happening in a particular manner, and not rely on the default in a program, thereby understanding the correct situation, which they can then relate and explain to their clients, and again, above all, manage their clients' expectations going forward; then the client will be best served.

GROWTH AND ENTRY INTO OUR PROFESSION: BUY VS. BUILD

Since many players in the industry are having a tough time finding a lead advisor to manage the process, firms have been opting to grow in our industry through the purchase of practices. This makes sense. The old adage "it is cheaper to buy than to build" does resonate with advisors. The advantage of buying a practice is that the system is already in motion and the infrastructure set. The process has been started, the employees hired, the technology, marketing, relationships, and other avenues are already in place. The planner takes that infrastructure, adds the personal "seal" or "brand" to it, and then expands upon it.

Building it can construct your model and originate the infrastructure in the exact way you are targeting, but getting through the learning curve and other detours may take longer initially. Advisors are going to continue to buy vs. build practices because it is cheaper to do so, says Harness. Building it would be more successful in the long run. He used a great analogy: "When you inject steroids into a racehorse, the horse will perform more quickly but ultimately break down." There are many services that specialize in acting as a broker in the purchase of a financial practice.

I have seen too many deals fail because the clients ultimately end up leaving the firm. For example, when addressing these issues during my classes and lectures, of the attendees who freely talk about their transition when purchasing their practices, many state that they overpaid for the practice. First, it is because the clients leave immediately or soon thereafter as there is no smooth transition. At any level, it's all about building and maintaining relationships. Generally, in these situations there is no real connection for clients to stay with the new planning firm. Many leave and go with another firm through a referral, proximity to their home or business, after rethinking what they are trying to accomplish, or simply for some other reason. Clients have to get to know you and where you are headed before they will continue to commit to a new practitioner.

One solid way to address that is to hire the seller and keep that planner on for a set period of time. I always caution with the minimum length of the installment sale. For example, if the buyer is to make payments over a five-year period, to ensure the likelihood that the existing database of clients will stay throughout the entire purchase period, have the seller become a new employee of your firm during that time. This enables the seller to introduce you to the clients as they visit the office. Many sellers even seek out that strategy because they need health insurance. Once the practice is sold, if the seller is under the age of 65 and cannot qualify for Medicare, they do not want to face a gap in coverage. Many like that approach because they may be able to negotiate with the purchaser to keep that particular health insurance. Some sellers may decide to try their hand at something else, but the overwhelming majority that I see are looking to perhaps do something different. As a result, many have a tough time accessing health insurance during that second career.

Second, I encourage advisors in this situation to pay for the seller's business based on client retention. For example, structure the deal over so many years – let's say three as an example – and adjust the price based on the number of clients who stay with the firm by the end of the third year when the payment stream is over. For example, two students of mine from Kentucky purchased a practice a number of years ago and overpaid for their business because they assumed 100% of the clients would continue as before with the firm. The firm had a good reputation, clients were satisfied, and the staff was top notch. But what they didn't realize was that they were in an older part of town, and clients did not know who they were or what they were capable of bringing to the table and so went elsewhere. The interpersonal skills had a huge disconnect after the sale. The client would say, "nothing personal," but it was not an ideal fit for many going forward. It took my students eight years to make up that overpayment.

Third, when purchasing a practice, you should include an attrition rate because not everyone will continue with the firm. Adjust it so that in three years, five years, or whenever the contract is for, based on client retention, the buyer is paying only for those clients who do actually make the smooth transition to the buyer's firm.

Carter adds that merger acquisitions will continue to grow to produce superior economies of scale.

CHANGE IN REGULATION

The regulatory environment is tough and getting tougher. Regulation Best Interest (BI) is a 2019 Securities and Exchange Commission (SEC) rule that requires broker/dealers to recommend to their customers only financial products that are in the best interests of those customers, and to clearly identify any potential conflicts of interest and financial incentives the broker/dealer may have with those products. It is closely related to the Department of Labor's proposed fiduciary rule. Its effective date is June 30, 2020. The CFP® Board revised its Code of Ethics to become enforceable on June 30, 2020.

"The public demand for fiduciaries is not going away and represents a global issue," says Dan Candura, CFP BOARD EMERITUS™ and head of Candura Group, LLC. Acting in the best interest of the client makes good business sense and is good ethics, and it is what the world wants now. You want to be proud of what you do. Candura gave a restaurant analogy: you can set up a quality restaurant to make money and establish loyalty, or a fast-food restaurant and make money on volume. He says we need to work with everyone. As people move toward retirement, they are more likely to ask for help.

Regulators are making moves toward adopting a fiduciary model. It is important for CFP® certificants to always do the right thing. You want to be proud of what you do for your clients, company, peers, and everyone else. The bottom line is that with or without any certification or licensing, you always want to do what is in the best interests of your clients. I tell my students that "Best Interest" is the automatic default.

An example of a potential game changer, says Beach, is if legislation is approved requiring the term "financial planning salesperson" or similar to be placed on a business card underneath the planner's name. Beach says this will cause more people in the industry to move away from this type of practice.

Game changes will result in a shift toward the fiduciary model and toward a revenue model that promotes payment for advice, says Harness. Consumers expect planners to be fiduciaries. Clients are looking for something more stable than a one-person shop. A fiduciary context could consist of using a team of 2–3 to diversify their approach. Segment those operations to see what the team members do best. Harness says human capital scalability is how we will navigate these waters. Greater certainty would include giving clients continuity after you have passed on.

HOLISTIC FINANCIAL PLANNING

Many of the larger firms are moving toward holistic planning. Holistic financial planning is the process of pursuing your life goals through the proper management of your resources. Life goals can include buying a home, saving for your child's education, planning for retirement, or leaving a legacy. Software is driving much of this process, with a few major packages leading the way.

Harness agrees with this assessment. "Some planners are not open to or do not recognize the value of holistic planning as it contradicts what the client may have vs. what they need." The trend today is that planners are understanding the value of globalization, which is seeing how one goal interacts with another. Our value is universal and needs to focus on how we market and differentiate ourselves.

From a holistic standpoint, Kitces states that we will need to be good on debt management, essentially the big items we don't normally get paid on, such as student loans, credit cards, car loans, etc. Fundamental advice we give to clients begins to change since it no longer hinges on product sales.

Garrett says the industry is focused on holistic planning. Through her network, Garrett is focused on helping human beings in whatever way possible. She wants her network to be seen as a protector and personal finance advocate.

As an advocate, Garrett says we need to be always ready in addressing client needs. We are life coaches dealing with therapy and behavioral finances. Financial planning should be simple. I ask clients, "I know you will be on the phone with a doctor, home health-care specialist, technical specialist, or someone else today. Do you want me to be on the phone call as well as a second set of ears?" Garrett says we need to break the mold that our relationship starts with the job and ends at retirement. Those subjects are too narrow. Our biggest breakthrough with clients is to help them expand their knowledge.

CHANGING OF THE GUARDS: THE EXPANDED FAMILY BASE AND ADDRESSING ADDITIONAL NEEDS

Many of us have worked with clients for many years. Those relationships are solid and in place. They almost seem foolproof and indestructible. What appears on the surface may not be the reality, however. More and more we are seeing that the client's extended family, essentially the children and others, tend to re-evaluate the situation with the planner after major events. New players enter and the existing planner disappears; certain family dynamics change. More often than not, they leave the existing firm. There are several reasons for that. One is that the firm does not do an adequate job of introducing the planner and other firm advisors to the client's extended family, who in fact will become the future decision makers. The interpersonal relationships with extended family members are virtually nonexistent and as a result, there is no bona fide reason for keeping the future soon-to-be inherited wealth of other family members within the existing advisory firm. Garrett believes we can prepare for these changes through financial therapy, coaching, and cheerleading.

Financial therapy is a process informed by the therapeutic and financial competencies that help people think, feel, and behave differently with money in order to improve their overall well-being through evidence-based practices and interventions. Full family involvement starts the process and can lead to others pitching in and helping out or families just working together. For example, many advisor offices have play areas for the children so the parents can give the planners their undivided attention. Others converse with their clients and over time their clients' children, grandchildren, and great-grandchildren who have a genuine interest in the family. The cheerleading factor occurs since everyone is on the same page with the client and all are rooting for common goals that represent a great, loving support system. It gets real personal in a hurry. The weirdness factor of having all of these parties attached to the process goes away pretty quickly.

"Seventy-four percent of our clients will continue to keep working well beyond age 65," says Robert Mauterstock, CFP®, Plan4Life, Brewster, MA. This also means that many older individuals will be at a better mental stage of health and can begin including their children and grandchildren in the process of managing their financial and health situations and what happens afterwards. Baby Boomers are in a much better framework retiring now vs. their predecessors. Mauterstock says that many of his clients begin a second career at age 60 and have an expectation of 30-plus years of retirement.

This also means that planners need to be ready to help clients prepare going forward during this stage of life, including intergenerational planning. This includes dealing with family matters with adult children, diminished capacity (including dementia and Alzheimer's), planning if one spouse enters an assisted living facility, and end-of-life planning. If this doesn't happen, 95% of the business you have been dealing with will be gone. A great quote from Mauterstock is "The day I retire, I lose my audience." Advisors should partner with elder care specialists to help make a difference in their clients' lives.

Even looking at your business as a "going concern," where it will continue indefinitely, again needs to account for the next round of players becoming a part of the process. Obviously, the client has to be fully comfortable with this approach. Continually coaching clients and lighting a fire underneath them to act, make decisions, and have others become involved will help expedite their decisions in an appropriate and timely manner.

This helps the planner create that long-term relationship with the "next batter up mentality." If this approach is not utilized, the risk for the planner is that these new, potentially long-term relationships do not help in understanding the client's current situation, the children's needs and expectations, the business's concerns, if applicable, and other issues out there that are not being addressed.

Planners should develop working relationships with other professionals to assist in the planning element, especially in the later stages of life. If the expertise is not located in-house, and no affiliates or associates of the firm can be called in, then working with a reputable group of specialists, perhaps as part of a network, will become necessary. Examples include elder care specialists, mortgage brokers, estate planning attorneys, and others who may become necessary to help clients figure out how to pay for the next stage of life.

PLANNER APPROACH: "CAUSE VS. EFFECT"

So what's happening now? "Ninety-five percent of the profession is chasing the effect vs. understanding the cause to address those changes," says Mitch Anthony, Founder and President of Financial Life Planning Institute, ROL Advisor.com, and Life-Centered Planners (U.K.). Anthony says the planner needs to focus on hearing and understanding the client's story first and then acting afterwards. Too many of us are focusing on bottom-line strategies which may or may not be imperative to what the client truly needs. Have the client alert you to events they anticipate so financial planning is in place. This uniqueness to each individual client takes away the cookie-cutter approach toward financial planning.

Anthony says it is better to prepare than to repair, and sums it up very well. "Hear the story first and then focus on the numbers afterwards. The planner needs to establish the context which helps the client resonate with them."

"We are judged by outcomes," says Mark Milic, CFP®, RICP, Partner, Relationship Manager, Douglas C. Lane & Associates, New York. For example, with the advent of TurboTax for mainstream tax returns, there is a demand and need for CPAs to work on tax returns at a higher level. That same rationale is developing for CFP® practitioners as part of the overall advice and knowledge we provide our clients. As we get paid, the company finds the cheapest product it can for the client. But when the focus is on how to maneuver our clients to a higher level, the reverse becomes true. The CFP® trademark is the de facto standard where the focus is on advice and not product, and there has been lots of rapid growth in this area.

Planning should start with the big picture and then compartmentalize by those disciplines that are essential for the client. The big picture will generate the areas of specialty and then help determine the funding necessary for each. It will help manage client expectations. Many planners gather money with the purpose of figuring out what the client will need those funds for.

Many times it works in reverse. Money goes in motion when life happens, says Anthony. All want to be ahead in money and the planner is at risk when money moves away. By then, it's too late. Financial planning needs to broaden the dialogue to all aspects of life and tie into the big picture.

When we are discussing client needs and wants, we need a system to help us generate that information. Digital tools can be useful in identifying what we should talk about. Clients need to realize the connection to their life and money and begin realizing the need for objective input, thereby broadening the dialogue. The advisor sits down with the client 15–20 years looking out. This financial lifeline needs to be populated with this dual effect. Essentially, the planner and client need to think it through from life/health to cradle/grave, says Anthony.

BEHAVIOR PATTERNS: MAKING SURE THE CLIENT "GETS" IT

What is the expectation for change with our clients? Today's profession needs to revolve around behavioral finance issues. In an era of constant change, planners need to focus on more of how this information will benefit the client and talk through the issues rather than relying on numbers dedicated through software. "We still need to see the human element and need to be concerned that artificial intelligence and technology do not replace it," says Jeff Tomerang, CFP® of Waltham, MA.

In many ways, the "talking" or "getting to know the individual" is missing in a more advanced technological age, especially in situations like financial planning. That approach should be at the forefront of what we do for our clients. How do you have that conversation with clients when they can't talk to their computers, asks Lawson. He adds that the value proposition is where we come in, otherwise you will lose the client. We make sure we do not use a "cookie-cutter" approach.

Having a clear dialogue between what the client states they want and the planner thinking through how it is most likely to work is important. "Clients make decisions based on behavior," says Susan Bradley, CFP® , CeFT®, Founder, Sudden Money Institute, Palm Beach Gardens, FL. Bradley states that many times it is a response to uncertainty. "We are more likely to see uncertainty being the norm. This can be triggered when clients ask what happens now, or I've retired, life stinks, or I've inherited more than I expected. Stress can drop the cognitive functioning."

Unexpected events can change client behavior patterns. For example, some crisis management issues began long ago while others have surfaced in the not too distant past. The Great Depression introduced protection for investors, 9/11 began establishing certain protocols, the 2008 financial meltdown led to a broad range of new actions by the Federal Reserve, the COVID-19 pandemic made many people realize that they were short on their savings, a low negative interest rate environment has been sustained, all of which can affect certain behaviors going forward. We have seen things shift on a dime and that type of managing future paradigm shifts will be more represented by firms and advisors alike going forward.

It's imperative to start developing a relationship with your clients, essentially becoming a "crisis management specialist," says Annalee Kruger, President, Care Right, Inc., Bonita Springs, FL. Aging is a very real process. Health care is already an expensive ordeal and since we face a health-care dilemma, parents having kids later in life, families that are smaller, the health-care pool will be smaller. Facilities will be different, with health care moving to virtual and automation, and using technology to cut down on health-care costs. The advisor needs to show the value that can be added over and above automation through the relationship with the client. "The media makes working with aging clients a problem no one wants to deal with," says Kruger. Aging crises needs to be in tune with what the client is going through personally. Early retirement, and how to prepare for that, and understanding family care giver issues can be overlooked.

Advisors should have offices geared for the needs of their older clients. For example, how many advisors think of having chairs with arms to help older clients get up? If you go virtual and they are not there in front of you, what happens if you don't drive to their house to meet with them?

The days of speaking one time a year with clients are over, says Kruger. Look at their needs and perhaps refer to other professionals. For example, include realtors, attorneys, and others as part of the planning process where the advisor can't provide competent service because it is outside their specialty.

Now is the time to show your older clients your value, that you care about them as a person. Help them relieve their fears. Reach out to the client's adult children and determine which of them wish to become care givers for their parents during this new free time. Are they willing to take care of their parents themselves? Do they live close by to help out? Reach out to the families. Technology can do the rest.

"Consumers don't seek out help or even see a shift in behavioral direction," says Kitces. For example, we don't wake up asking someone to change us, or to save us from ourselves. Our goal is to help clients implement better decisions in becoming more successful. Clients will ask whether they will actually end up in a better place due to changes in lifestyle to make a value-added difference. Our role is helping clients with outcomes and being held accountable and judged in the future by influenced persuasion decision making.

Bradley states that the financial planning profession will no longer operate in a three-step process whereby we coach the client with respect to getting an education, settling down, and getting a job. Things are changing rapidly. "If the client is age 65 or older, it's a whole different way that we need to learn. Clients hire planners to lead a better life. We have to be really in it with our clients," she says.

Bradley emphasizes that we have to know how to have disruptive conversations with our clients. Using the leadership triage (ask questions, be quiet, deep listening) helps structure conversations. Paraphrase the client's response so you can tell what they are doing correctly or not. Sort and organize to discover the best path to enter uncertainty, and determine whether there are any immediate threats to the client's well-being. It takes longer, but you can end up with a matrix on how partnering with you can resolve many of these issues. Have meaningful conversations and trade-offs during this time and use them as pivot points. It's sort of a make-it-or-break-it time.

Bradley says, "We are not getting better at fulfilling an implied promise of financial planning. We need to talk with clients about their readiness to move forward. Keep conversation client centered and personal to have a deep connection. If you see inconsistencies, try to stay aware and present. People will see this more in 10 years and will initially be happy, and then something happens that will change all that." What happens when you stop addressing the issues with the client on a regular basis? You can make it their fault, or you can lean in and help them find a new entry point.

"Pay attention to those clients who have or are part of families with unique disabilities, such as autism, whereby you have to make trips to the school or other facility to talk about personalized client gifts," says Milic. Focusing on niche marketing whereby specialty-type advisors establish and gain the client's trust, which could take as long as 1–2 years for them to really open up to the advisor, could generate satisfied clients for life.

Carter believes in education and more education for the client. "We need to connect with them both emotionally and intellectually so that if we only deal with them by phone or videoconferencing, we can educate them on the other side."

McClanahan states that we spend 80% of our time helping people plan their future and 20% on things going on now. This needs to become part of the planning process, if it is not already, to provide psychological and financial resiliency. Disability will change, with policies going to age 90 if people are healthy and productive for that long.

McClanahan says that retirement won't be as important since clients will be working longer and will use their money to enjoy life. Therefore, retirement life expectancy is stagnant. We will have more obesity, diabetes, epidemics/pandemics, and a population explosion, with people living in more concentrated areas. We need to quit talking about retirement. We need to start talking about transition and resiliency. Maintaining the ability to work as long as possible and making yourself useful so you are not out of a job will be key. That will help keep you mentally and physically ready.

Changing your disciplined approach requires an adjustment, adaptation, or reinvention which will provide the client with a new starting point for the next time life changes. "If you keep giving advice and they are not taking it by the third offering, then they are less likely to act," says Bradley.

When working with our clients, we need to incorporate the entire family, where possible. Many advisors do not think about these issues, needs, or other concerns outside of the core client, and that could have severe consequences. For starters, many children leave the parents' current advisor after something happens to the parent. If the parent client is amenable to including successive generations as part of the discussions, it may be a good idea to include them, so they know what the issues are for the parent client going forward.

This second generation could include children, parents, and others. Milic provides an example of how it works in his practice. "Many of my largest clients today are those that started out as fairly small clients by today's standards and we grew together. When my relatively new client asks if I will also manage his daughter's smaller account, I emphatically say, 'It would be our pleasure,' and I know what I just committed to from a time perspective. I need to spend time speaking with my client's child and making sure we are addressing the child's needs. As a general matter, I find that the second generation wants to have completely different dialog than their parents. They are in very different stages of life and are far more concerned with planning surrounding their 401(k) allocations, insurance needs, general wills, and planning for college. Knowing the family dynamics, and especially the emotions surrounding money for all of the players involved, is crucial to serving the family at a high level.

"Technology is enabling advisors to streamline the client experience," says Lawson. He adds that more clients are deciding that they wish to remain in their home during firm/client interviews. This allows Lawson to frame his meetings from the behavioral side. He says, "We are constantly focusing on listening to our clients and truly understanding what their intentions are. We ask them, 'What's on your mind?' We constantly reframe and rephrase client responses to ensure that we understand where they are coming from."

Carter concurs with this assessment. "We lean toward smaller offices, especially in light of what is going on now. I believe the commercial real estate industry will ultimately be affected. Most of our staff do not need to be in the office currently. It's easier to do remotely now because of the relationship we have with our clients. In fact, our firm has increasingly used video-conferencing, which cuts down on overhead, and then the savings can be applied toward client service, improving phone, writing, and speaking skills, and enhancing staff salaries."

Carter still arranges regular staff and client get-togethers. He provides fun gatherings with his clients "since people are social beings and want to be a part of our office family and mingle with the staff and our other clients on a regular basis." In addition, for staff outings, Carter is partial to his Ft. Worth Stock Rodeo since he is a rancher. He has his staff pick two charity days per year, wherever they would like to go and whatever they would like to do, as long as the firm is together as a group.

COMMUNICATION AND PEOPLE SKILLS

McClanahan says, "Good communication classes need to be more in the mainstream, incorporating speech and psychology and learning how to listen." She adds: "Say what you do and do what you say." She responds to her clients within a set period of time. "I call back my clients within one day and send emails within two days." A copy of Carolyn's "Client Engagement Standards" is given in Chapter 2.

"Create resiliency for clients and yourself. Too many people get locked into when they are going to quit," says McClanahan. Regarding her business plan, when communicating with clients she goes out one year by putting actions (compared with outcomes) in only to get clients to act toward their goals.

Scott Kahan concurs with McClanahan. "The most important issues affecting our industry are communication and people skills. People want hand holding and relate best when talking with an advisor. They want what used to be the family doctor." Many clients are looking for one-stop shopping. They want the advisor who can be the "initial go-to person" to either help them out, or work with other advisors, or be the source for referrals so that the individual has a handle on those future issues.

"We have found that many clients enjoy meeting with young planners. It helps the clients experience a different perspective and differing world views," says Lawson. "We have our staff work in silos. We all meet with the client initially and then it goes to a primary advisor."

"We have many clients who travel to Omaha and/or meet with us live virtually. We found that younger clients tend to meet with us virtually and consider it a waste of time to visit our office," says Carson.

When I meet with clients and students, and in my lectures, I love to use my whiteboards. The more the better! Like me, Carson likes to be able to write on the wall, whiteboard, or easel as a way of making sure clients follow along and get involved in the meeting. He has different teams consisting of 4–6 staff in the office – a senior, junior, customer service manager, with an emphasis on subject matter experts, all in house. Carson meets with clients often early on to make sure all are on the same page. Once the relationship becomes mature and runs well, require meetings at least annually. Carson always communicates with clients and meets with them at least once per year.

"The investment side is the easiest part of our business. The most time consuming is working on the consumer side due to the personal connection that is necessary to make the plan a reality. We should never, ever forget what we bring to our clients' lives," says Kahan. There are ways to use technology to enhance our people skills, but that should not be the governing force. Downloads are fine, but we need to see the people sooner rather than later. As a training exercise, I have our interns and other new planners listen to other planners' client phone calls to help them gain an understanding of how to approach the issues.

On the technology side, there are several major platforms out there. "Sensationalism causes panic," says Kahan. Look at what has transpired with COVID-19. Sure, it takes a while for things to get back to normal. But they have in the past. Just look at the last few unexpected triggers within the last 20 years, such as 9/11 and 2007/2008 – the Great Recession. Just like many clients thought this would be it, the markets rebounded and then some! The major difference between this and the Great Recession is that that was an infrastructure problem, whereas in this case it put the whole world on hold. It also provides a reality check for many who have never experienced market downturns of this proportion.

The way in which Kahan has his staff approach these issues and be able to influence behavior can be summed up as follows: "Our biggest change we can make is the team of professionals, since human contact in walking clients through this scenario is expected by clients and must be done. Even the Zoom conference model, or other tech-oriented platforms where advisors can still see their advisors and advisors can see the behavior of clients, is key. One of the biggest issues I have seen with this latest unexpected world turn of events is that some younger planners don't want to take this on themselves. The planner needs to step back and not take it personally. You have to remember that you can't control this. We will get through it."

Mark Milic discusses why it is critical to be better prepared than the competition. He says, "Many of my clients have relationships with other advisors at outside firms and in most cases they share this information with me. I recognize the reasons for this and greatly appreciate and respect the value of relationships. When I walk into a meeting with my client, whether outside advisors exist or not, one of my personal goals is to be better prepared than any other advisor within my client's universe. This means that I read and re-read the copious notes I've taken from past meetings. I'm recalling the kids' names, ages, occupations, grandkids, states in which they reside, etc., prior to walking into that meeting. I don't believe in 'winging it.' My financial plans have more scenarios than I actually discuss during my meetings, just in case my client asks about alternative opinions. All of this not only helps in crafting a productive meeting but it also shows command and understanding of the family relationship. This same level of preparation applies if I'm meeting a prospective client for the first time, if I'm giving a presentation to a small or large group of people, or if I'm part of a panel discussion. I often-times will practice and rehearse a week in advance. Working hard and being well prepared will get you 90% of the way there."

CHAPTER 2

How to Structure Your Practice

Now that we have determined some of the major infrastructure issues that may affect the way we practice financial planning, and have gained an understanding as to the potential macro-level changes expected for the balance of this decade, let's switch to the tactical approach of how to develop your firm going forward.

There are many ways to structure your financial planning practice. The first question you need to address is, what market do you wish to serve? You can't be all things to all people. There are so many variations that many planners get lost starting in one market and then drift off to another, only to realize afterwards that they are not set up properly or do not possess the proper infrastructure for maximum effectiveness to develop their chosen market.

Vincent Rossi, CFP®, Founder, President, and Chief Investment Officer, Intelligent Capitalworks, Scottsdale, AZ, says it is important for planners to "pick your lane and work hard to own it." Know what lane you are in because you cannot be too many things to too many people. Focus on the depth and breadth of your lane and do it well. If you say you are going to do it, then do it! Many younger planners are not taught to do this. To quote noted asset allocation expert Roger Gibson, "The beginning stage is the most important part of the work. Either way you are going to do the work. If more is focused on the back end, the client will become angry."

Structuring your practice in an appropriate manner is critical for maximum effectiveness. Many advisors I have shared this with ask for total employee involvement in how to grow or what changes to make. Give everyone a stake in the success of the business. If employees stand to gain from what is being created and they feel a sense of ownership and pride, they will be on board and are more likely to become an integral part of the process in building the proper infrastructure. It will also allow you to remove some of the staff learning curve and get things done quicker and more efficiently. It's the old adage, "As a manager, you are only as good as the players you have playing for you."

The first thing the firm needs to address is making sure the planners and others comply with the rules. Assuming you have the licensing, regulatory, and other compliance requirements at hand, make sure you adhere to your appropriate Code of Ethics. (For a more complete guide to regulation, please see Chapter 1.) For CFP® certificants, the CFP Board's Code of Ethics is a strong reference for planners operating in our field. The cornerstone of the Code and Standards is centered around fiduciary duty. At all times when providing financial advice to a client, a CFP® professional must act as a fiduciary and therefore act in the "best interests" of the client. For planners, I would hope and assume that is the norm. Again, that is your default – always. A full copy of the resources on the CFP Board's new Code and Standards can be found on the CFP Board website at CFP.net/code.

The Making of the Office Environment has been broken into my most important concepts within our profession. Once you have the infrastructure in place and know how you wish to proceed, you can go out and gain the specifics for working through the process and identifying the issues, exposures, and recommendations at hand for each of the technical disciplines.

Rattiner's Secrets on "The Making" of the Office Environment

1. Office Procedures Manual
2. Office Expectations Strategies
3. Accountability and Monitoring Client Progress
4. Determining the Type of Practice You Are Looking to Run
5. Operational Thoughts
6. The Setup: Establishing Your Business Entity
7. Development and Follow-through of Your Business Plan

8. Development of a Marketing Plan
9. Life Coaching and Changing Behavior
10. Intellectual Capital/Structuring the Model Firm for the 2020s
11. Marketing

The strongest businesses have the best infrastructure setup. That means corporative initiatives are well thought out before they are put into action. Accountability is noted and staff members know how to handle day-to-day activities and problems before they erupt and possibly explode. Everyone understands their responsibilities to the firm, in relating with their peers, and in servicing their clients.

All the office players essentially are playing a part – almost like a movie role – to allow for the smoothest sailing, consistency, and continuity. This is easiest when each of the employees knows their specific responsibilities. The best way for that to happen is to provide each employee with the opportunity to contribute to the creation of a universal office publication. In business terms, that is the development of an office procedures manual.

OFFICE PROCEDURES MANUAL

To me, an office procedures manual is the key to maintaining the ultimate organized and orderly business environment. The manual describes the role of each individual in whatever capacity in the practice. It specifies what each employee's functions are. It ties the employee to a department and appropriate oversight and shows how it all connects. It contains protocol on how to act internally with other staff regarding division of responsibilities, the importance of operating on the same page, and the teamwork involved in working together.

In a financial planning firm, based on the structure of the firm, there could be many different divisions, all with multiple responsibilities. Enabling everyone to agree on the way the office should be run is critical for the practice's long-term success and possible expansion. It also provides guidance to prospects and clients as to how the firm runs, what they can expect, and the process(es) conducted by the firm.

To me, everyone has to have "buy-in" to the process. Firms I have consulted with have had the partners and senior management start with an outline or table of contents of the initial draft. This allows each item to be placed appropriately. Organizational charts of departments and positions within the company should be included to make sure manual readers can connect the dots.

Describe the specific responsibilities for each department and each staff person assigned. Ensure what the protocol procedure should be. Positions as well as names should be incorporated throughout. The manual should include contact information for the person who owns the process. This helps facilitate questions, and direct comments or concerns, if need be. It shows the chain of command. It provides guidance on the responsibilities of core members by assigning their job responsibilities and outlines how to do that particular function. In a pinch, it could temporarily enable one staff member to fulfill the responsibilities of another.

Key elements should be stated in bold, followed by bullet points and then descriptions. Bullet points help with organization and ensure staff can follow the essential details. If the manual has links for searchable PDFs, those will enable employees to get more information if necessary. There should be continual updating to perhaps change certain procedures if no longer applicable. Also, if there are some specific or technical procedures that need to be followed, defining them throughout would make sense. If aspects need to be changed, there should be a process in place to gain approval by running those changes by others.

Once the document contains the core elements, it should be circulated to the managers and then to support staff for their input. This enables everyone to see how things are supposed to run and the functions for each particular staff person. Any client issues that may arise have specific solutions on how they should be addressed and by whom. The procedures manual should always be updated to reflect changes in process, new divisions, and new delineations or spans of control that have been changed or formed over time. The manual should be updated at least annually, or whenever business procedures, significant responsibilities, or other updates occur.

Bill Carter cross-trains all staff in order to ensure that all client responses and expectations are the same. He wants his clients and staff to internalize their experiences at the firm by going over the issues to always provide the best solutions.

A shortened version of the office manual in an executive summary format should be provided in advance to each prospect thinking of doing business with the firm as well as to those clients already associated with the firm. This enables clients to know what the next procedural step should be when issues come up. It all helps to set and manage your clients' expectations, which as we said earlier is the main reason for disagreements among planners and clients.

To keep the staff on track and make sure all important office issues are spelled out, another important document that should be circulated just for staff is the Corporate Engagement Standards.

OFFICE EXPECTATIONS STRATEGIES

For your office to run well and to make the client experience enjoyable, there are many ways to ensure that everyone is on the same page in the office. The team has to act in unison to make what the firm is communicating viable and attractive for clients who join the firm. These actions should not be glossed over by the powers that be but should be learned and incorporated into the culture of the firm.

There are certain basics, what I would call nonnegotiable items, that always need to be present. Displaying a positive and respectful attitude, working with honesty and integrity, reliability, and accountability, flexibility in responsibilities, and representing the organization in a responsible manner, both on the job and off the job – these are what I would call givens. Managing staff expectations is all about being on the same page. It is important to know what is expected from the employees and teams, and to set realistic, reasonable tasks and deadlines to make it happen. A "next player up" mentality needs to surface, which as explained earlier provides homegrown team players to help out where necessary. Performance expectations should be clear from the day that someone accepts a position with the company. Specificity and clarity as to expectations and how you will measure them help manage the expectations. The overall purpose of performance expectations is to move toward a specific company goal and to create workplace accountability from one employee to another.

Employees should ask for help when they need it and should never be accused of stating "It's not my job." The chain of command needs to ensure "everyone gets it." Employees should be encouraged to ask questions and clarify unnecessary confusion and answers that seem vague or redundant.

A positive way to communicate this is for the supervisors to step into the staff's shoes to ensure they understand the process. Promote dialogue and communication. Focus on the company's core mission and values. In fact, many companies have new staff start at the bottom, learn the basics, and then grow into positions of authority and supervision.

This mental preparation will go a long way in helping to set firmwide expectations, making employees feel valuable, and ultimately inspiring and rewarding them. Most employees want to climb up the corporate ladder and get promoted, which could lead to earning more money, taking on more responsibility, and ensuring the firm's values are being carried out. Sharing ideas for improvements and presenting new opportunities helps the morale of team members. All employees want to feel good about what and how they are doing things to promote the public good, especially at the office.

In a perfect world, most employees opt for a work/life balance. That's a tough one. Employees who get the sense that the firm cares are more likely to put their heart and soul into the position and do a better job. Avoiding unnecessary stress and aggravation goes a long way toward a civilized approach to the role assigned by the firm.

Decisions need to be made about where to set expectations, with an understanding as to why. The firm's employees need to recognize and agree to accept what is required by them in this capacity. This should be done first in writing. They can agree to meet and discuss the process, with general thoughts being presented and then each person chiming in as to what they like and don't like, in order to get buy-in on the same page when staff members are ready to put it all into operation and take it into the work environment. To streamline the process, perhaps software can be used to provide uniformity and eliminate mistakes in the approach of the staff.

Everyone at the firm should sign off that they understand, agree, and will abide by the office expectations. They need to be motivated by thriving on the internal dynamics of the firm. The persons discussing rules, procedures, client mishaps, and other aspects that can arise need to make it clear for everyone who has a vested interest in the firm. Rewarding employees for exceeding expectations will make for a strong and positive environment where everyone is rooting for the success of the other staff members.

Supervisors should meet with employees on a regular basis to discuss ongoing and new projects that are scheduled to arise and hold one-on-one meetings to display caring and professional leadership. As someone who is a big one-on-one person, which is my approach, I believe this gives the team member the opportunity to express in confidence whatever ongoing issues they may be experiencing, and it allows for direct resolution of issues to help pave the way for an even more productive work environment. Since employees are all different, tact and discipline need to be factored into the ongoing communication.

The approach used should stem from a positive outlook rather than a negative one. Don't start with what is wrong or failing; rather, focus on what is right, how things can be tweaked to make them even better, and how those experiences can be taken to the next level. People want to learn and strive to do better. Constant feedback and evaluations from superiors would help reinforce the actions of the staff member.

All of the above issues can also be summarized in an employee handbook, which should be updated at least annually. Another approach is to go over these items with employees through corporate engagement standards so that everyone is fully aware of what is expected of them.

This Corporate Engagement Standards program is provided with permission from Carolyn McClanahan, M.D., CFP®, Life Planning Partners, Inc., Jacksonville, FL.

Life Planning Partners, Inc.
Corporate Engagement Standards

Our purpose is to provide practical financial life planning that enhances and simplifies our client's financial life. A great work environment is important to achieve this goal. Engagement standards provide clear directives on how we operate as a company and how our team is expected to interact with each other.

What we expect from each other:

_____ PLEASANT WORK ENVIRONMENT – We like to have fun at work and strive to maintain a pleasant working environment. We enjoy laughing, jokes, and anything else that brightens the day.

_____ PASSION FOR EXCELLENCE – We have a passion for excellence in all that we do.

_____ COMMUNICATION – We have an open door policy with honest, direct, and clear communication. If something bothers or offends a team member, they need to share that information. If there is a criticism of another team member or the way things are done, we listen to each other from a place of learning, empathy, and goodness and work to resolve the situation through consensus.

_____ UNCERTAINTY – All questions are good questions. If you are uncertain, ask. When you don't know the answer for a client, say "That's a good question and let me get back to you."

_____ LIFETIME LEARNING – Continuing education is valued and expected. We agree to mentor each other in our areas of strength to allow us to learn and grow as a team.

_____ TEAMWORK – We encourage collaboration of ideas and actions. We also share in the work that has to be done. Everyone pitches in when needed.

_____ A BALANCED LIFE – Balance is important when creating a great life. Taking care of us first helps us take care of others better. We are encouraged to take time off for fun and family matters. We provide $250 per year for participation in athletic events or classes. We also like to give back to the community – we allow two days off per year for community service or other charitable work.

_____ RESPECT FOR OTHERS – We are all valuable. Our relationship needs to be reevaluated if we ever stop enjoying or respecting one another.

_____ ERRORS – Mistakes are human. We take full responsibility for any errors made and we learn from them. We agree to make each other aware of errors as soon as they are discovered. We do our best to minimize errors and immediately remedy errors that occur. Our goal is to make the client "whole."

_____ RELIABILITY – We rely on each other to do what we say and say what we do.

_____ INTEGRITY – We follow high ethical standards. We are a fiduciary for our clients and we will do what is best for the client even if it is hard.

_____ VERIFICATION – We trust and verify. We have checks and balances to make certain crucial tasks are completed.

_____ DELIVERABLES – We are consistent with the services we deliver to clients. We develop and refine client service procedures to maintain efficiency and quality. It is expected that all employees will follow the same procedures.

_____ HOURS OF OPERATION – Life Planning Partners, Inc. keeps flexible hours for clients as well as for our staff. Deviations from the normal schedule are communicated through voicemail or email messages.

_____ DRESS CODE - Life Planning Partners, Inc. dress code is casual on days we do not have client meetings and on weekends. Clients are welcome to visit the office unannounced and are informed that we may be in casual attire. When we have client meetings we will dress in proper business casual attire.

_____ CELEBRATIONS – A job well done should be rewarded and celebrated.

I understand and agree with these awesome engagement standards. Any questions have been answered to my satisfaction.

Agreed to and accepted by:

Team Member: _____

Signature: _____ Date: _____

Life Planning Partners, Inc., Carolyn McClanahan, President

Signature: _____ Date: _____

ACCOUNTABILITY AND MONITORING CLIENT PROGRESS

"Accountability is essential. This is putting the office procedures manual into action. Organize your practice by discipline, function, or some other aspect," says Ross Levin, Chief Executive Officer and Founder at Accredited Investors Wealth Management, Edina, MN. In Levin's firm, every employee is responsible for a separate area, called a strategic planning area, which consists of a specialist or outside specialist (staff who don't have individual responsibility) of the firm. Over time it is a stronger setup because the staff has been there a long time and fully knows what has to happen and by whom. The arena of pure generalists, where staff is everything to everyone, is becoming increasingly more difficult.

In his landmark book, Levin presents the _Wealth Management Index_™ (a book I referred to often when I got started in this business and still use today), an innovative tool for financial advisors to quantify their clients' success in financial planning. The index helps financial advisors establish rational goals with their clients and measures their progress toward achieving goals. In the accounting world, it is similar to the work program that helps provide guidance on what CPAs are doing.

Some advisors focus on the front portion of the process with little regard for its completion. It is impossible to measure the progress you are making with these clients. If clients wanted quick "go-to" answers, they can purchase a software program, input what they need, and buy what is suggested or follow the course of action identified. The financial planning process is not about that. It is about identifying the issues, determining potential exposures, and providing thought-out recommendations to address outstanding concerns. Our reality is we help manage and monitor the process throughout to ensure that clients are always staying true to their objectives.

Because wealth management encompasses a variety of disciplines – the management of personal risks, prudent investing, reduction of income taxes, and ensuring appropriate estate distribution, to name just a few – traditional performance measures can be misleading and ineffective. Having a guide to showcase what needs to happen and when for the client's financial situation to become effective assists in that process.

DETERMINING THE TYPE OF PRACTICE YOU ARE LOOKING TO RUN

There is a huge distinction between "fast work" and "slow work," says Levin. Fast work, on disciplines such as tax, investments, retirement, and estate, can be achieved through artificial intelligence. Slow work happens when the client asks how much they can afford to spend on a house if they move and you have a long discussion around what they want their lives to look like, how they wish to raise their family, how they imagine living, before you ever reach for the spreadsheet. Slow work happens when the client asks what type of entity they should set up for a business they are exploring with a friend and you have a discussion around going into business with a friend and all the things that entails.

Industry changes and artificial intelligence are helping resolve the back-office challenges of managing client data. Rossi talked about software evolution and cautioned, "Once you have deployed a piece of software, it can be brutal to migrate out of it." Many pieces of software were brought to market as "stand-alone" offerings years ago. Today, much of that stand-alone software has been integrated into "ecosystems" and the integrators understand that the more modules a planner uses in their ecosystem, the more the planner sticks to their integrated software. Planners need to recognize that as integrators scale up, they will likely be "captured" in the integrators' ecosystems.

Many advisors I know set up their firm by splitting up the technical responsibilities by function. The attorney handles estate planning issues, the CPA handles tax issues, the insurance advisor(s) perhaps life and health and/or property, the casualty advisor handles insurance issues, the investment advisor designs and maintains investment portfolios, and the behavioral specialist, chief communicator, or someone else may deal with sitting down, designing, and meeting with the client to establish, maintain, and monitor the financial plan.

One of the analogies I use that is also shared by Evan Beach is that in order to run a successful practice, you need to align yourself with skilled players at each position. For example, for a baseball game, you have nine starting players whose positions and responsibilities to the team are all different. They essentially complement one another. There is certainly some overlap, but everyone needs to be trained and skilled in the field, for example, in their respective position to help play their position. Having nine shortstops on the team with no one in the outfield capable of catching a fly ball is not going to help that team succeed. The same analogy can be brought to the test here in the financial planning world. Having a diverse skill set where everyone has their key position and can potentially be a backup for other positions is a good way to groom the future championship team!

Part of this analogy, too, are activities used to create energy vs. drain energy. The synergy necessary to breed success can be contagious and certainly worthwhile in determining the type of practice you wish to run.

If the firm gets into other niches where in-house specialists are not available, other experts can be brought in to be responsible for providing services such as aligning with a mortgage broker, education planner, divorce professional, or perhaps someone else, if there is a strong faction of those types of services within the practice. These planners may be handed the realm of responsibilities in their particular field only. It keeps the firm in alignment by delegating client issues to planners of authority who become involved in those specific areas only. As an added bonus, it provides structure for the clients and for the owners of the practice. In Levin's firm, because of his setup using strategic planning areas, all clients belong directly to the firm and not to the individuals who work at the firm.

A practitioner meeting can evolve for multidimensional clients whereby each of the professionals within the firm can discuss the specific concerns of the client from their relative context. This type of practice sharing consists of all wealth managers getting together and talking about the outstanding issues. Essentially, your clients cannot get the plans you are delivering for them in this context from any other type of service.

Rossi refers to what he calls the 10 allied disciplines of wealth management:

- Financial planning
- Life underwriting
- Investment consulting
- Investment management
- Estate planning

- Philanthropic counsel
- Trust services
- Tax
- Accounting
- Law

To create a structured visual of this view for his firm and clients, Rossi presents the workflows within these 10 allied disciplines using chemistry's periodic table of the elements framework. The workflows in the table of elements help the client see and learn the advisory firm's view of the wealth management process and help the client begin to self-identify and articulate where their problems are and how they interrelate with the client's bigger picture. This process helps Rossi's team and his firm's clients begin to "see" the scope of engagement they need, and how they will establish their value proposition and price for it. This is not easily scalable stuff. Many planners think they are practicing at this level, but few do, and fewer do it well. Rossi relates this type of work to practicing medicine as a doctor. It is impossible to do when your firm is positioned and built for pharmaceutical (read "financial product") sales. To succeed at this type of work, you need to be in the business of "learning medicine" (acquiring and applying intellectual capital across the 10 allied disciplines for the benefit of clients). It is analogous to the commitment of lifelong learning required of doctors and other professionals.

A great quote from Rossi is this: "If you truly do this kind of work, you will have a deliverable (or study) in your file for each workflow and not just notes on a note pad." People can build their own portfolios for free. They pay us to manage much more than money. They pay us to help them solve the problems they are facing and help them get to where they want to go as safely as possible.

Being a pure generalist is becoming more difficult. A good generalist identifies what the problems are. You know what you know, and you know what you don't know. As a result, you know where to look for help regarding those issues you do not feel comfortable assisting the client with. The generalist would then be responsible for connecting the client to a specialist for these types of issues to be appropriately addressed.

OPERATIONAL THOUGHTS

"The whole world is changing. Firms will change the way the game is being played now. Take copious notes for support staff to understand," says Mitch

Anthony. Enable all members of the team to be on the same page through the broadening of one's capacity, which is the other side of planning.

I like to start with the development of a mission statement representing my core business belief system and from there develop other tools to support the mission statement. A mission statement is a short statement of why your practice exists, establishing its overall goal and identifying the goal of its operations: what kind of product or service it provides, its primary customers or market, and its geographical region of operation.

Because many planners look to expand with additional offices within their main city as well as into other cities, that approach could be a drain on human capital and cost. "It's easier and more efficient to run one office and have clients congregate there vs. having the responsibility of running multiple offices," says Levin. One reason is that many client meetings occur on Zoom as distance meetings where we can still see the client and react to their body language and their thoughts accordingly.

Planners are enamored with the concept of buying their buildings. "In essence, you are limited by the size of the plant's pot," says Levin. And since a limited amount of office time may be spent with clients, I kind of equate it to a plant's pot.

Regarding pure technology, you can have success in the model you are comfortable with, but where planners get messed up is in changing their model. It's hard, however, to create a relationship with technology, because software can't replace curiosity!

Regarding stimulus packages today, it may be better to have more leverage to work with tax rates that will be more favorable for the client in the future. As more investments move into the insurance and annuity arena, it will be intriguing and interesting to see the 4% distribution rule work in a "0%" interest rate environment.

The new norm regarding longevity and people transitions is that as our business changes and moves online because of the environment and cost, you will have to figure out the type of business you plan on running going forward. Mega firms try to be all things to all people. Pick your niche and stay focused.

THE SETUP: ESTABLISHING YOUR BUSINESS ENTITY

Those starting out should envision probable losses initially. In order to absorb and make use of those losses upfront against other types of income, a pass-through entity such as an LLC or S corporation probably makes the most sense. With a one-person S corporation, as a one-person business (which more than 90% are), you are running a corporation as a pass-through entity, with income and losses passed down to your personal return along with limited liability.

One benefit of pass-through losses is that if you are married, your spouse's income can offset your pass-through losses, resulting in a smaller tax liability. Ideally, it's all about making money, but it could help out in the early years. With an LLC, you have fewer restrictions on the structure. Both setups work best for those starting out and those already established in their practices. Regardless of entity structure, you should always have errors and omission (E&O) insurance as a backup.

Running your practice as a sole proprietor just doesn't make sense to me. The unlimited liability resulting from the business itself, which could jeopardize not only your personal income but your family assets since the owner and taxpayer are one and the same, is a tough pill to swallow. Add to that the filing of Schedule C (the most audited tax form) and that scenario doesn't quite do it.

As a one-person firm, an S corporation makes sense. In states that allow one-person LLCs to operate, they could also be effective as long as the S corporation tax election is made. If you are in business with someone else, the LLC or the S corporation would be worthwhile entity types, and certainly better than a general partnership. As a general partner, again, you have unlimited liability. Even as a small minority owner, for example, as a 1% owner who is a general partner, you could still be hit with 100%-plus of the partnership liability. In other words, you are liable for the mishaps, deliberate or not, of your other general partners. There are just better ways to organize your practice. A potential downside of an LLC as a one-person owner is that if you don't elect to be taxed as an S corporation, by definition (meaning you are not part of a partnership) you will be taxed as a sole proprietorship completing Schedule C, since you are a one-person entity.

DEVELOPMENT AND FOLLOW-THROUGH OF YOUR BUSINESS PLAN

You can't start planning without a plan, in any walk of life! Depending on where you intend to offer and deliver your practice, the current market trends need to be addressed and thoroughly researched. Using your mission statement (discussed above) as your backdrop, you will need to determine the trends that will dominate in the future. You'll need to figure out the overall market(s) being served, a profile of what the practice will look like, and the need for the product or service, and that will allow you to service the operating environment, dissect the market, analyze and distinguish the competition, minimize the likelihood of failure, figure out what you are missing or lacking in your service, and be ready for opportunities and challenges to successfully compete in your targeted marketplace.

One way to assess the situation is through the development of a SWOT analysis. SWOT stands for strengths, weaknesses, opportunities, and threats. This analysis helps the firm see where it is strong and where it is weak compared with the competition, and how to improve on those areas to put yourself in a position to successfully compete in your market space.

Strengths

Strengths are the backbone of what your company does extremely well. They are transparent so that you and others can see your firm's advantage, and how well you dominate your existing and perhaps new market space. They give rise to your firm, and employees, becoming a major player in your targeted universe.

Weaknesses

All businesses have weaknesses and you'll need to be able to identify them and how your competitors see them so that they don't create a rift or setback for your firm. Areas such as procedures, offerings, cash flow concerns, staffing, communication, and follow-up need to be identified and targeted to improve. You can't choose to ignore these exposures because they can be devastating to the development and continued success of the firm.

As such, you'll need to fully identify your weaknesses, then figure out how to address them and how to turn them into potential strengths. Failure to be successful in this area will impede your firm's advancement to the next level. You'll need to focus on your core attributes, or in certain situations leaving that space.

Opportunities

Opportunities are potential gaps in the existing marketplace, potential trends you may uncover through your research in a variety of areas, from a new way of addressing certain needs, technology possibilities, future trends, political actions, or other areas that help you to identify and immediately act in these small windows. They can help you gain the advantage you need to compete more effectively in the environment.

Threats

Threats are any negative external issues that could adversely affect the success and even survival of your practice. These could include staffing concerns, change in marketplace and servicing conditions, massive technology restructuring, regulatory element changes, and other aspects that could affect your ability to continue your practice as a going concern.

Running your practice should not be done in a vacuum. Always know where your firm stands in the marketplace and more importantly where your competition stands. Be ready to meet any potential challenges head on and to make key decisions. It doesn't mean your firm needs to make changes immediately, but you need to think about and ultimately tackle those issues when moving the firm forward.

When following up on the business plan and performing the next steps, start with a macro perspective and then get into the micro initiatives. Run the numbers to develop a cash flow statement, a balance sheet, and an appendix of supporting documents and statements. Determine how the practice will look at the maximum valuation point and include a potential exit strategy for the business.

Spell out how much money and resource commitment will be necessary to get the business off the ground. Based on that landscape, determine the objectives for success. Objectives quantify in dollars and time when things will be met. Look at the resources necessary to help you achieve those objectives spelled out in the document.

Examine the potential contingencies you will have to overcome. Determine the implementation necessary for the business to become a reality. The basic discussions of where the business is now (Point A), where the business needs to go (Point B), and the road needed to connect the dots as the game plan should be determined.

In today's world, it is important to make your business stand out from your competitors. Include potential answers for those interested parties reading the document, such as partners, potential investors, and staff. Once all the prep has been done and the document written, include a one-page executive summary at the beginning that explains the rationale for the business's success.

DEVELOPMENT OF A MARKETING PLAN

Once you develop your business plan, the development of the marketing plan is the next logical step in the sequence. The key to the successful development of a marketing plan is for the document to be focused. Undertake a market analysis. Identify and develop macro- and micro-level strategies for the target market(s). Business development is always going to be one of your main focal points.

Targeting the right client business and not necessarily all client business goes a long way in the satisfaction of running and growing your successful practice. To accelerate the process, target and create strategic working alliances, both on a national and a local level, to provide you with a better product/service offering. Once determined, develop an action plan.

Work within the budget you establish. It does not have to be expensive to make it work better. It needs to be efficient and pinpointed. Determine pricing. Ask yourself whether you want to provide an a la carte, high-end, or more personal and subsequently more expensive service, or are you looking to price things at a lower rate to gain market share by securing volume? Whichever approach(es) you plan to take, keep score! Audit the results from a quantitative standpoint and provide client satisfaction surveys to adjust your game plan as you move forward. See pages 51–60 for a definitive game plan for marketing your practice.

LIFE COACHING AND CHANGING BEHAVIOR

This decade will turn more financial planners into life coaches by intertwining life issues with financial issues in the development of their practices. Coaching involves getting the most from your clients. It's one thing to help clients plan financially; it's another to have them learn and understand the issues and to achieve what they'd like through the course of changed behavior. Clients will want and expect their planners to be receptive and to bring that skill set to the table.

Coaching involves helping the client to move in the direction they wish. A more well-rounded planner requires a broader capacity and skill set to allow for a better understanding of the client, which can then lead to more effective counseling and coaching. This will enable the planner to gain an advantage and incorporate these behavioral areas into the development of appropriate recommendations. This type of focus embodies more than just the numbers representative of planning but instead enables the planner to guide and manage those kinds of client conversations going forward without feeling awkward, says Mitch Anthony.

You can broaden financial planning into understanding your clients and then helping them to change. Cam Marston of Generational Insights, Mobile, AL, states that planners need to develop more intimate and interpersonal relationships with their clients. Clients, in turn, need to learn how to think about many aspects, including the three keys to happiness: family, friends, and faith.

Marston says the planner should address the following issues with their clients. "Advisors may feel reluctant and not trained in this capacity, but tying in monies with what clients want to achieve is a good way to get clients on track. Will clients hire left-brain thinkers who may be able to relate and connect better as compared to right-brain thinkers who tend to be more analytical?" asks Marston. This is more of an immediate client need and not a timed goal to get to the future. One way for advisors to accomplish this is to spend more time talking, visiting, and being attentive with clients and less time on the spreadsheets.

"A basic premise is, what are people going to pay you to do in 10 years? Also, what changes need to be made sooner, such as in six weeks perhaps, to get started on those most critical issues? You need to lay the groundwork for how and what your clients will be thinking.

"One way to make your practice relevant through the re-architecture of financial services is to pay attention to the changing demographics. A good approach is to share duties and responsibilities and do things for clients that others could not do based on the nature of the relationship."

There are many generational differences in financial advising. Marston says, "A major factor in building successful client relationships is the likeability factor, which emphasizes the advisor's ability to establish a connection or rapport consistently with both prospects and clients." We need to understand a one-size-fits-all approach toward marketing will simply not work due to where each generation is currently. Marston goes on to state, "Part of the issue is that each generation has a different investing and financial outlook according to their life and career stages. In addition, each has different attitudes toward different financial instruments, strategies, products and means of investment planning and savings." The bottom line is that the planner needs to develop a specific niche-marketing and technical approach when reaching out to these different target markets.

There's a much harder balance for parents, though. Marston says the client needs to keep their "eyes on the prize." Parents may have contributions in a variety of capacities for their children under the age of 30, for a much longer period of time, and until later ages. Focus on children/education and retirement. For example, according to the *Journal of Abnormal Psychology* in 2019, an analysis of a federal survey showed increasing rates of teen and young adult respondents reporting a major depressive episode in the past 12 months. Rates have stayed more consistent among older adults.

"It's all about relationships and hand holding. That's what clients want and desire," say Rick Konrad and Vicki Fillet of Roosevelt Investment Group and Wealth Management, New York. Konrad and Fillet use an integrated approach. In coaching their clients, they start with education, build trust and client longevity, and learn how to tailor aspects specifically for the client vs. using a robo/outside-the-box approach. They do not use a cookie-cutter approach. They adhere to their clients' needs. "Many times, we see women prefer to work with women advisors of the firm because they may be more open to share information they may not be comfortable providing to a man," says Fillet.

Scott Kahan says when coaching and communicating with clients, never ask questions starting with "Why?" Planners must develop listening skills which will help in understanding the behavioral aspects of clients. Kahan learned this a long time ago. The last person to speak loses! Say what you need and then have the client communicate their issues and concerns to you.

"Some people care about their money more than their life. You need to solve a problem for the client, not sell a product. Help them be a better person by helping them make better choices with better information. That's how big the opportunity is," says Cheryl Holland of Abacus, Columbia, South Carolina. Either you understand it or you don't. And if you don't, you won't be here in this profession long enough. You will never hear a doctor say, I'll be on the golf course today at 2pm. Financial planners shouldn't do that, either, because you'd be doing a disservice to the profession and to your clients, and would be incredibly dishonest to yourself.

Industry change and artificial intelligence are helping resolve the back issues of information. Helping clients understand and sort through this is the challenge. Rossi talks about using software and concludes that once you get into it, it is brutal to get out of it. It was set up a la carte back then. Companies understand the planner's overreliance on it.

"There is a tremendous demand for what we do vs. the tremendous supply, which is why our pricing remains intact. The need for advice is not going away," says Holland. "People want to sit down with someone. The evolution will be toward niche oriented." There are two types of people in this world, says Rossi: people with problems and people who will have problems. Figure out what your main thing is. Intergenerational clients tend to be older and have more components for you to deal with. In either case, "choose a lane where you can add value and own it," suggests Rossi.

In designing her firm, Holland does a good job of defining her niche, developing strategy, and developing people. She says, "Our culture is strong and recognizable to provide a meaningful and unique fit. Either you fit or you don't. Makes for a better team environment and a highly processed driver."

In the next 10 years, Holland sees a trend toward virtual teams vs. physical teams as a way of accommodating behavioral transitions of clients. She says, "We will continue going toward a silo model creating vertical teams, solving needs that are unique to that client. Whoever comes on deck takes care of work that comes in. Software is getting more expensive since many models are going toward pay per user. With fewer people because of technology, the cost of it is getting more as a result. I think more state regulation will take shape." Lastly, Holland's hope and assumption is that the planning profession will become a more gender-equal and diverse group of advisors.

"From 40-odd players in 1983 to three major players today, we act as price takers and not price makers. Businesses don't change. We are here to help clients solve their financial problems. The nature of these problems has changed over time but there are still and will always be problems. That's why it's important for us to be on top of behavior modifications, which will help us to continue to evolve into an intellectual capital business," says Rossi. If you want to solve problems, you will have to know how it works. Life is not an algorithm. Be thoughtful about pricing intellectual capital.

INTELLECTUAL CAPITAL/STRUCTURING THE MODEL FIRM FOR THE 2020s

Intellectual capital is a great way of describing the value of our practice and what we bring to the table. It is a combination of objective and subjective measures. Objectively it is the value of all the knowledge, financial, and physical assets on the balance sheet, skill sets represented, industrywide training, including firmwide capability and capacity, ideas of the staff within the practice, and other informational resources the practice has at its disposal. These factors can then be used to drive and increase market share and profits, maintain the best office staff working environment and the customer base, provide new services, and revisit products.

It is also comprised of subjective measures since it puts a dollar value on a host of intangibles (not fully defined with a specific dollar amount on the company balance sheet), including goodwill and environment. This gives us a competitive advantage in an organization, a working environment, benefit to society, and a return of capital. The transformation of human capital (discussed previously) into a structural capital environment can be considered the mission of intellectual capital.

"Seeing the consolidation from some 40-odd players in 1980 to a handful of major players today, we live in a world where there are fewer price makers and more price takers," says Rossi. "Client needs haven't fundamentally changed. We are here to help clients solve their financial problems. The technicals of their problems have changed over time but their fundamental problems haven't. This profession will continue to evolve into an intellectual capital business." If you want to solve problems, you will have to know how to solve problems. Portfolio construction and management may be addressed by AI and algorithms, but clients' lives are not algorithmic. Build your intellectual capital, learn how to solve more complex problems, and you'll be in a better position to price for it.

MARKETING

1. Know your target market
2. Set up a professional advisory board
3. Set up a client advisory board
4. Be dedicated in getting to know, understand, and motivate your clients
5. Find a qualified mentor
6. It's all about referrals
7. Obtain a professional designation
8. Host a client event
9. Send out birthday cards, personal notes, and thank-you letters
10. Write articles, be featured in industry/trade publications, and speak to industry/trade groups
11. Make your website professional
12. Become an industrywide consumer speaker starting with local employers.
13. Start a blog
14. Use social media
15. Provide regular/weekly contact to clients

What's the outlook for marketing during this upcoming decade? A continued reliance on technological and social outlets for starters. Marketing does not automatically become easier through the use of technology. If anything, it may require more responsiveness and awareness to consistently advertise your services. Here are some ways to begin thinking about getting your firm to the next level.

Know your target market

In your existing practice, spend some time deciphering the types of clients you have attracted since you became an advisor. Many business owners have not broken down their constituencies into different groupings. One of the chief benefits of this approach is you'll determine which types of clients you like working with, begin to focus on them, and not make overtures to the others. As we consistently learn in life, you can't be all things to all people! It is much more advantageous to be focused on those niches that make the most sense for the type of practice you run.

Set up a professional advisory board

When I set up my initial business structure, including an advisory practice of which education, industry consulting, tax and financial planning, and conference planning were all part of the conglomerate, I wanted qualified individuals with professional expertise to act as a sounding board for my suggestions and rationale. Mind you, this was my first experience of going into business on my own, back in 1997. I have had the good fortune to know many movers and shakers nationally from all over the United States whom I asked to be a part of my professional advisory board and I ran through with them my ideas for going out on my own. We would meet by phone once a month for several months in the beginning.

I wrote out my mission statement, business plan, and marketing plan for each of them to review. I asked general questions, sought guidance on detailed explanations of industry-specific issues, asked what each did right and wrong when they went into business for themselves, among other things that I should be concerned with.

Before I left my employer at that time (the Institute of Certified Financial Planners (ICFP) in Denver, CO) and tried to make it on my own, I wanted good, objective feedback, both pros and cons, and have them basically tell me the way it was! As a New Yorker, I am straightforward, direct, and blunt in my thoughts and assessments, and am not appreciative of beating around the bush. (My CFP® education classes, CPA CE classes, and general lectures are run like that, too!) And the board members whom I counted on were as well. They told me what made sense and what did not, what they liked and what they didn't, what I wanted to hear and what I didn't, and what they would pursue and what they wouldn't. All great information, certainly overwhelming. They were not shy and I was most appreciative. I could not have paid money for formal consultations and received better advice. When it was all said and done, I made the move. Best thing ever! As I say always in life, sometimes you just got to go with your gut. And I did.

One of the points worth noting was a one-on-one conversation I had with my board member, the legendary Harold Evensky. He said to me, "Jeff, don't try to overthink this. You have great ideas on paper and a very specific purpose that you need to focus on and stay away from the rest. You have the right background. You know many of the players. You need to give it a shot. And in a worst-case scenario, if it doesn't work, you'll go out and get a job!" I thought to myself, wow, what a revelation. How simple and profound. And he was right! If it didn't work out, I would go back to what I know. I have consistently worked Harold's mantra into much of what I consult on and for others to whom I give advice.

Set up a client advisory board

Taking strategy 1 to another level, this is a personal favorite of mine. Here's a very practical approach. Take all of your existing clients and label them into three groupings, "A," "B," and "C." The "A" clients are the ones you love to work with. You can't have enough of them! The "B" clients you like to work with. They are fun and satisfying, but not at the same level as the "A" clients. The "C" clients you'd like to put on irrevocable waivers. There is a disconnect there between the client and yourself, but they are still holding on for whatever reason.

Ask 12 clients (couples or singles) to volunteer and help you grow your business. You alert them that you wish to add personal financial planning services to your business repertoire, or perhaps add other ancillary types of services to your existing practice. I did this initially with my existing tax clients so I might expand into providing personal financial planning advice to those same clients and potentially others. I had five As, five Bs, and two Cs on each board. The reason I had two Cs in there was to help see the disconnect. I was interested to know what else they would like to see or experience and perhaps what they were expecting that I wasn't providing them at that point.

In exchange for their commitment, I provided them complimentary financial plans for the first two years or for the length of service on the board. I had six clients rotate off the board each year. Some of the initial group were asked to serve for three years, others two years. They gave me strong definitive advice which came from the heart, both pro and con, which I particularly like and treasure. Everything from expectations, communications, pricing, services, to follow-up, etc. would be discussed. We would meet quarterly for breakfast or dinner, which was on me.

The results were phenomenal – they showed what I was doing right and reassured me, and brought to my attention things I was doing wrong for each of these groups. It also confirmed why I loved working with As, liked working with Bs, and what I could do to help transition my C clients into Bs or As as a potential longshot. Probably most beneficial to these volunteers was that I'd honor them at the annual dinner in front of all my clients. And when they rotated off the board, I'd make a short speech about their service or interests and honor them with a plaque for all their help. You can't imagine the line of clients approaching me during that evening and asking me to serve and help in that capacity.

Be dedicated in getting to know, understand, and motivate your clients

In strategies 1 and 3 above, have ongoing contact with the clients on the issues pertinent to them. Many clients want to go through the formal process, but others are looking for the relationship to feel safe. Begin by asking them personalized questions, like what can money do for you, how important is it to attain the amount of money you want at that particular point in time, how do family decisions factor into the equation, and do you want to be fully involved in the actual planning process? Constant contact in getting to know your clients involves monitoring the financial plan, monthly phone calls or live meetings, or other aspects where you and the client are in constant communication. The more involvement and contact, the better the working relationship will be.

One way to accomplish this is to customize service for your clients. You need to know the reasons behind where your clients are coming from and where they wish to go in order to best customize your service. You can't wing it. Most firms don't take it up to this level to properly get to know and understand their clients. It's not about the money. If you focus on what's listed here, the objectives outlined, the activities and events that are relevant, and the order of each, it will assure where the money will come from. Understanding the strategies we have outlined in the behavioral finance section represents a great starting point.

Find a qualified mentor

I'm a huge believer in learning on someone else's nickel. To me, it's not about the money upfront. Getting a proper framework and understanding the landscape you are operating in, how to approach issues, how to listen and understand, and how to follow up are critical components for success. As I tell my students, this isn't rocket science. You will learn it. But you need to be smart about it. Put yourself in a position to succeed. Having a solid game plan to start off and get running is important.

Having someone show you the ropes is key even if it means sacrificing money up front or leaving it on the table. Remember, there is plenty of money to go around. Sometimes learning from someone else and paying a little upfront to reduce the minimal production time allocation necessary to commence is the most valuable lesson you can take from getting started or deciding to work in a different area or platform. Doing it for a year and then going on your own with a game plan to follow is important. This will also shorten the learning curve and help you come out of the game running. Asking your existing professionals about mentoring, contacting a trade or membership association, from a local university advisor or financial planning program housed at the school, or even on the web, are good starting points for meeting with, interviewing, and determining whether you see the world the same way and thus are able to use an approach you believe is consistent with what you want to achieve. The better you know your audience, the more focused and on top of your marketing you will be.

It's all about referrals!

I never have any issues about asking for referrals. I have used that approach with all of my CFP® Fast Track classes over the last 31 years as well as my tax and financial planning clients and other industries in which I operate. The bottom line is I tell my clients, students, and others that if you like what I have done for you, I would truly appreciate you referring me to someone who can stand to benefit from the services I provide.

I have found that people genuinely like to help out, and if clients and students truly like you and want to be part of the process to help you grow your business, they will want their friends and family to benefit from your expertise. Many clients will graciously take you up on that and recommend your service to friends and family.

Obtain a professional certification

The CFP® certification at www.cfp.net is the highest level that encompasses the financial planning process. There are other designations available and specialty off-shoot designations and certifications as well that deal with related areas within the financial planning process.

Host a client event

As I mentioned earlier, having an annual (or perhaps more frequently) client appreciation dinner is a wonderful display of connecting with your clients. Examples could include a charity or fun golf outing, dancing and dining event, local chamber of commerce event, or something relevant and important from your community that holds meaning. These would be great ways to continually reconnect with your clients.

Other times attending a live local networking event can provide you with exposure and show how you would like to be identified in the community, and help you in meeting key centers of influence. Online networking enables you to search the name of your community to find local online groups and associations. When you correspond in those settings, your name will pop up to everyone else as someone with similar interests. It is a very efficient way to meet new individuals, and to market yourself while growing your professional network.

Send out birthday cards, personal notes, and thank-you letters

Unfortunately, this does not occur much anymore. Yet with technology where it is, this should be pretty easy to maintain and follow through with. Personalizing notes as if you are a regular member of the family or simply as a good friend carries a lot of weight. It adds a sense of loyalty and trust where bonding becomes more prevalent. Certainly, after you are hired or referred by the client, sending out a couple of sentences as a handwritten and sincere thank-you letter will go a long way.

Write articles, be featured in industry/trade publications, and speak to industry/trade groups

When I was employed as the Technical Manager at the AICPA's Personal Financial Planning Division in New York City in the late 1980s and early 1990s, I learned the key to getting ahead and rising to the next level was through my writing, speaking, and becoming known in the industry. As a result, I worked on getting published for those reasons. I thought showcasing myself as an expert and aligning myself with industry players would enable me to climb up the ladder and secure other writing assignments and speaking gigs. I also decided that becoming a financial trainer for some of the larger financial services organizations, and becoming an industry consultant would help me accomplish these objectives. I was right.

Doing these things allows you to become known as "the specialist" in your chosen field, someone who truly understands what the issues are and how to keep a sharp eye and focus on the opportunities that arise every so often. Many times, trade publications are looking for fresh content, so they will be willing to showcase a new and/or different point of view. Push and defend several ideas on ways you can reach your targeted audience through the publication or event. Don't be a generalist but make it specific to the trade or industry you are trying to reach.

Local clubs and organizations are constantly looking for speakers to visit their groups. Consider charitable groups, educational institutions, companies experiencing downsizing, and other venues that could help those in need or provide a framework on how to do certain financial things going forward. Your role is to come off as the "go-to expert" in that particular area.

Make your website professional

If you plan on taking this business seriously and want to grow it based on our discussions thus far, spend the time to make your website look professional. First impressions, which can be formed in virtually no time, will dictate how seriously viewers will take your business. You can also try out new and different elements on a regular basis to see what sticks and what is well received. Working with an outside designer or even someone to provide you constructive feedback would be a great place to start. Having your face present on the website will help increase conversations and generate a human emotional connection.

Become an industrywide consumer speaker, starting with local employers

When I moved to Denver from New York to take a job with CFP Board, I was afforded the ability to continue working on tax returns as I had done in New York while at the AICPA. One of the things I did was to make myself known around my new home. I approached municipalities, unions, and other businesses in the area and explained to them the benefit of having me present to their employees and explain their company retirement plans, essentially as an extension of human resources. I did not charge fees for being there to present. We did lunchtime presentations once or twice per month. Sometimes it carried over to cover other relevant and integrated topics.

At that time, before the internet, other than handing out a business card (what's that?), my presentation included all of my contact information on the cover page. Attendees tended to keep the handout after the presentation. What that did for me was make me the informal go-to person from that company. Bottom line was that even though I was never officially recommended by any of the companies I presented for, when employees had an issue (and there was always something that came up) with any financial topic, including insurance, investing, retirement, education, and taxes, to name a few, the employees called me! I built a business using that approach. And now with technological follow-up better than ever, getting to know and communicating with these types of workers should be even easier.

Start a blog

Blogging gives your prospects and clients a cheap way to get across a targeted message on a regular basis. This marketing approach, which can be updated as often as the advisor wants, even daily if you have time, gives advisors the ability to develop content that will resonate with the wants and needs of their target audience. Blogging lets your clients know who you are by essentially branding you with opinions, stories, anecdotes, photos, videos, and other ways of having your personality shine through to your clients. It makes those prospects and clients who are interested in what you have to say to catch on by following you live and reading or listening to your updates. It can create streamlining opportunities for those who have a genuine interest in a particular category by allowing the end user to type into the search bar select key words to gain additional relevant information.

You can make those individuals aware of what is happening in your practice or in current events right now, and more importantly how that will impact them. The content could become an asset of your practice. It could also encourage community engagement by giving the reader the opportunity to voice their opinion about the ideas you have produced and chosen to focus on, and encourage social media usage by having that content shared through various social media channels. It also gives readers a vehicle to ask questions about your services or even offer feedback. Having a blog provides credibility in your niche specialty.

Incorporate social media. Social media marketing involves using social media platforms to connect with an audience whereby you can build and showcase your brand, increase sales, and drive website traffic. This will enable you to reach all of your connections at the same time in one swift, single action. From an efficiency standpoint, it doesn't become any easier than this. It is a more effective and productive way of sharing information and communicating with clients.

As an added plus, it can introduce you to new connections based on common interests you have identified. You would accomplish this through the publication of strong content on your social media profiles, listening to and engaging with your followers, analyzing your results, and running social media advertisements. Some of the benefits you can achieve through social media are establishing social media goals and objectives, researching the competition, and creating a social media calendar. It may be advisable to hire an individual for your firm to stay on top of this channel.

Provide regular/weekly contact through meetings, calls, chats and other means with your clients. There is nothing like repetition. We have all heard the more times we get up to bat, the more hits we are going to get. In business terms, the more we approach our clients and let them know we are with them, the better it will be for connecting with and ultimately benefiting them, which in turn will benefit us.

To continue this regular contact, I encourage advisors, students, and even clients to hire their children to work for them to head up their social media component. It's effective and cheap! Let's face it, young people are well versed on most things technological, including perhaps running your social media operations. What I've done in my tax and financial planning practices is to create a weekly letter to provide a discussion piece for marketing purposes – essentially, letting the client know I am there, I care, and please bring me your thoughts if I can be of any assistance to you. Then give that letter to your child and have him or her do a mass mailing for you, perhaps once a week, to your clients. In addition, if surveys are offered, responses are requested, or other immediate feedback is needed, the child can tally the individual responses and keep track of them.

This reaching out to your clients on a regular basis, essentially creating this "drip marketing" campaign, provides constant communication and helps reinforce the planner–client relationship. The cost and time commitment for the child is minimal. Children enjoy being a part of helping and contributing to the family in its core business.

And best of all, instruct the advisor that whatever the children earn remains theirs, to use to fund college, for instance, as savings for other objectives, now or in the future, and to set them up with a nest egg for their personal use. As a legitimate business expense, it can count as an ordinary and necessary deduction for the advisor and as taxable income for the child. With this reportable earned income, the child can contribute to an IRA, SEP, etc. to shelter some of the money and tax hit and to truly have savings for a rainy day. It is clearly a win/win for the planner and for the child.

Remember, you don't have to pick any one marketing idea. Marketing is all about trying many alternatives – as we used to say in New York, "Throw the spaghetti against the wall and see what sticks!" Certainly, working through as many ideas as possible will enable you to get the most from the process, which is putting your name, company, and specialty in front of others all of the time.

CHAPTER 3

Developing a Well-Thought-Out Personal Financial Plan

The purpose of the financial planning process is to provide a well-thought-out plan based on the planner gaining an understanding of client wishes and desires to help determine whether they can then become client realities. An understanding of what those client issues are, coupled with any exposures that may put them at a greater risk, and the ability to find appropriate solutions to determine a path toward those objectives, makes for a well-thought-out plan. Our role as an advisor is to understand and realize those paths.

Clients need to seek a coordinated approach to the multiple facets of the daily and lifetime financial needs of clients. Some clients may be too busy to learn what they need to know, some may want to defer to the experts, others simply want you to do it with minimal involvement from them. That certainly is the wrong way to proceed.

Like the financial planner, the client should understand what is expected of them up front and as a part of entering into the relationship with the planner. To be successful, clients need to have "skin in the game." They have to proclaim ownership. They have to understand the ins and outs of the financial decisions affecting them. As I say to my students, your clients need to use a similar approach. It's one thing to be a part of the process; it's another to receive direction without a true understanding of how it could affect them if things don't go as expected. Clients cannot be at liberty to state that if something doesn't work, who can we blame?

As the hired financial planner, we develop a well-thought-out plan to bring the different components together. As the "quarterback" or coordinator of the different functions that clients need to address, we can help ensure that the process is working as well as possible. The client benefits from having one "go-to" person in their corner who can work with the various experts required to develop a comprehensive financial plan, and who can help them understand the language of those experts. Financial planning consists of six major components: cash flow management, insurance, investments, income tax planning, retirement planning and estate planning, and perhaps a variety of outside areas relevant to a particular client. These components track the financial concerns of the client and are discussed in detail in the following chapters.

As stated, the hired financial planner must act for the exclusive benefit of the client at all times and must put the interests of the client ahead of the planner's own interests, essentially representing the duty of a fiduciary. If the client does not trust the planner (or will not take their advice), they are better off working with another planner. The reverse is true as well.

This is one of the most rewarding professions out there. You get to see the output of what you helped the client create and strive for. With the clients I started with a long time ago, it is personally satisfying to help them out. An example would be working with them when they first got married, to having children, to advancing in their careers, to attending their children's college graduations, and knowing that you were able to assist them in achieving their stated objectives. The list goes on and on.

Before financial planning became a profession, individuals typically sought the advice of many specialists, who too often did not communicate with each other and whose advice sometimes created conflicts with the advice of other advisors. This haphazard approach often meant that the plans prepared by one advisor could not be carried out because of the work of another advisor. Our purpose here is to eliminate those concerns by providing useful, thought-out ways of approaching client dilemmas and concerns.

The following concepts provide the basis for planning discussions and opportunities on what we need to do in providing a better financial planning experience for our clients.

Rattiner's Secrets on "The Making" of the Client Experience

Getting Through to Our Clients: Making Sure We Are on the Same Page

Relating with Clients
Communicating with Clients
Nonverbal Behaviors
Listening Skills
Steps in the Personal Financial Planning Process

GETTING THROUGH TO OUR CLIENTS: MAKING SURE WE ARE ON THE SAME PAGE

In speaking with thousands of advisors, from the results of my own practice, and lecturing for the past 30-odd years, the one common and consistent denominator for planner/client success is in "managing our clients' expectations." It sounds so simple . . . and it is!

Managing client expectations means they are fully expecting what will happen and won't be surprised by the reality and the fine print. Clients will be ready for the outcome since they were prepped in advance to understand this could be an actual occurrence. I always tell my students that the sure sign of a successful financial planner is when the market goes down by 20% and you get no client phone calls! Why? Mama says there will be days like that! The fact is that the market has gone up and down throughout our measurable history. It's not "if" it goes down but "when." On the flipside, managing these expectations can alert the client to the possibility that if things go in a certain direction, such as down, it may present them with a great buying opportunity in the not too distant future. The point is, they won't be alarmed and won't go into panic mode and begin listening to the media signs they will be bombarded with.

For example, have you ever gone out to purchase a car and thought you negotiated a deal in the showroom only to find that when you got behind the closed door of the financing arm, it didn't look quite the same as you envisioned just a short while ago? That's the concept of managing client expectations. As a result, that client/car buyer is likely to walk out of the showroom without a deal.

Mark Milic thinks it's crucial to manage expectations from day one as you don't want to let down your client before having a chance to even serve them. He says, "It's like striking out before you even had a chance to bat. Many clients have had poor relationships prior to entering your office, and understanding where things went wrong in their previous relationships will give us a chance to serve them at a higher level. You will only know the answer to this by asking many open-ended questions, including using the phrase 'Tell me more' constantly." Milic adds the following, which I feel is right on target: "The vast majority of my initial meeting is listening, probing, and asking questions and trying to find 'the need behind the need.'"

Milic goes on to say, "Recognizing the type of prospective client you're about to spend the next 60–90 minutes with is incredibly important for the advisor because it will dictate the tone and direction of the meeting and you only find this out by listening and asking questions up front."

Managing client expectations isn't just important at the start of the client relationship; it is part of the ongoing process where both sides know what is expected and where things stand. Incorporating that approach will surely make everyone operate on the same page and reduce the potential for damaging lawsuits.

RELATING WITH CLIENTS

Part of managing expectations with clients means gaining an understanding of where the client is coming from and where they would like to be. The client and the planner need to discuss attitudes, values, and built-in biases since clients are not always rational and may have limits to their self-control. It is necessary to consider these behavioral finance concerns since each client is starting out from a different planning position. This formalized process looks at what the client has experienced throughout their lifetime. The planner's objectives are to hear the client and translate that information into a more defined process through the development of a personal financial plan.

"We need to ask questions of the client that make them comfortable in providing pinpointed answers," says Derek Lawson. Begin with "Mr. and Mrs. Client, what's on your mind" and other leading questions to get them to start opening up, says Lawson. Allow them quiet time. Frame your discussions and meetings from the behavioral side. You don't want to go too fast, where the responses are "Yes, but . . . ." The clients won't get it. Rephrase and reframe their answers to ensure that you are understanding and listening to their responses. Provide that value proposition where you are relying on their output vs. deferring to a computer.

The setting of the meeting can also have an effect. Lawson says sometimes it may be better to meet clients in their homes, or perhaps virtually, where you can still observe their body movements and see their immediate surroundings. That could provide you with a better perspective of who the client is and where they are coming from. Have the conversation revolve around the client's goals. What's really valuable to them? Don't use a cookie-cutter approach. "The planner needs to communicate with clients to increase their motivation, otherwise you will lose them," says Lawson.

It becomes tougher than it looks because the client is approaching the table with unexpected attitudes, as is the planner. Many examples come into play.

- Clients from foreign countries may have values and behaviors that are different from those of the planner.
- Family background can create certain expectations for an individual concerning budgeting and saving, in many categories, such as raising and educating children.
- Divorcing clients may generate anxiety. Perhaps the individual who had nothing to do with the finances previously now needs to become involved and take responsibility. Further, the reduced resources available coupled with a shorter time span to accomplish specific objectives make it quite challenging.
- Nontraditional and blended families may not be accustomed to a sudden change in funding. An example would be the lack of health and retirement benefits that could be available to more traditional families, thus requiring additional planning scenarios to fulfill the family's needs. The end result is a way to overcome those biases and boundaries and for the planner and the client to be on the same page.
- Emotional issues simply cannot be dismissed because they were formulated for whatever reason over a period of time. This could affect budgeting and savings capabilities. They need to be included into the goal- and objective-setting process of the financial plan.
- Younger clients may not see the urgency of saving for later-term objectives, such as retirement, or perhaps planning their estate. Many of them may prefer to live in the present.
- When attitudes conflict with the attainment of select objectives, that could pose a challenge for the planner. An example would be the "market timing client" wanting to ignore the planner's advice and do their own thing. Or for those who have had a bad experience with a planner and the market, giving them the opportunity to overcome their

experiences in order to gain an understanding of how financial planning can be used for their benefit could prove the ultimate reward.

- Conflict may arise if a younger married couple with children start the financial planning process and disagree over issues such as education funding, purchasing a car or house, and even retirement. How to organize those objectives which could conflict with the savings mechanism could pose a challenge.

- Planners need to consider clients' capacity for risk and their ability to overstate their acceptance and tolerance for risk. Not everyone has the same tolerance for risk. Much of that can be determined through past experiences, age, and clients' ability to rebound and up the ante at a later date. Risk appears in all areas of financial planning. Many clients call themselves "risk averse." I don't believe that is a legitimate term. To me, clients are loss averse, where they don't want to realize losses and assume they can make significant gains by taking perhaps unnecessary chances. For example, in investment planning I say to the client, "How will you feel if tomorrow the market goes down by 20%? Will you lose sleep over that?" And unfortunately, that is a reality, as we have seen in the recent past. Clients need to buy into the philosophy and realities of investing. Another example is in insurance. Can the client have a plan for managing risk that does not include the purchasing of insurance? If not, can they withstand losses? In retirement planning, how will the client feel if they end up underfunding their retirement objectives? In estate planning, what happens if the right people don't receive the right assets? You can certainly go on with different disciplines and varying tolerances for risk.

- Value-driven planning clients seek to develop a financial plan that serves goals and objectives reflecting the client's spiritual, emotional, and personal needs in addition to their financial needs. The reflection of one's priorities and needs is the key. For example, asking a client what they would try to accomplish in life if they had sufficient cash to do what they would like to, or if the client were likely to pass away soon, how they would live their life going forward.

Milic states that it is imperative to watch your client's reaction as you discuss these important topics. "Too often the client's eyes will glaze over and they will not process the important point you are trying to make. We need to use every tactic possible to help the client process the most relevant points within the financial plan, which can include a dramatic pause during your presentation or directly challenging your client to be certain of the point you are making."

COMMUNICATING WITH CLIENTS

Communication is a critical skill for financial planners to master. There are proper ways to help clients during this process and to ensure the information you receive is relevant in the planning process.

Interviewing is the primary method for gathering data and retrieving relevant information about clients. Information to be gathered includes the identification of the client's financial goals and objectives. The financial planner may need to ask follow-up questions to make certain that these goals are clearly and fully communicated. Many planners use a data-gathering questionnaire/fact finder to consolidate the information needed during the process. This helps set the stage in step one of the financial planning process, discussed below.

Planners may directly ask the clients matter-of-fact questions which generally control the direction and pace of the questioning. These "closed-end" questions can be an appropriate way of attaining information in an efficient way. Examples include where the client works, job title, occupation, and names of family members. Unfortunately, they do not allow for the sharing of thoughts and feelings.

To really understand the circumstances surrounding the client, use open-ended interview questions enabling the client to control more of the pace and direction of the dialogue, flow, and exchange of information. This enables the client to expound on ideas, opinions, feelings, and desires. The planner is more flexible in this setting by enabling the client to provide more in-depth responses and explanations.

If the planner gives more specific direction to the client, that is called advising. Advising can be beneficial where the planner has expertise in a particular area. If the planner shares in a two-way communication for the purpose of establishing a working alliance, that is called counseling. Here the planner is collaborating with the client to find ways to reach financial goals and is not just directing the way the client should approach a particular solution.

NONVERBAL BEHAVIORS

Nonverbal behaviors are ways to communicate without words. The body, through facial expression and eye contact, and the voice, through tone and pitch, are the primary sources. For example, body movements can communicate subtle messages to a planner who pays close attention, and body movements are often more straightforward than verbal statements. Facial expressions and eye contact help express fear, suspicion, trust, self-esteem, or even concern about what the planner is doing. Voice tone can be loud or soft, pitch can be high or low, which may show anger, hostility, or excitement through a high voice, or shyness, fear, and depression with a low voice. This inconsistency between what is said and what is not said helps determine whether the planner recognizes when there is a lack of harmony.

During this decade there will be a bigger push to meet virtually with clients, and this may not relay this nonverbal behavior as freely as would a live meeting. With telephone calls and other auditory devices being used more frequently as well, all of this is missed, and the planner loses a golden opportunity to be able to read the client and plan adjustments that may need to be made.

Milic says that when he talks about sensitive topics such as spending, sometimes he witnesses different body language coming from different types of clients, and often these subtleties give him an insight as to who the spender is.

LISTENING SKILLS

Active listening requires the planner to focus on what the client is trying to communicate. The recognition of verbal and nonverbal signals is important for planners to have empathy for the client's feelings, to understand the message from the client's perspective, and to be able to respond in order to facilitate client understanding. "When the client is not listening to you, they are reducing their trust in you," says Lawson. I subscribe to this approach by providing a restatement response, essentially paraphrasing or repeating what the client has said in their own words, to ensure that I have interpreted the client message correctly before moving on. "By taking an active listening approach, the client can really hear what you are talking about," says Lawson.

STEPS IN THE PERSONAL FINANCIAL PLANNING PROCESS

Once the planner and the client, or even the prospect, begin to understand one another, they are now in a position to work together with minimal interruptions. Many players in our industry have their own definition and steps within the financial planning process. To make it a logical and easy-to-follow method of operation, I will be incorporating seven steps in the financial planning process. There are some similarities to other methods of teaching the process, including some overlap with those discussed by CFP Board in its revised Code of Ethics. My steps can be summarized with the following acronym.

(LIADPIM):

1. Learning and Understanding the Client's Personal and Financial Circumstances.
2. Identifying, Evaluating, and Selecting Objectives.
3. Analyzing the Client's Current Course of Action and Potential Alternative Course(s) of Action.
4. Developing the Financial Planning Recommendations.
5. Presenting the Financial Planning Recommendations.
6. Implementing the Financial Plan.
7. Monitoring the Financial Plan.

Within each step, we'll break down the components by discussing and answering the question "What is it?" (the premise behind the issue), and share the "exposures" (to the client) and Rattiner's Secrets to be considered when addressing them.

1. LEARNING AND UNDERSTANDING THE CLIENT'S PERSONAL AND FINANCIAL CIRCUMSTANCES

What is it? The financial planning process is made up of seven important steps. Each step is critical for a successful client relationship, even if the activities taken in each step vary from client to client. Establishment of the client–planner relationship sets the expectations of the parties and lays the groundwork for developing the trust required for successful financial planning.

What is the exposure to the client? Effective planners are trusted advisors. This first step is critical in establishing this trust along with determining general expectations as to how the process will benefit the client. If the client enters into the process with a planner who is not trusted, the process will likely result in a failure to implement the recommended plan and a dissatisfied client.

You need to be bold and direct. If a client's expectations are off-base and not realistic, you need to say so! State that based on your initial review of their financial situation, there is little, if any, likelihood that their objectives can be accomplished. If the client's sole purpose for visiting your office is to look for the next phenomenal stock and other little-watched investments that are likely to become part of the Fortune 500 inductees, you need to tell them that it's very unlikely to happen. I go further and state that if I knew how to pick these types of stocks, don't take offense, but I'd be doing this on my own account and not for anyone else!

In my personal tax and financial planning practice, I turn down about 80% of the prospects that enter my office because of what I have been repeating: I will not be able to manage their expectations. Think of it this way. If you and the client are starting off in different places, then you are likely to end up in different places. It's not worth the hassle, headache, or potential lawsuit implications. There are more than enough qualified clients out there. Enough said.

Be blunt and direct with the client. The client is coming to you because there are potentially issues they need assistance with. If that were not the case, they could deal with those concerns themselves. As stated, we have to know where our clients have been and where they need to go. They need direction, guidance, and flat-out help.

I explain it like this to a client. Say you want to drive from Los Angeles to New York. You know you need to travel east and north. If you start out on I-10, you can probably wing it and figure out how to get there. But wouldn't it be easier and more effective to follow a map, or even better, a navigation system? It would be more efficient since you would get there quicker, and cheaper, incurring less money for fuel, hotels, meals, etc. That's the point! I tell them that's what we will be doing for you. We are providing that navigation system to make sure you get to where you need to go in one piece, with proper guidance, in a manner that is conducive to helping you achieve your objectives.

Rattiner's Secrets: Take time to define the scope of the engagement. This includes:

- identifying the service(s) to be provided
- ensuring that the client realizes that if they change the nature or the scope of the engagement without follow-up written authorization to revise the engagement letter (to be discussed shortly), the financial planner will not expand into those areas

- disclosing the financial planning practitioner's compensation arrangement(s)
- determining the client's and the financial planning practitioner's responsibilities
- making sure the client provides the financial planner with all necessary information to complete the engagement, and that the planner does not guarantee any of that information
- establishing the duration of the engagement
- alerting the client that they have a limited window to provide you with the necessary information to complete their financial plan on a timely basis, otherwise the planning engagement will be terminated
- providing any additional information necessary to define or limit the scope

Practical example: Jacque has been doing financial planning for over 10 years. With many satisfied clients, he wanted to find a way to shorten the process. To reach this goal, prior to the first meeting he sent an outline of what a client could expect from him and what the client was expected to do. When Jacque and the client first meet, data gathering is the first order of business, and Jacque often has to tell the client to drop off various financial and legal documents. Having worked with hundreds of clients over his career, he is also aware that virtually every client wants certain things, so to save time, he assumes all clients want those same things. Within a few months, Jacque noticed that his newer clients were not implementing their plans and weren't even returning his phone calls. What happened? From the beginning, Jacque had no rapport with his clients. They didn't know what to expect from him and too often had no idea what he expected from them. Additionally, he started treating individual clients as part of a group of clones, with certain identical needs and wants. Every client deserves the full attention of the planner, and while some clients may want what practically everyone else wants, they don't want to think of themselves as part of a homogeneous group. Jacque was attempting to shorten the process. Every step is important. With some clients, certain steps take more time than with other clients, but eliminating steps seldom works.

As a part of establishing the client–planner relationship, the financial planner enumerates in writing each task or responsibility that they are assuming for the client. This is the preface for an engagement letter. Have the client initial each item when an understanding is reached on that item.

Without this in writing, the financial planner may miss or improperly understand what is expected of them (and of the client), likely leading to problems in the future.

Engagement letter

There is no better way to make sure your clients are on the same page as you than using an engagement letter. Back in my CPA days, some 40-odd years ago, I learned about the importance of a properly constructed engagement letter and I have been hooked on it ever since.

An engagement letter is a written agreement that describes the financial planning relationship that is about to be entered into by the client and the financial planner. The letter details the scope of the agreement, its terms, conditions, and costs. It spells out the rights and responsibilities of both parties. Essentially, it states the parameters in advance of entering into a formal engagement.

The benefit of the engagement letter is that it minimizes potential disruptions and situations since all the specifics of the relationship between both parties are covered in writing. A carefully drafted agreement, initially with an attorney's help, essentially represents a meeting of the minds by both parties. And of most importance is that the engagement letter is used to set and manage expectations on both sides of the agreement.

An engagement letter is less formal than a contract but still a legally binding document that can be used in a court of law. The client gets the reassurance of knowing when a service will be completed and how much it will cost. The letter also makes it clear whether other costs are involved that are not covered in the agreement, such as required software that must be purchased separately by the client.

The engagement letter spells out the scope of the engagement for services to be performed, whether financial planning (see below) or something else, as well as setting boundaries on the work that is expected to be performed. The letter may also cite services that lie outside the current agreement but may be added in the future as needed, with an estimate of the costs of these additions.

If the relationship is long-term, many companies require their engagement letter to be updated and signed again by the client on an annual basis. This allows for any changes in the business relationship over time and strengthens the legal standing of the document. It also reminds the client of the scope of the agreement, perhaps forestalling "scope creep."

Engagement letters can be obtained through your broker dealer or RIA, online, and through your E&O provider. E&O providers have a strong incentive to provide you with one since it can help reduce the number of claims going forward.

Below are two examples of letters (client communication strategies letter, Figure 3.1, and a sample financial planning engagement letter) representing the types of information you may wish to gather from the client or provide to them in advance of beginning your working relationship to help avoid potential misunderstandings later on. All the information necessary to begin the working relationship needs to be spelled out by you and accepted by the client in its entirety to avoid misunderstanding and to help manage your client's expectations.

You may wish to work with an attorney to help generate your engagement letter to cover the points you wish to include in any type of service you will provide to the client and for any documents that you will be relying on. The purpose for drafting these documents is based on the expectation the client will read, understand, and sign off before you get started. The examples below should not be used as shown but rather as a starting point for items you may wish to include in the preparation of client letters.

Client Engagement Standards

Our purpose is to provide the best financial life planning possible and to build excellent long term relationships with our clients. We believe that the secret to any successful relationship is to have clear expectations from the beginning. We ask that you read the tenets by which we operate, what you can expect from us, and what we expect from you, as our client.

Our Tenets:

I. Financial Life Planning is an ongoing process involving: goal-setting, cash flow planning, risk management, investment management, asset protection, healthcare planning, tax planning, and estate planning.

FIGURE 3.1

   II. Good communication is critical for a mutually beneficial relationship.

  III. We employ a systematic approach to achieve thoroughness and efficiency in providing comprehensive financial life planning services.

  IV. A terrific plan requires a time commitment from you as well as from us.

   V. We believe in a disciplined investment approach based on long term asset allocation. We do not believe it is possible to time or predict market movements.

  VI. We enjoy working with great people who appreciate the true value of our services.

 VII. Everyone should have the opportunity to live a great life. Our goal is to help people achieve this.

VIII. Our fees are based on the complexity of your needs. The fixed annual fee covers all continuing planning services, including investment management. We receive no compensation from any entity other than you.

What We Deliver:

   I. We look at all aspects of your life to create an ongoing financial life plan that fits your goals, values, and resources, as well as maximizes your opportunities.

  II. We assist you all along the way with the "heavy lifting" process of implementing your plan. Then we monitor your plan regularly to make certain that all parts stay relevant and updated.

  III. We keep all your information confidential, safe and secure. Our client portal and office systems employ advanced security features and protocols to protect your data. We share information only as needed with attorneys, accountants, and other professionals with whom you may be working, in order to effect services, quote coverage, or review accounting, insurance, and/or legal service options.

  IV. We strive to return all phone calls within one working day and emails within two working days. We will inform you of any short term deviations from this policy.

   V. We have regular meetings to keep up to date with your plan. We review each of the following at least once a year:

     A. Insurance and risk management

     B. Investments and your investment policy

     C. Estate planning and asset protection

     D. Goal planning and projections, tax planning and cash flow planning

        In addition, we address any issues of concern to you throughout the year.

  VI. We are highly flexible in both the timing of when we are available and methods of communication to make meeting participation convenient for you.

 VII. We manage your accounts within our investment philosophy and process, to help meet your goals in a cost effective manner.

VIII. We commit to always doing our best on your behalf. We are proud to serve in a fiduciary capacity for you. We love what we do and take pride in doing the best job possible.

  IX. We are compensated by client fees only. Our fees are fully disclosed to you and we do not accept any commissions or referral fees.

FIGURE 3.1 *(Continued)*

What We Expect From You:

(Please initial each section to indicate that you understand these statements.)

_____ **I am willing to participate in the Financial Life Planning process as described above on a continuing basis.** Each part of the process is interdependent and requires information or participation.

_____ **I am willing to delegate the implementation and monitoring of my plan to Life Planning Partners, Inc.** Acting without our input or knowledge may affect our ability to provide appropriate advice. You are hiring us to help you enjoy life more fully, and part of this process is to let us do what we do best.

_____ **I agree to be responsive to emails and phone calls within a reasonable period of time.** Many financial planning issues are time sensitive, most especially tax items.

_____ **I agree to provide requested data and documents in a timely fashion.**

_____ **I agree to receive documents electronically either via e-mail or the Client Portal.**

_____ **I understand that Life Planning Partners, Inc. only accepts clients that agree with their investment philosophy and process.** Diversification, asset allocation, and a long-term focus are keys to sound investing. Chasing returns, following tips, giving in to hunches and listening to predictions do not fit our philosophy. We encourage questions to develop comfort and trust with the <u>delegation</u> of investment functions.

_____ **I understand that Life Planning Partners, Inc. will only provide advice on investments selected through their research.** We utilize a large number of investment research sources. It is not time or cost-effective for us to investigate investments that do not fit our investment philosophy.

_____ **I appreciate that Life Planning Partners, Inc. keeps flexible hours for clients as well as for staff.** Deviations from the normal schedule are communicated via company newsletter, email response, and/or through voicemail outgoing message.

_____ **I appreciate that Life Planning Partners, Inc. dress code is casual on days there are no client meetings and on weekends.** Clients are welcome to "drop by" the office but we may be in casual attire.

_____ **I understand that Life Planning Partners, Inc. takes full responsibility for their errors.** You agree to make us aware of errors as soon as they are discovered. We do our best to minimize errors and correct all errors to the best of our ability to make you whole.

_____ **I agree that our relationship needs to be reevaluated if we ever stop enjoying or respecting one another.** We are committed to living our lives from a place of joy and kindness, and hope to have long-lasting, healthy relationships with all of our clients.

_____ **I understand that fees are due on a quarterly basis and are deducted from my account or paid directly by me.** Life Planning Partners, Inc. sets client fees at the end of every even year (2018, 2020, etc.).

FIGURE 3.1 *(Continued)*

My initials above indicate that I understand these statements and have had any questions answered to my satisfaction.

Client Signature: _____ Date: _____

Client Printed Name: _____

Client Signature: _____ Date: _____

Client Printed Name: _____

Advisor Signature: _____ Date: _____

Advisor Printed Name: Carolyn S. McClanahan, CFP®, President, Life Planning Partners, Inc.

www.lifeplanningpartners.com

FIGURE 3.1 *(Continued)*

Client Engagement Standards is used with permission from Carolyn McClanahan, M.D., CFP®

Life Planning Partners, Inc., Jacksonville, FL 32217

Always Be Prepared, Inc., Sample Engagement Letter

February 1, 202X

Mr. and Mrs. Client
123 Main Street
Anywhere, USA

Dear Mr. and Mrs. Client

Always Be Prepared, Inc. (We) are pleased to provide Mr. and Mrs. Need-help Fast (You)/(Your) with the professional services described below. Please review this letter carefully as it outlines the specific services *Always Be Prepared, Inc.* will provide you. This letter covers any and all services we will provide to you as part of this engagement, verbally through consultations, and/or detailed reports in writing.

Our responsibilities to you

1. We will develop a comprehensive personal financial plan for you based on the subject matter listed below under Scope of Engagement. We estimate that the preparation and presentation of this financial plan will take us 10 hours to complete. Our billing rate is $300 per

hour. The $3,000 fee for the development of this financial plan will be broken down as follows:

- 50% due and payable upon the signing of this engagement letter
- 50% due and payable upon the presentation of this financial plan

2. We will meet with you for approximately two hours to complete an interaction data gathering and prioritized objective meeting to allow us to gather the information we will need to complete your personal financial plan. Within five days after this initial meeting occurs, we will provide you with a list of outstanding items we need you to follow up on. Your plan will be completed and ready to discuss with you 30 days after we receive the last outstanding item from you.

3. In constructing the financial plan, we will analyze your financial situation and provide recommendations to satisfy your objectives, when and where appropriate. After we have completed the financial plan, we will meet again with you to review the plan and resulting options.

4. Our recommendations will be only as good as the information you provide us. Specific issues not addressed by you or information not provided to us will directly impact these recommendations.

5. Should you want us to implement the recommendations uncovered from this financial plan, or if you prefer to have other professionals implement the findings from our plan, we will accommodate your request. If we assist with the implementation, we will not receive any commissions or overrides on any transactions.

6. Because of the time frame indicated in satisfying and fulfilling our obligation to you in this engagement, we are not under any obligation to notify you regarding changes in the financial planning landscape, including but not limited to changes in financial markets, changes in tax or other laws, valuations from investment-related products, or landscape/environmental conditions.

7. This engagement concludes at the delivery of your financial plan.

8. Please initial those areas below that you want us to evaluate.

Scope of engagement

We will prepare a financial plan to include the following specific concerns you have brought to our attention:

1. Cash Flow Analysis and Management
2. Insurance Planning Review
3. Education Needs Analysis

4. Investment Planning Review
5. Income Tax Planning
6. Retirement Capital Needs Analysis
7. Estate Planning Analysis
8. Other. Please list _____

Your responsibilities to us

1. We expect you to provide us with all information that we view as necessary in order to successfully complete your financial plan. A listing of additional information not initially provided, but necessary, will be provided to you within five days after our initial meeting. All information will be kept confidential.

2. We are relying on the accuracy and completeness of the information you provide to us in addressing any of the following areas you may want our assistance with, including but not limited to the data-gathering questionnaire and any and all supporting data you provide to us in rendering professional services to you. We do not guarantee the accuracy of any information you provide to us and we are not liable for any errors of fact or judgment on any information provided by you to us as long as we act in good faith.

3. If you provide our firm with copies of brokerage, investment advisory, retirement plan, education/529 statements, insurance policy declaration pages, income tax returns, estate planning documents, budgets and other statements in written and/or read-only access to your accounts, we will rely on the accuracy of the information you provided us in these statements, and we will not undertake any action to verify this information. We recommend you receive and review all statements promptly and carefully, and direct any questions regarding account activity that we are not in a position to answer to your banker, broker, investment advisor, attorney, CPA or other professional, if applicable.

4. You are responsible to pay our fee at the appropriate time stated above and any expenses incurred by us at the time of plan delivery.

Other considerations that are part of this engagement letter

1. You understand that the responsibility for any and all financial decisions rests with you.

2. You are under no obligation to follow through on any of the recommendations made in this personal financial plan.

3. We will not initiate any financial transaction on your accounts without your prior approval.

4. This agreement may be terminated at any time by either party. If you terminate this agreement within 72 hours, you will be refunded any fees paid by you. After that time period, you will not be entitled to any refunds. If you terminate this agreement, all investment recommendations stop immediately.

5. We reserve the right to withdraw from the engagement without completing services for any reason, including if information we request is not received by us by specify the date.

6. You may request that we perform additional services that were not originally spelled out in this engagement letter. If this occurs, we will communicate with you regarding the scope and estimated cost of these additional services. Engagements for additional services may require that we amend this letter or issue a separate engagement letter to reflect the increased responsibilities and obligations of both parties. In the absence of any other written communications from us documenting additional services, our services will be limited to and governed by the terms of this engagement letter.

7. If any portion of this engagement letter is deemed invalid or unenforceable, such a finding shall not invalidate the remainder of the terms set forth in this engagement letter.

8. If we, in our sole discretion, believe a conflict has arisen affecting our ability to deliver services to you in accordance with either the ethical standards of our firm or the ethical standards of our profession, we may be required to suspend or terminate our services without issuing a financial plan.

9. We will return to you all original records and documents that you have given us at the conclusion of this engagement. Our workpapers are the property of our firm and will be maintained by us in accordance with our firm's record retention policy and any applicable legal and regulatory requirements.

10. If a dispute arises out of or relates to this engagement letter, or the breach thereof, and if the dispute cannot be settled through negotiation, the parties agree first to try in good faith to settle the dispute by mediation administered by the American Arbitration Association before resorting to arbitration, litigation, or some

other dispute resolution procedure. The costs of any mediation proceedings shall be shared equally by all parties.

11. This engagement letter, including any attachments, encompasses the entire agreement of the parties and supersedes all previous understandings and agreements between the parties, whether oral or written. Any modification to the terms of this engagement letter must be made in writing and signed by both parties.

12. This letter confirms our understanding of the terms and objectives of our engagement and the nature and limitations of the services we will provide. The engagement between you and our firm will be governed by the terms of this letter.

* * * * * *

We appreciate the opportunity to be of service to you. Please date and sign the enclosed copy of this engagement letter and return it to us to acknowledge your acceptance and agreement with its terms. It is our policy to initiate services only after we receive the executed engagement letter.

Very truly yours,

_____

I.M. Ready
President

Always Be Prepared, Inc.
ACCEPTED BY:

_____   _____
Signature – *Client Name*   Signature – *Client Spouse's Name*

_____   _____
Print *Client Name*   Print *Client Spouse's Name*

_____   _____

2. IDENTIFYING, EVALUATING, AND SELECTING OBJECTIVES

What is it? The crux of financial planning is in the data-gathering and goal-setting step of the process. *No other step is as important.* Adequate data and a clear understanding of the client's objectives are "the roadmap" for the financial plan. This step involves identifying and listing all possible goals the client has an interest in pursuing. Evaluate the relevance and feasibility for attainment of each. Then prioritize the list since clients have limited resources and an overabundance of objectives they wish to pursue. I purposely use the word "objectives" rather than "goals." Goals are open-ended broad statements that the client wishes to achieve. An example of a goal is the client wanting to be rich. Well, what does that mean? How do we define rich? For example, a client may say they wish to retire at age 65 with $2 million in the bank. Another client may say they want to retire at age 60 with an income stream of $200,000 per year. Objectives therefore are quantifiable and definitive. There is a dollar amount and a time attached to each. And since clients have limited resources, it is imperative to prioritize them from most important to least important to make sure the big-ticket items are identified, evaluated, and ultimately selected for attainment.

Rattiner's Secrets: The planner needs to obtain comprehensive financial and personal quantitative data on the client as well as their objectives, needs, and priorities (qualitative data). By the time the data gathering is complete, an experienced planner will have a good idea as to the route to each client's financial success. Assessing the qualitative data tells the planner what motivates the client and why the client will or will not follow the plan.

Here are some examples of both quantitative and qualitative data. Sources of quantitative data:

- all assets and how titled
- all debt – balance, periodic payments, maturity date, and interest rate
- all income and sources
- all outflows and expenses
- all life insurance – type, ownership, insured, death benefit cash values, dividend options, premium, beneficiary, and loans
- earmarked income or assets
- will and trust information
- all other insurance information and particulars
- budgeting information
- all tax and retirement plan information
- personal information
- employment benefits

(continued)

(continued)

Types of qualitative data:

- risk tolerance level (difficult to ascertain accurately for most planners)
- wishes for transfer of assets at death
- all income continuation desires for heirs
- retirement plans – age at retirement and income desired
- inflation and before-tax rate of return estimates
- attitudes about providing education for children and estimated costs
- feelings toward charity
- anticipated income increases throughout career
- changes in lifestyle anticipated, particularly during retirement
- other relatives who may become dependent upon the client in the future
- financial planning goals and priorities
- interests in activities/hobbies
- major capital expenditures in the future
- current and anticipated health

What is the exposure to the client? The primary exposure a client has through this step in the process comes from incomplete or inaccurate information. Most clients have their own field of expertise and do not often understand or remember all of their financial and legal dealings. For example, overstated income expected from a defined benefit pension plan results in inadequate preparation for retirement. Incorrect data about asset ownership can defeat the intent of estate or gift planning documents or plans.

Rattiner's Secrets: Do not shortchange yourself or the client in the gathering of data, qualitative or quantitative. Quantitative tells you where the client is and what it will take to get them to a specific financial goal. Qualitative tells you why they want to reach the goal and what will make them work toward it. Qualitative data will also tell you what they are not likely to do.

Practical example: Paul and Lisa Mumford have an estate in excess of $14 million. They also expect their retirement plans to provide more than double what they will need in retirement income in about three years when Lisa retires. Since there is no assurance that the estate tax will remain at a higher level, their planner has suggested they begin a substantial gifting program to their three married children and seven grandchildren. Even though their estate assets are earning much more than the annual gifts would require, they don't want to follow the planner's advice. Why not? Paul and Lisa are afraid they will need the money in case they get sick. Ridiculous? Of course, from a quantitative point of view, but completely logical and appropriate from their qualitative viewpoint. A planner who neglects to adequately assess a client's qualitative information will be dismissed by the client.

Here is an example of a preliminary questionnaire used by planners as a starting point to help gather data and client information. It can be sent to the client in advance or worked on in the waiting room before the first office visit.

Preliminary Questionnaire
To Determine Client Financial Planning Needs

Name: _____

Please take a few minutes to complete this checklist. Any "no" or "not sure" answers can point to potential problems that we may be able to help you resolve. (This questionnaire should be completed prior to meeting with the client.)

Monthly Income and Expenses

1. Do you use a budget?   Yes No Not Sure
2. Do you have any financial problems that require   Yes No Not Sure
   immediate attention?

Retirement

1. Are you saving for retirement?   Yes No Not Sure
2. Do you know what rate of return you need to   Yes No Not Sure
   maintain your lifestyle and keep ahead of
   inflation and taxes?

(continued)

(*continued*)

Children's Education

1. Have you planned for this expense?	Yes No Not Sure
2. Is the ownership of your education savings designed to reduce taxes?	Yes No Not Sure

Your investments

1. Are they well diversified?	Yes No Not Sure
2. Are you satisfied with their performance?	Yes No Not Sure

Risk and Insurance

1. Will your insurance cover your family's needs in the event of death or disability?	Yes No Not Sure
2. Do you have an umbrella liability policy?	Yes No Not Sure

Estate Planning

1. Are your wills current?	Yes No Not Sure
2. Is your estate designed to minimize taxes and fees?	Yes No Not Sure

3. ANALYZING THE CLIENT'S CURRENT COURSE OF ACTION AND POTENTIAL ALTERNATIVE COURSE(S) OF ACTION
Statement of financial position

What is it? A statement of financial position or "balance sheet" is the basic financial statement for everyone. It is a summary of assets and liabilities, what the individual/family owns and what he/she/they owe. The bottom line is the "net worth" (assets minus liabilities) of the client. It is a financial snapshot of a moment in time (usually calendar year end). It is the document that tells a client where they are financially.

All assets consist of three categories: cash/cash equivalents, invested assets, and use assets. These are shown at fair market value as of the time of preparation of the statement. This is in contrast to a balance sheet prepared for a business, which is constructed using historical cost or "book values."

Optimally, the balance sheet will also include the titling of the assets and liabilities, such as sole ownership or joint tenancy with right of survivorship. This is particularly important when using the balance sheet for purposes of estate planning.

What is the exposure to the client? Without a balance sheet, the financial planning process is pointless. If you don't know where you are, it isn't likely you will ever get to where you want to be.

> **Rattiner's Secrets:** Emphasize to every client the importance of providing complete and accurate financial information. It is the base on which all financial plans are built. Absolute accuracy isn't possible since many assets do not have an easily ascertainable value, but every effort should be made to reflect current values.

Practical example: Adam Tompkins brought his checkbook, mutual fund statements, savings account information, last year's accumulation values in his 401(k) plan, and his most recent mortgage statement to his planner's office and asked her to put together a balance sheet for him. The planner took notes regarding the information provided, made a few copies, and handed Adam a list of other information that she needed. Adam had not provided anything indicating the current market value of his home, his automobiles, the antiques he had in his home, his coin and stamp collections, a couple acres of land in Aspen that his uncle left to him, current bank statements, current quarter's 401(k) statement, a current statement with respect to his rollover IRA, the balance due on his auto loans, his credit card statements, the balance due on another unsecured loan, and a few other items. A balance sheet does not provide useful information unless it is as complete as it can be.

Statement of cash flow

What is it? The cash flow statement shows where money came from and where it went over a certain period of time. There are two types, historical and "pro-forma," although usually "pro-forma" or expected income and expense statements are constructed by businesses only. This topic covers historical cash flow. Personal cash flow statements typically separate fixed from variable expenses. In addition, tax obligations – income taxes, FICA taxes, and/or self-employment taxes – are often shown separately as a third category of expenses.

What is the exposure to the client? A cash flow statement shows a client how money coming into the household (inflows) is being managed. Most people do not really know where all of their money goes. They know how much is being spent on the mortgage or rent, groceries, utilities, phone, and some other relatively fixed expenses. However, they don't often know how much is being spent on variable or discretionary types of expenses, such as clothes, entertainment, lunches, and all of the small expenses that are paid with cash, checks, or debit cards. A client can't make changes in spending habits and gain control of their cash flow unless the current spending pattern is known. As we keep saying, you need to know where you are coming from to know where you are going. Identifying the nature of expenses as fixed or discretionary can help a client better manage money. Is a cable TV bill fixed or discretionary? The alternatives and level of use might cause one person to consider it fixed and another to consider it discretionary.

> **Rattiner's Secrets:** Have clients create a budget for a 12-month rotating period. As one month matures, delete that month and add the next month so the client is always going out 12 months in advance. The client should also keep a spending log on their phone or on a memo pad for a month or two on a daily basis. This log is to record any and all spending. The log serves three purposes. First, it helps establish a budget to which expenses can always be tied. Developing the budget enables the client to know how much money they have to work with. Second, it helps in developing the cash flow statement, which specifies where pocket cash is spent. Third, it makes the client(s) think about every expense. Most people don't think much about the extra $2.00 for a soft drink, or $10.00 for lunch, or money spent on snacks, an extra magazine, the office pool, lottery tickets, or dozens of other items people spend money on. These "little" expenses can easily add up to thousands of dollars per year. A client who has specific financial goals, and who has not been able to make progress in achieving them, can benefit from knowing where money is being spent and appropriate choices can be made about how those funds are used.

Practical example: Rene needs a new car, but she just can't seem to put together a down payment. In talking with her, you determine that she buys her lunch every day, spending between $9.00 and $15.00 depending on where she goes. She often has a drink after work with some of her co-workers, and she really enjoys exotic beer. Because she is so busy, she picks up fast food for dinner about four evenings a week, and the rest of the time she rummages through the many pre-packaged meals in her freezer. Her grocery basket is typically filled with pre-packaged meals and whatever looks good when she goes shopping. Rene could likely reduce her lunch costs by $30 per week by taking her lunch with her. A typical fast-food meal may cost as much or more than a steak dinner cooked at home from scratch, and it isn't as healthy. Pre-packaged meals are often rather expensive relative to scratch-made meals, and again, they are less healthy. Even the pre-seasoned chicken is healthier and less expensive than the pre-packaged meals. Many less expensive foods are also easy and fast to prepare. Exotic imported beer costs more than the everyday pedestrian brands, so a few more dollars per week can be saved there without giving up the social contact. Going to the grocery store without a shopping list usually results in spending more than is planned for or necessary. It is likely that Rene could save a couple of thousand dollars a year simply by making a few changes in her personal cash management habits.

Effect on Financial Statements

It is important to know the effect of everyday transactions on personal financial statements. For example, the only effect a loan has on the personal cash flow statement is to add an outflow. The balance sheet is where the biggest effect comes in. In the case of a leased or rented asset, there is no entry on the balance sheet except to the extent that a lump sum may have been taken from one of the listed assets as an initial payment to secure the leased asset. There is no debt shown nor is there an asset recorded.

If an item is purchased, there may be a number of changes in the balance sheet. First is the addition of the market value of the asset. Depending on the accounting method used by the client, it may be listed at its purchase price or at its present value. There will likely also be a reduction of some asset, typically a liquid asset that was used to make the purchase. If there is a loan that was secured in order to purchase the asset, it will show up as a liability. The difference between the asset value and the outstanding debt related to it is its contribution to the net worth of the client. Over time, the balance sheet *must* show either depreciation or reduction in value of the asset, if in fact it is going down in value. Depreciation is generally applicable to assets used in business.

The following is a prototype balance sheet and cash flow statement to help you visually understand how these numbers can affect the client's financial situation.

CONSTRUCTION OF STATEMENT OF FINANCIAL POSITION

Joseph and Emily Bauer
Statement of Financial Position
As of December 31, 202X

Assets		Liabilities and Net Worth	
Cash/Cash Equivalents		Liabilities	
Checking	$_____	Short-term Liabilities	$_____
CU Savings/Passbook	$_____	Long-term Liabilities	$_____
Money Market Accounts	$_____	Total Liabilities	$_____
Life Insurance Cash Value	$_____		
Total Cash/Cash Equivalents	$_____		
Invested Assets			
Stocks/Bonds/Funds	$_____		
IRAS	$_____		
Vested Retirement Accounts	$_____	Net Worth	$_____
Total Invested Assets	$_____		
Use Assets			
Residence	$_____		
Vacation Homes	$_____		
Personal Property	$_____		
Total Use Assets	$_____		
		TOTAL LIABILITIES	
TOTAL ASSETS	$_____	AND NET WORTH	$_____

Footnotes
all assets are listed at fair market value
all liabilities are listed with the outstanding principal balance and accrued interest if applicable

CONSTRUCTION OF STATEMENT OF CASH FLOW

Joseph and Emily Bauer
Cash Flow Statement
For the Year Ending December 31, 202X

INFLOWS: (1)

Gross salaries	$_____	$_____
Dividends/Interest	$_____	$_____
Etc.	$_____	$_____
TOTAL INFLOWS		$_____

OUTFLOWS:

Savings and Investments (2)		$_____
Fixed Outflows (3)		
Mortgage Payments	$_____	$_____
Auto Payments	$_____	$_____
Insurance Premiums	$_____	$_____
FICA Taxes	$_____	$_____
Etc.	$_____	$_____
Total Fixed Outflows		$_____

Variable Outflows		
Federal and State Taxes	$_____	$_____
Consumer Debt Reduction	$_____	$_____
Etc.	$_____	$_____
Etc.	$_____	$_____
********	$_____	$_____
********	$_____	$_____
********	$_____	$_____
********	$_____	$_____
********	$_____	$_____
Total Variable Outflows		$_____
TOTAL OUTFLOWS		$_____

Footnotes
(1) gross inflows
(2) including reinvested dividends and interest relatively predictable, recurring and little control
(3) can be fixed or variable

What is it? Analysis of the data and creation of financial statements is the process of organizing the collected data into a usable format. It provides a clear picture of where the client currently stands financially. It also provides the basis for the qualitative recommendations and financial projections. The analysis goes beyond mere financial statistics. It includes any special needs, insurance and risk management, investments, taxation, employee benefits, retirement and/or estate planning.

What is the exposure to the client? Without preparation of financial statements, the planner runs the risk of missing important information. This puts the client's plan at risk. Analyzing and evaluating is the financial diagnosis phase of the process. As in medicine, without a diagnosis there is no way to develop a plan of action. Without a good diagnosis, the plan of action may be inappropriate or even harmful.

Rattiner's Secrets: A planner needs to work diligently to include all relevant facts in their analysis. If facts are missing from the gathered data when the analysis is being done, the planner must either contact the client to obtain the information or come to a mutual agreement on any assumptions required, or use reasonable assumptions to complete the process, keeping in mind that those assumptions must be disclosed when presenting the plan. This step cannot be skipped or shortchanged. Failure to do an adequate job here leaves open the possibility that strengths and/or weaknesses in the existing plan, if any, will be overlooked.

Practical example: Planner Penelope Z. Swift has many years of experience and prefers to scan the quantitative data to get an idea where a client is financially and then focus on the qualitative issues. In the case of her client, Ginnie Swan, she was aware of substantial investments in her portfolio. What Ms Swift failed to notice was that they were primarily – 90% – in the technology sector and over half of those were in the over-the-counter, out-of-favor types of investments. She then focused on Ginnie's desire to remain conservative in her investment portfolio. Her recommendations did nothing to address the lack of diversification and relatively high risk of Ginnie's current investments. Further, she failed to recognize that all of the life insurance Ginnie had to protect her family was through her employment, and she planned on leaving her job and starting her own consulting firm.

Ms Swift merely checked to make sure the amount of life insurance Ginnie had was adequate to meet her life insurance needs. In this case, Ms Swift failed to do an adequate analysis of Ginnie's quantitative data to recognize severe conflicts with the qualitative information.

4. DEVELOPING THE FINANCIAL PLANNING RECOMMENDATIONS

What is it? The development of the plan is the creation and explanation of recommendations and solutions to problems that spring from the analysis of the data and the client's objectives. There is no single correct plan for any one client. Rather, there are always alternative approaches. However, there is also the problem of presenting too many options to a client and having them do nothing for fear they are making the wrong choice. The planner must evaluate the alternatives and choose those that best serve the client's long-term interests and are likely to be accepted by the client. Since good financial plans involve many integrated components, the planner needs to consider those parts in relation to their importance, urgency, and the desires of the client to establish an order for implementation and a timetable that can be followed in establishing the plan. Once these steps are completed, it is time to present the plan, with its schedule for implementation, to the client.

Developing the plan involves the exploration and discovery of many components, one of which is the proper use and involvement of technology as a means to an end, essentially comprising just one element of the bigger picture. Unfortunately, I see many decisions made by planners today that are based solely on information found with the assistance of technology. The human element or behavioral aspects need to be the leading factor.

What is the exposure to the client? A client must have confidence in a plan before they will "buy into" it. A plan that is poorly developed or that doesn't address the client's needs, wants, and desires will fall on deaf ears. Every client believes they are unique. The plan they see should reflect the mutually defined scope of the planning engagement; the mutually defined client goals, needs, and priorities; the quantitative data provided by the client; the client's personal and economic assumptions; the practitioner's analysis and evaluation of the client's current situation; and any alternative(s) selected by the practitioner.

Rattiner's Secrets: Use an established or personally created checklist to make sure nothing is missed. Most clients will not tell you they are unhappy. You find out when they don't pay their bill or fail to follow any part of the plan. The word "overkill" is aptly used when related to a financial plan. Most of the financial planning software can provide a very thick printout that will cause the client to fall into a frozen state of inertia, doing nothing because there is too much to comprehend. The plan that is presented needs to have easily digested sections. An example might be:

- Financial statements
- Personal goals (wants, desires, retirement, charitable giving, family plan, etc.)
- Life insurance goals and recommendations
- Financial goals and recommendations
- Plan of action

Practical example: Jerry Jackson just purchased the best financial planning software he could find. It included a 14-page data-gathering questionnaire and allowed him to create phenomenal presentations. He put together a fantastic plan for his new clients, Frank and Fran Friendly. When he sat down with them to go over the plan, he was sure they would be as excited as he was. He started on the introduction page that reiterated what his firm was all about and described the entire financial planning process. The rest of the introductory section included neat graphs of the economy, percentages of people who retired financially secure, and other useful information. Section Two was the fact-gathering questionnaire, which Jerry quickly reviewed with the clients over the next 30 minutes. Section Three listed the Friendlys' qualitative goals and a discussion as to how those affected different portions of the plan. Next was a section on general retirement and estate planning that Jerry used to emphasize the importance of starting early. Finally, at Section Five, Jerry got into the insurance planning section. He had some excellent comparative analysis diagrams and summaries regarding the policy options. He showed an annual income and expense flowchart that spelled out how life insurance proceeds would be distributed. Page 23 of that section showed the breakdown of the life insurance needs analysis. Pages 24 through 27 showed comparisons of various policy combinations that would provide the needed coverage. Section

Six began with "the Friendlys fell asleep." Jerry realized that people often use a financial planner because they know they need to deal with these issues but are not particularly excited about them. They rescheduled the appointment, Jerry moved the unnecessary information to a back-up binder that the Friendlys could take or leave, and then presented them with a six-page summary with lots of whitespace that clearly told them what they wanted and needed to know. The plan is now on its way to full implementation.

5. PRESENTING THE FINANCIAL PLANNING RECOMMENDATIONS

Presenting the plan is our second formal meeting with the client. At this point, we reconnect with the client and confirm where they have come from, where they are going, and how we are providing that roadmap, that blueprint, that navigation system, essentially the personal financial plan to help get the clients to where they would like to proceed.

Behavioral finance issues come to the forefront. We need to listen to the client during the presentation, making sure we are addressing their concerns and providing guidance for what the client needs to do in order to be satisfied. I have learned from experience that handing the client the plan, having them read through this huge document, and asking them to contact you with questions is a complete waste. There has to be buy-in from both parties, so that everyone is always on the same page. One of my favorite sayings in my classes is "know what you know, know what you don't know." Take it upon yourself to get up to speed in those critical areas that may provide you with the toughest time or present the biggest obstacles for achieving success.

We are not getting better fulfilling an "implied promise" of financial planning during the presentation stage, states Susan Bradley. We need to talk with clients about their readiness to move forward. Bradley says, "Keep conversation client centered and personal to have a deep connection. If you see inconsistencies, try to stay aware and present. People will see this more in 10 years and will initially be happy and when something happens that will change."

What happens when you stop? You can make it their fault, or you can lean in and help them find a new entry point. Helping them change their discipline model will result from the client wanting to move on from the occurrence of a prior event(s). This requires an adjustment, adaptation, or reinvention and the new normal, which will provide the client with a fresh starting point for the next time life changes. "If you keep giving advice and they are not taking it by the third offering, then they are less likely to act," says Bradley.

6. IMPLEMENTING THE FINANCIAL PLAN

What is it? Implementation is the action step. It begins the process of connecting the dots – from Point A to Point B. If this doesn't happen, the plan is truly not worth the money. I have seen many clients get the plan, love it, and then file it. That doesn't help them clear the hurdles they need to experience for success.

Many times this happens because they don't have the time, can't be bothered, or just become the ultimate procrastinators. This is where the planner works with their clients to start the process of making the changes that need to be made for the plan to work. This step includes:

- identifying activities necessary for implementation
- determining division of activities between the practitioner and the client
- referring to other professionals
- coordinating with other professionals
- sharing information as authorized
- selecting and securing products and/or services

During the course of a financial planning engagement, the planner may find it necessary to refer the client to other advisors, such as an estate planning attorney or tax accountant, or perhaps to agents and brokers who already work with the client, such as a property and casualty insurance broker. However, if doing so, the planner should be sure to thoroughly explain to the advisor what services they are expected to perform and in what time frame. The planner should also be sure to monitor the relationship between their client and the other advisor, sometimes going so far as to sit in on all meetings between them.

Finally, the planner should emphasize to the other advisor that the referral of a client is just that: the referral is their client and only secondarily the client of the other advisor. In other words, the planner should be sure to *control* the relationship as much as possible.

What is the exposure to the client? A plan that remains on paper has no more value than a plan that is not created. This is the test phase. If the client follows the recommended implementation plan, the planner passes the test. If the client doesn't implement the plan, the planner has failed. The biggest risk to the client is inertia. The planner needs to help the client take the steps required for implementation. It may require only listing the activities that the client must do or it may require regular coaxing and encouraging. In some cases, the planner may have to schedule appointments with the client's lawyer, accountant, investment advisor, and/or insurance agent. Many clients use a financial planner because their self-image includes being financially incompetent. Many use financial planners merely because they don't have the time to delve into each area to determine their best options. These factors will affect the assistance they will require to get the plan implemented.

> **Rattiner's Secrets:** Work with your client to develop an implementation calendar. Tell the client you will be happy to do as much or as little as they want you to do. Check with them regularly to confirm that the plan is being implemented. Remind them of the reasons they had the plan done.

Practical example: Planner Gray worked hard to develop a comprehensive financial plan for Dr. Conway. The good doctor told planner Gray that he would get right on the implementation. Eighteen months later when planner Gray met with Dr. Conway for his annual plan review, only a couple of minor parts had been implemented. Dr. Conway explained that he was just too busy and had put off the meeting for six months because he was embarrassed that he hadn't done more. It wasn't because Dr. Conway wasn't smart enough to take the steps, or even understand what needed to be done. It just wasn't what he wanted to be doing. In a case like this, planner Gray needed to be much more involved in keeping Dr. Conway on track to get the plan in place.

7. MONITORING THE FINANCIAL PLAN

What is it? Monitoring of the financial plan consists of periodic contact with each client to determine whether any of the factors that were used in the development of their plan have changed. Typically, a regularly scheduled semi-annual or annual appointment is sufficient to keep up to date.

What is the exposure to the client? Financial plans are not finished products. The economy as well as family and business dynamics change over time; the world landscape can change on a dime, as we have experienced. As a result, every plan requires periodic review and adjustment to stay on track or to redirect the process as needs and/or wants change. It's hard to believe that smartphones first came into the mainstream about a decade or so ago. One of the best bull markets over time literally stopped overnight in March 2020. This is just a sliver of the many factors that continually change the face of the future. Assumptions made when the plan was created or thereafter may not be valid assumptions going forward.

Rattiner's Secrets: At the beginning of a financial planning engagement it should be mutually agreed that the relationship does not end with the presentation of a plan, or even the implementation of a plan. Periodic reviews should be agreed to in advance of completing the initial plan. Whether the reviews are every six months or once a year, this should be discussed and established up front. Here is the rationale.

At a minimum, meeting with the client annually will shed new light on things that are relevant at that particular future time. I ask one pointed question to the client: "Mr. and Mrs. Client, since we last met, what has changed in your life that we need to address and perhaps work into your financial plan?" I then sit quietly while the client reflects and provides me with the detail. It is amazing how much they say just since the last time I met with them. If I compare this new scenario with the existing plan I created earlier, the results may be totally different.

My point to the client is simple and direct. The shortest distance between two points is a straight line! I then mention that if we can address any changes to the original game plan as soon as you get off track to ensure you get back to that straight line, it will be easier, more efficient, and cheaper for you to address the modifications needed going forward. If we wait for many years to even begin reviewing the document, it may have changed so significantly, or it may not be relevant any longer, which both pose the risk that the client is no closer to adequately addressing their situation going forward and may have to start the process all over again.

Practical example: Karen and Stan had a well-developed financial plan. They established education funds for their two children. They were funding their retirement plans and had an emergency fund in place. Their wills and insurance programs were current. Then Karen found out she was pregnant with their third, and quite unexpected, child. Their financial plan needed some modification. Shortly after that good news, Karen's uncle died and left her a piece of income-producing property in another state. The property basically made enough to pay for its taxes with a little left over, but it became another reason that their plan needed a revision. Their neighbor, Carlton, used the same planner and also had a great plan. Then, his job was eliminated and he started his own consulting firm. This one change created several reasons for review and revision of his plan.

As you can see, the development of a personal financial plan is a challenging task. If approached properly, by both the planner and the client, it can be a rewarding experience all the way around.

CHAPTER 4

Dispensing Advice on Cash Flow Management and Budgeting Concerns

"It all starts and ends with cash flow!" Clients can have grandiose plans for gathering assets and tying their objectives to meet the accumulation of these assets over their lifetimes, but if they are not identified clearly and funded appropriately, that will probably not happen. Our role is to help plan out recommendations and build a strong foundation that can enable clients to fund throughout the planning process. Cash flow is the magic key for future success. I tell clients all the time that you can't pay bills without having sufficient cash flow to help during the process.

Part of managing cash flow is to have a handle on debt management. It is too easy to lose track on minimizing or eliminating debt, so careful attention needs to be present here. Debt can come in short-term or long-term denominations, which could generate a very different game plan when managing. In addition to the obvious, the problem with accumulating too much debt is that it could affect credit scores, which ironically will make it more challenging and more expensive to borrow funds to cover the debt, which is the purpose to begin with.

CASH FLOW PLANNING

Cash flow planning ties into the seven-step financial planning process discussed in Chapter 3. The essence and foundation of financial planning can be found in the proper management of cash flow. This is the beginning and should be done for all clients during every planner–client review, regardless of net worth and income. After review, if the cash flow looks well, then we know that the client is on the right track. We won't know that until we perform the cash flow analysis. If not, we know where to start working with our clients. If the numbers don't work out, referrals for debt management counseling can be made. Many times, the client's personality, attitudes, values, and financial background can be important considerations that are necessary to gain cooperation in this area. This is where strong communication, coaching, and behavioral finance issues by the planner can be of help. Talking through these issues, identifying both good and bad past experiences, can make the client realize what is necessary to get on the right path. I have seen many wealthy clients essentially cash poor and have seen clients with a moderate income do extremely well because they are tied to the cash flow management process.

Cash flow statements should be done at least annually, perhaps quarterly, but ideally monthly. Since this is the measuring stick for the attainment of objectives, analyzing cash flows more frequently will help ensure that the client doesn't get too far off course. If they do get off course, we need to tell them that something has to give! It's really not a hard concept. Either they pare down their objectives to make them more realistic and attainable based on their current financial situation, or they should spend less; they could save more, they could restructure their liabilities, reallocate their assets, or invest differently. That could mean perhaps taking a little more risk, but you would need to be careful with this last possibility. If the client is not willing to make any necessary changes, it would be an impossible situation to work with them and manage their expectations.

The process used to manage cash flow is the same for most everyone, but since people are on different ends of the pay scale, resources accumulated, future inheritances, and other possibilities, the numbers will appear to be different for each of our clients. Our job as advisors is to help them understand and recognize how to work within their budget.

> **Rattiner's Secrets:** My client explanation in this area is pretty direct. Moneywise, whatever comes in goes out. When it leaves, it can either be saved or spent. That's the process (assuming clients pay their bills on a timely basis). Inflows come from a variety of sources, include active,

passive, portfolio, and other types. Outflows consist of savings and expenditures. Expenditures can be further broken down into fixed and variable (discretionary) expenditures. The rule of thumb I use for clients is that if they can save 10% of their gross income each year for approximately 20–30 years, they should be able to retire on roughly 80% of their current expenditures. I tell my clients they are never too young to begin saving. And if they are older, it's never too soon to begin. What I have seen from clients is delayed savings ultimately leads to delayed retirement.

In breaking down the client's outflows, we may be able to offer some guidance and direction based on the category type. With fixed expenditures, the client has little option in manipulating these. Payments for mortgage, rent, car, home equity loans, student loans, other fixed-payment loans, and perhaps other expenses where there is little maneuverability to change are a foregone conclusion. However, with discretionary expenditures, this is where the client may have the most control and opportunity to make changes, which can enable us to help make a difference to have things happen appropriately for the client. Savings is where the client is pulling their money to accomplish those objectives identified during the financial planning process. The objective here is always to max out when possible.

This is where the heart of the discussion rests with my clients. The secret to success in financial planning is to minimize the discretionary expenses, take those previously allocated funds and re-route them into the savings category, and then earmark those funds specifically to accomplish the prioritized objectives we discussed in Chapter 3. With objectives being defined as definite and measurable, meaning each with a specific time frame and dollar amount, clients will realize that this type of planning is relevant and extremely possible in satisfying those objectives designed for immediate and long-term success.

This is the initial discussion for my clients before anything else regarding funding objectives occurs. As we keep saying, it's all about managing your client's expectations and there is no better way to alert your clients that they are on the right path or not anywhere near it. I don't beat around the bush with clients since if we don't start off at the same point, we will end up differently in both availability and accessibility of funds needed to make the intended targets.

Sometimes it is a struggle for younger clients who are not there yet because it is too far down the road. But there is no time like the present to begin planning. Many times, I will take out my HP12C calculator and do rough calculations on the spot. For example, if a client saves $6,000 per year in an IRA, and over 40 years earns at a reasonable 6% return, it will amass into $928,572 at retirement. Not bad! I demonstrate that type of concept with various scenarios in the hope the client will act upon it sooner rather than later. I encourage them to save for the rainy day, as life has many curveballs, as explained below. Another effective strategy is to print out the numbers and give them as a spreadsheet under different scenarios so the client can see the various possibilities, react to them, and take them home as the necessary objective to help them begin their planning opportunities.

The practical thing with assisting your clients with cash flow planning is that technology can greatly assist in this area. It could occur as a reporting mechanism where cash flow is entered manually, can be tracked electronically, or can happen piecemeal electronically as purchases and other things happen for the client. But before cash flow management can occur, the client needs to set up their system of controls properly. That's where budgeting comes in.

Managing Cash Flow

Cash Flow Planning
Budgeting
Change in Cash Flow Alignment
Emergency Fund Planning
Debt Management Ratios
Consumer Debt
Housing Costs
Total Debt
Savings Strategies
Debt Management
Secured vs. Unsecured Debt
Buy vs. Lease/Rent
Mortgage Financing
Types of Mortgages
Home Equity Loan and Line of Credit
Refinancing

BUDGETING

A budget is used to plan and evaluate the income, expenses, and spending patterns of an individual or couple. It should provide a realistic estimate of the individual's income and expenditures, prepared using actual historical information and considering the individual's financial goals and time frame for achieving those goals. It then serves as a control document to compare actual spending to desired spending.

There are three stages of the budgeting process:

1. Estimate income (gross or "net" after taxes).
2. Estimate expenditures (both fixed and variable expenses, while also keeping inflation in mind).
3. Budget for savings (should be planned as an integral part of the budget and not just as a "hoped-for" residual amount).

The resulting savings at the end of the budget period are sometimes referred to as "discretionary cash flow" since this is the amount that remains for investment *after* payment of all monthly expenses (including taxes). It's important to reflect taxes into the calculations because our clients will generally not have choices to defer or eliminate. Clients will have to pay for their expenses after taxes are figured into the calculation, from the net amount. Lastly, it is impossible for a client to grow their net worth without having some discretionary cash flow that is available to them for investment purposes.

Rattiner's Secrets: When developing a budget, it is important to determine the necessity of certain daily, monthly, or annual expenses. The "why" of certain expenses can make it a discretionary (tending to be a variable) or a non-discretionary (fixed) expense. Ask the client questions about expenses that don't easily fit on the non-discretionary expense side to determine whether they are indeed necessary. Finally, recognize that items that are discretionary for some clients may be non-discretionary or fixed expenses for others.

I tell my clients to constantly go out 12 months in the budgeting process. First, the client can see the natural progression of expenses moving forward. Second, it allows the client to stay on top of their spending habits, so it does not get out of hand too quickly. When one month ends, remove that month and add the new 12th month out. This allows the client to always keep looking forward for 12 months at a time. This will also impact where the cash flow statement goes, which as we'll see takes the final results from the budgeting process. Monitoring the budgeting process enables the client to stay on a better course for attaining objectives.

I have developed a master budget/cash flow statement and balance sheet for all of my clients. The reason is simple. This allows all clients to follow the same format, though not necessarily using the same accounts. Since the numbering system is universal, if a client has a question, anyone in the office can help answer the question since all the clients' statements are set up in the same manner. For example, for the balance sheet, assets are listed in the 1000s, liabilities in the 2000s, and net worth as 3000. Under cash flow, inflows are listed in the 4000s and outflows in the 5000s. You can have many different account titles under each heading and subheading, and the client just addresses the ones that are relevant to them. See Figure 4.1 for a sample cash flow statement and Figure 4.2 for a sample balance sheet.

CASH FLOW STATEMENT
B. Prepared Right
For the Year Ending 12/31/2X

INFLOWS: (1) - GROSS INCOME	Account Number	Amount
ACTIVE INCOME - EARNED INCOME: #4000	**4000**	
W-2 - #1	4010	$
W-2 - #1	4020	$
W-2 - #1	4030	$
W-2 - #1	4040	$
Self Employment - 1099 Misc - #1	4050	$
Self Employment - 1099 Misc - #2	4060	$
Bonus/Commissions - #1	4070	$
Bonus/Commissions - #2	4080	$
Alimony - #1	4090	$
RETIREMENT INCOME SOURCES: #4100	**4100**	
RMD #1	4110	$
RMD #2	4120	$
Pension #1	4130	$
Pension #2	4140	$
401(k)/403(b)/457 #1	4150	$
401(k)/403(b)/457 #2	4160	$
IRA #1	4170	$
IRA #2	4180	$

FIGURE 4.1 Sample cash flow statement

INFLOWS: (1) - GROSS INCOME	Account Number	Amount
PASSIVE INCOME: #4200	**4200**	
Real Estate	4210	$
Property/Limited Partnership #1	4220	$
Property/Limited Partnership #2	4230	$
Property/Limited Partnership #3	4240	$
Property/Limited Partnership #4	4250	$
Property/Limited Partnership #5	4260	$
Property/Limited Partnership #6	4270	$
Property/Limited Partnership #7	4280	$
Royalty Income	4290	$
PORTFOLIO INCOME: #4300..#4599	**4300**	
Interest #1	4310	$
Interest #2	4320	$
Interest #3	4330	$
Interest #4	4340	$
Dividends #1	4350	$
Dividends #1	4360	$
Dividends #1	4370	$
Dividends #1	4380	$
Capital Gains/(Losses) #1	4410	$
Capital Gains/(Losses) #2	4420	$
Capital Gains/(Losses) #3	4430	$
Capital Gains/(Losses) #4	4440	$
OTHER INCOME: 4500..4699	**4500**	
Social Security #1	4510	$
Social Security #1	4520	$
Disability Income #1	4530	$
Disability Income #2	4540	$
Gambling Income (Loss) #1	4550	$
Gambing Income/(Loss) #2	4560	$
Game Show/Other	4570	$
State Refund	4580	$
Miscellaneous	4610	$
Miscellaneous	4620	$
Miscellaneous	4630	$
Miscellaneous	4640	$
TRUST & ESTATE INCOME	**4700**	
Trust Income #1	4710	$
Trust Income #2	4720	$
Estate Income	4730	$

FIGURE 4.1 (*Continued*)

INFLOWS: (1) - GROSS INCOME	Account Number	Amount
POTENTIALLY TAXABLE INCOME	**4800**	
Sec 125 Cafeteria Plan Contributions	4810	$
Employer Health Care Sponsored Premiums	4820	$
Other Pre-Tax Benefit Expenses	4830	$
Tax-Sheltered Retirement Plan Contributions	4840	$
NON-TAXABLE INCOME	**4900**	
Alimony (2019+)	4910	$
Child Support	4920	$
Allowances	4930	$
Gifts	4940	$
Grants/Scholarships and Loans	4950	$
Qualified Roth IRA Distributions	4960	$
Other	4970	$
TOTAL INFLOWS		$
OUTFLOWS: 5000		
SAVINGS AND INVESTMENTS	**5000**	$
FIXED OUTFLOWS: 5100...5599	**5100**	
Mortgage Payments (Principal and Interest) #1	5110	$
Mortgage Payments (Principal and Interest) #2	5120	$
Rent Payments - #1	5130	$
Rent Payments - #2	5140	$
Auto Payments - #1	5150	$
Auto Payments - #2	5160	$
Student Loan Payment #1	5170	$
Student Loan Payment #2	5180	$
Insurance Premiums: 5200...5399	5200	$
Life Insurance #1	5210	$
Life Insurance #2	5220	$
Disability Insurance #1	5230	$
Disability Insurance #2	5240	$
Health Insurance #1	5250	$
Health Insurance #2	5260	$
Long-Term Care Insurance #1	5270	$
Long-Term Care Insurance #1	5280	$
Homeowners/Renters Insurance #1	5290	$
Homeowners/Renters Insurance #2	5300	$
Automobile Insurance #1	5310	$
Automobile Insurance #2	5320	$

FIGURE 4.1   (*Continued*)

FIXED OUTFLOWS	Account Number	Amount
Excess Umbrella #1	5330	$
Excess Umbrella #2	5340	$
Other Insurance #1 . . . ...#10	5350	$
Real Estate Taxes #1	5380	$
Real Estate Taxes #2	5390	$
Payroll Taxes	5400	$
FICA Taxes #1	5410	$
FICA Taxes #2	5420	$
FWT #1	5430	$
FWT #2	5440	$
SWT #1	5450	$
SWT #2	5460	$
Other Taxes #1 . . . .#10	5470	$
Etc.		$
Total Fixed Outflows		**$**
VARIABLE (DISCRETIONARY) EXPENSES:	**5600**	
5600..5999		
Utilities (Water, Sewer, Gas, Electric, Etc.)	5610	$
Cable and Streaming Services	5620	$
Telephone	5630	$
Subscriptions	5640	$
Communication - Other	5650	$
Meals/Food - Home	5660	$
Meals/Food - Away from Home	5670	$
Vacations	5680	$
Entertainment	5690	$
Accessories	5700	$
Transportation	5710	$
Car Expenses - Fuel #1	5720	$
Car Expenses - Fuel #2	5730	$
Car Expenses - Vehicle Maintenance #1	5740	$
Car Expenses - Vehicle Maintenance #2	5750	$
Car Expenses - Parking & Tolls #1	5760	$
Car Expenses - Parking & Tolls #2	5770	$
Car Expenses - Registration, Licenses, All Else #1	5780	$
Car Expenses - Registration, Licenses, All Else #2	5790	$
Commuting Expenses	5800	$
Child Care/Babysitting	5810	$
Credit Card Payment #1	5820	$
Credit Card Payment #2	5830	$
Professional Fees	5840	$

FIGURE 4.1 *(Continued)*

VARIABLE OUTFLOWS	Account Number	Amount
Education/College	5850	$
Hobbies	5860	$
Club Dues	5870	$
Health Care - Unreimbursed Medical/Doctors	5880	$
Health Care - Prescriptions	5890	$
Personal Care	5900	$
Elder Care	5910	$
Personal Property Tax #1	5920	$
Personal Property Tax #2	5930	$
Alarm/House	5940	$
Pet Grooming & Other Expenses	5950	$
Household Maintenance and Repairs	5960	$
Domestic Help	5970	$
Laundry and Drycleaning	5980	$
Lawn/Yard	5990	$
Total Variable Outflows		$
TOTAL OUTFLOWS		$

FIGURE 4.1 *(Continued)*

BALANCE SHEET
B. Prepared Right
As of 12/31/2X

ASSETS (#1000s)	Account Number	Amount
CASH AND CASH EQUIVALENTS (#1000-#1090)	**1000**	
Checking	1010	$
Savings	1020	$
Money Markets	1030	$
CDs	1040	$
Cash Surrender Value - Life Insurance	1050	$
T-Bills	1060	$
Commercial Paper/Bankers Acceptances/Eurodollars	1070	$
Other	1080	$
Total Cash and Cash Equivalents		$

FIGURE 4.2 Sample balance sheet

ASSETS (#1000s)	Account Number	Amount
INVESTABLE ASSETS (#1100-#1990)	1100	
RETIREMENT ACCOUNTS (#1100..#1390)		
Pre-Tax Retirement Accounts		
QUALIFIED PLANS	1110	$
Defined Benefit Plans		
PV - Pension/Defined Benefit Accounts	1120	$
PV - Cash Balance Plans	1130	$
Defined Contribution Plans		
Money Purchase	1140	$
Target Benefit	1150	$
Profit Sharing	1160	$
401(k) Plans	1170	$
ESOP	1180	$
Stock Bonus	1190	$
Post-Tax Retirement Accounts		
Roth - 401(k)/403(b)	1210	$
Roth - IRA	1220	$
Personal Retirement Accounts		
403(B) Plans	1230	$
IRAs	1240	$
SEPs	1250	$
SIMPLEs	1260	$
Non-Qualified Plans		
Deferred Compensation Plans - Salary Reduction	1310	$
Deferred Compensation Plans - Salary Continuation	1320	$
457 Plans	1330	$
Stock Options - ISOs	1340	$
Stock Options - NSOs	1350	$
Restricked Stock Options	1360	$
Stock Appreciation Rights	1370	$
Phantom Stock	1380	$
ESPPs	1390	$

FIGURE 4.2   (*Continued*)

ASSETS (#1000s)	Account Number	Amount		
AFTER-TAX INVESTMENTS (#1400..1590)				
Equities - Individual Stocks	1410	$		
Fixed Income - Individual Bonds	1420	$		
Mutual Funds - Equities	1430	$		
Mutual Funds - Fixed Income	1440	$		
Exchanged Traded Funds	1450	$		
Mutual Funds - Other	1460	$		
Real Estate - Investments	1470	$		
Passive Type Investments/Limited Partnerships	1480	$		
Annuities	1490	$		
Alternative Investments	1500	$		
Managed Accounts	1510	$		
Derivatives/Options/Futures/Warrants	1520	$		
College Fund/Sec 529 Plan/Other	1530	$		
Total Investable Assets			$	
PERSONAL USE ASSETS (#1600..#1990)				
Primary Residence	1610	$		
Secondary Residence	1620	$		
Automobile #1	1630	$		
Automobile #2	1640	$		
Watercraft	1650	$		
Personal Property	1660	$		
Collectibles	1670	$		
Other	1680	$		
Total Personal Use Assets			$	
TOTAL ASSETS				$
LIABILITIES (#2000..#2990)	**2000**			
SHORT-TERM				
Accounts Payable	2010	$		
Debts Maturing in One Year or Less	2020	$		
Credit Card #1	2030	$		
Credit Card #2	2040	$		
Credit Card #3	2050	$		
Consumer/Personal Loan	2060	$		
Car Loan Within One Year	2070	$		
Other	2080	$		

FIGURE 4.2 (*Continued*)

ASSETS (#1000s)	Account Number	Amount
LONG-TERM (#2100 - #2200)		
Mortgage #1	2100	$
Mortgage #2	2110	$
Car Loan Greater Than One Year	2120	$
Other	2130	$
TOTAL LIABILITIES		$
NET WORTH (#3000)	3000	$
TOTAL LIABILITIES AND NET WORTH		$

FIGURE 4.2   (*Continued*)

Practical example: A six-pack of your favorite soft drink will cost between $2.50 and $3.50. Six cans of the same soft drink out of a machine usually cost between $6.00 and $12.00. Buying lunch every day will probably cost at least $25 per week and may go over $60 a week when including tips and transportation. Spending a few minutes putting together a lunch to take to work will likely cost much less. If debt reduction and creation of an emergency fund are important, then why lease a new, top-of-the-line Acura if you can buy a used Honda Accord with payments that are half as much? Just because a person can afford something out of cash flow doesn't mean they should. Of course, if they spend too much out of cash flow, there will be no discretionary amount available for savings or investment.

CHANGE IN CASH FLOW ALIGNMENT

"What you'll see when we start shifting away from being retirement centric will be to a focus and alignment with cash flow which will enable spending advice to be aligned with personal life goals. That resolve will provide clients with the comfort, determination, and will to live until we can't anymore," says Michael Kitces. It will be much more powerful and impactful. "We won't be able to help the client who doesn't know where their money is going," states Kitces. We won't need product knowledge but rather advice knowledge. This is a change of pace for us since historically our competencies have been built around products we used to sell.

From a holistic standpoint, we will need to be good on debt management, essentially the big items we don't normally get paid on, big ticket items such as student loans, credit cards, and car loans. Fundamental advice we give to clients begins to change since it no longer hinges on product sales. In today's world, debt management is coming to the top of most people's concerns about making things work out in the long run. The only positive that hopefully will come out of this current crisis is our clients realizing that they may not have sufficient resources to cover the things on their "To Do List" and they may now have to accelerate these ambitions into overdrive.

EMERGENCY FUND PLANNING

What is it? The emergency or contingency fund is part of the foundation of any good financial plan. Liquidity is the ease of converting assets into cash without a significant loss of principal. Marketability is the ease of buying or selling an asset. The assets that constitute an emergency fund should always be liquid in nature and, preferably, marketable. However, of the two, liquidity is the more important attribute of any emergency fund. Thus, cash and cash-equivalent assets are the norm when constructing the emergency fund. Such assets also tend to have a maturity date of no more than one year from the date of purchase or acquisition.

Why is this an issue? Life happens! Unfortunately, we don't have a fool-proof roadmap to help us perfectly navigate our way. Your client could lose their job, become sick or unhealthy, need to take care of a sick relative, have issues with children and other loved ones that require a financial outlay, etc.

There is also the question of how much (what amount) should be kept in the emergency fund. This is a particularly important question given that short-term and/or safer (more liquid) assets also tend to have a lower rate of return.

What is the exposure to the client? A client without an adequate emergency fund may be forced to liquidate securities when their market value is down. Further, they may have to cash in an IRA with its attendant tax penalties if the owner is under age 59 years and six months, or they may have to sell some property or assets that they otherwise would wish to retain. That's why I tell the client either way you'll have to make do...it's better to be proactive rather than reactive! In an emergency, with short notice, borrowing may be quite expensive, and if the emergency is a disability resulting in a loss of income, borrowing will only make the problems worse.

> **Rattiner's Secrets:** Evaluate each client's financial circumstances and come to an agreement about the appropriate amount to keep in an emergency fund. Three to six months of monthly expenses is typically a reasonable range. For one-income families, a six-month level may be more appropriate. For two-income families, a three-month level may be adequate. If your crystal ball is clear and working, you can tell your clients exactly what will happen and when. That will make the process easy. Until that time, being a little conservative is not a bad idea.

The category where these funds are kept, the cash and cash equivalents section of the balance sheet (as explained in Chapter 3), is the client's safety net for emergencies. The client wants to withdraw only from these accounts and not from the investment assets account, because that could have an effect on the entire investment portfolio. The cash and cash equivalents section is designed as a safety net, meaning the client will never get rich from accumulating all assets in these types of investments, but it should be the primary source for working through the current financial crises of the early 2020s, and for unforeseen emergencies, such as loss of a job, paying rent, mortgage, car loan payments. This account should be the client's starting point.

In planning for my clients, I tend to lean on the conservative side, meaning I would rather have too much in reserves than not enough. Another good way to combat a lack of immediate cash is to take out a home equity line of credit (HELOC), which represents a potential backup plan if money becomes scarce. With a HELOC, if you don't use it, you won't incur any fees, and if you do, it's there ready to be activated if need be. If you do need it, you probably can draw an appropriate amount, based on how it was initially set up, to cover that temporary shortfall or lag of funds. This allows the client to access 3–6 months of emergency funds first and then, if necessary, access hopefully a large enough base to draw from if needed.

When a client who needs six months of income in an emergency fund has accumulated three months' worth of cash or cash equivalents, slightly less liquid assets, such as a 90-day certificate of deposit or similar type of investment can probably be used. These will provide an increased return, and the slight restriction on cashing them in will help them stay in place for emergencies. Life insurance cash values may also be used in emergencies where there is a likelihood that the loans will be paid back. Lines of credit that are available with the use of a credit card are also possibilities, although the client should be sure and apply for the line of credit before they actually need it.

Practical example: Dirk Mathis earns $70,000 per year and his wife Darlene earns $92,000. Annually their net income is about $110,000. Their monthly expenses are close to $9,000. They never seem to have enough money left at the end of the month and have virtually no savings or investments beyond small 401(k) accounts. As a result, if either Dirk or Darlene has to be away from work for even a month without pay, their financial lives would likely be turned upside down. This couple needs to find out where all of their money is going and get some control of it. They also need to have at least three months' worth of expenses in an emergency fund. To set aside well over $20,000 will not be an easy task with their spending habits, but with good planning, Dirk and Darlene can reduce their monthly expenses and begin to build the necessary emergency reserves.

DEBT MANAGEMENT RATIOS

Debt management ratios for personal financial planning are very important in assessing the financial strengths and weaknesses of a client (their overall financial health). The following ratios and guidelines can assist in the evaluation of a client's debt position:

- The client should have sufficient liquid assets for an emergency fund (generally 3–6 months of fixed and variable outflows).
- **Rule of thumb:** consumer debt, such as credit cards and auto loans, should not exceed 20% of net income (gross income – taxes).
- **Rule of thumb:** monthly payments on a home (including principal, interest, taxes, and insurance) should be no more than 28% of the owner's gross income.
- **Rule of thumb:** total monthly payment on all debts should be no more than 36% of gross monthly income (PITI (see below), credit payments, alimony, child support and maintenance).
- The client should attempt to save at least 10–15% of net income, not including reinvested dividends and income.

Debt management can make or break a client's finances. Every day the print and broadcast media are full of offers to lend money. Practically every adult, and many students, regularly receive solicitations in the mail for another credit card. Many marriages end because of money problems, and they almost always stem from excessive debt. Many people do not know when they have too much debt until it becomes a serious problem.

CONSUMER DEBT

Consumer debt is any loan that is made to purchase a consumer item. This would include credit card purchases, auto loans, loans to buy furniture, and in-store revolving lines of credit. It might even be a bank line of credit.

Not only does such debt add to a client's debt service (and, therefore, increases their debt ratios), the interest paid on consumer debt is specifically non-deductible for federal income tax purposes.

You should help clients understand the differences in interest rates and how much it costs to borrow money using the various options available. Show them examples of the interest cost differences between their options. Unfortunately, many clients do not ask for your assistance until they have already entered into the contract.

Practical example: Sue Ellen and Charlie are buying a new bedroom set. They can charge the $5,000 expense at 17% or borrow $5,000 from the bank at 8.5%. What is the difference? If they pay $100, 2% of their initial balance, each month on the credit card, it will take over 87 months to pay it off at a total interest charge of almost $3,759. Alternatively, if they borrow from the bank and pay it off in 60 months, their payment will be $102.58 and the total interest they would pay would be slightly less than $1,160. This is a saving of $2,600. If they were to pay the $102.58 on the credit card each month, they would have it paid off in just over 84 months and the total interest paid would be about $3,560, $2,400 more than getting the bank loan. However, it is also worthwhile to point out that by buying the furniture on credit, they are paying at least $6,160 for $5,000 worth of furniture. Accordingly, maybe saving before making the purchase would be a better option.

$5,000 to purchase bedroom set			
Source of payment	Amount of payment	Total paid	Total interest
Credit card 17%	$100/Mo.	$8,758.95	$3,758.95
Bank 8.5%	$102.58/Mo.	$6,154.96	$1,154.96
Credit card 17%	$102.58/Mo.	$8,552.59	$3,552.59

HOUSING COSTS

As noted, an individual's expenditure for housing costs should not be more than 28% of their gross monthly income. However, you should note that the only form of taxes included in this ratio are property taxes on the home and that the only form of insurance included is homeowner's insurance. Thus, the commonly referred to acronym of "PITI" stands for:

- Principal on the home loan or mortgage
- Interest on the loan
- Taxes (property taxes)
- Insurance (homeowner's insurance).

TOTAL DEBT

Also, as noted, a client's total debt ratio should not be more than 36% of gross monthly income, thereby including the subcomponent housing and consumer debt ratios. Of course, it is entirely possible that this total debt ratio may exceed the standard for any one month (usually because of high credit card interest payments), but, long term, if the client continues to exceed the recommended amount, they will likely need to seek the services of a credit counselor or other debt management specialist.

Practical example: Penny and Art Stone have a monthly PITI (housing cost debt) that is 32% of their gross income. However, their two cars are paid for and in good condition, and they manage to carry a zero balance on their credit cards into each month. They have no other debt. Hence, while their housing debt is a bit high, the complete lack of other debt makes it an acceptable situation. (Note that this would likely not be the case if Penny and Art did not manage to pay off their credit card debt each month.)

SAVINGS STRATEGIES

What is it? Part of the base of any financial plan is the emergency fund. This fund doesn't just appear; it must be built, typically through some planned savings program. An example is to establish a direct deposit account with your bank and then have your employer deposit your check in the bank and have the bank transfer money to a savings account before depositing the balance in a checking account. Money market mutual funds may also be set up to draft a fixed amount from a checking account monthly.

Saving strategies must also be built with time frames in mind. Short-term saving goals may use different strategies than medium- or long-term saving goals.

What is the exposure to the client? For clients to build an emergency fund, they need a method that works (and that they will follow). Promising to save whatever is left at the end of the month rarely, if ever, works. A financial planner with an established client who does not have a savings plan has not served the client well. If the client will not work on even this basic facet of a financial plan, they will probably be better off finding a planner who is able to find what will motivate them to act.

Rattiner's Secrets: Some clients view financial planners as magicians who can tell them the "big" investment to make them rich! This is unrealistic. Planners should tell their clients that the process of achieving financial goals requires commitment and effort on their part. Financial independence takes time to achieve; it does not happen overnight from some lucky stock pick.

Practical example: Tom and Joleen have been trying to build up an emergency fund for years. It seems that whenever they get a few thousand dollars in the fund, something comes along, like wanting a new car, needing a washer and dryer, or having the house painted, and they "have to" spend it. Kami, their planner, suggests setting up a savings account at their credit union, where Tom's paycheck is automatically deposited, and then having $100 from each of his paychecks deposited into it. That account will be devoted strictly for emergency fund purposes only. Saving for other purposes will be created by Joleen having the same thing done at the bank where her paycheck is deposited. They then sit together to determine when they will next need to buy a car, whether any appliances may need to be replaced in the next few years, and to identify any other major expenses that could be expected.

DEBT MANAGEMENT

Debt management is a key issue if the client has any chance of meeting their objectives. You should be addressing both long-term and short-term debt.

Long-term debts are those amounts with a maturity date of beyond one year. Short-term debt is debt having a maturity date within the year. Generally, since there is a positive relationship between the maturity date of an obligation and its "duration," longer-term debt is more interest rate sensitive and, therefore, riskier.

Short-term debt may be used in the construction of the emergency fund since it is generally relatively liquid. An example of such debt is a certificate of deposit (CD) that has a maturity date within the year.

SECURED VS. UNSECURED DEBT

When money is borrowed, the lender expects that it will be repaid (indeed, the lender can take legal action to enforce repayment by the borrower). To make sure that it is repaid, lenders (usually banks) often require the borrower to offer an asset as collateral. That means if the borrower doesn't make payments, the lender may take the collateral, sell it, and keep the amount that is owed. When collateral is used to protect a loan, it is called a secured loan. Typically, the collateral offered for a loan is the asset for which the money was borrowed. When a borrower merely promises to pay the lender and offers no collateral, it is referred to as an unsecured loan.

BUY VS. LEASE/RENT

Which is more cost effective, buying an asset or leasing it? There are many factors that go into the decision. Among these are the following:

- Cash flow
- Obsolescence
- Expected life for user
- Tax issues: marginal tax bracket of the purchaser or lessee, deductibility of interest payments
- Comparison of inflows vs. outflows
- Savings rate of return
- Lending rates of return
- Types of leases: closed-end lease and open-end lease. (Note: a closed-end lease is also known as a "walk away lease" since it allows the lessee to "walk away" from the lease at the end of the period without any further obligation. Alternatively, an open-end lease obligates the lessee to purchase the asset – usually, an automobile – at the end of the leasing period.)

The calculation for a lease payment is really a fairly simple time value of money calculation. The calculator is set for 12 payments per year. The I/YR is the annual interest rate charged. The total cost of the asset, for example, an automobile, is the PV; the residual value is the FV; and you calculate for the payment. If your state charges sales tax on the payment, you add it to the result. If your state charges sales tax on the full price (most states), you either add it to the price of the car or pay it when you register the car. The next step applies if the car is used for business purposes. Determine the net cost by multiplying your payment by 1 – your marginal tax rate. It is important to remember that if a car is used solely for business, the entire lease payment is deductible. When purchasing a car for business, however, only a limited portion of the value of the car is deductible. If a client likes to keep a car for many years, buying is typically a better option. If the client uses the car for business and replaces it every few years, leasing makes more sense.

> **Rattiner's Secrets:** We will see in Chapter 7 that owning can have better tax benefits than leasing. In addition, through proper management, owned assets can be kept longer and thus have the future payments wiped away for a period of time.

Practical example: Steven Client is planning on getting a new car. He asks you, as his planner, whether he should buy it or lease it. At the same time, his wife, Gail Client, is shopping for a new car. Steven's car will be used for commuting to work and probably for most of the family's personal driving. Historically, Steven has kept a car for these purposes for about 10 years. Gail, on the other hand, uses her car for her work as a real estate broker. Her car will be a luxury car and have a lot of miles put on it. She will likely keep it only three years. In this case, it probably makes more sense to purchase Steven's car and lease Gail's car. Leasing makes little sense when a car is to be kept for 10 years, and buying a luxury car limits the deductions that are available when the car is used for business. Further, the calculation for buy vs. lease will show that for a three-year period, leasing is generally more cost effective.

MORTGAGE FINANCING

A mortgage is a promissory note or agreement signed by the purchaser wherein they pledge their home as security for repayment of the loan. The term of this obligation is usually either 15 or 30 years, although recently some 40-year obligations have also been used to finance the purchase.

Typically, the purchaser must "qualify" to borrow money via a mortgage and then must make a down payment of 10% or more of the purchase price.

Some clients desire to do a cash-out refinancing, which enables the client, after qualifying for a larger mortgage, to pay off the existing mortgage and to consolidate other debts into the mortgage balance. Examples could include personal loans, car loans, credit card balances, and the like. The problem here is that if this amount becomes too large without proper restructuring in other areas or another type of approach to achieve long-term objectives, it could backfire and leave the client saddled with more debt. I would advise looking at this option carefully to see whether there are any benefits here.

> **Rattiner's Secrets:** I'm a big advocate of shorter loan periods, if possible, for a number of reasons. First, many times the interest rate can be 1/4–3/8% less for a 15-year loan vs. a 30-year loan. Second, the client pays less interest over the life of the loan (assuming the client stays at the property for a good portion of the loan duration). Third, yes, you hear the argument that the client can pay it off sooner if they want to but they are not forced to do so. What happens is that other things come up, many unexpectedly, and the money being used to pay off the mortgage might be used to cover other expenses later on, such as a health issue, job loss, longer period than anticipated during retirement, or children issues. I view this as a forced savings element which helps clients attain their target objectives sooner.

TYPES OF MORTGAGES

There are many types of mortgages, although most break down into either a fixed-rate obligation or an adjustable-rate obligation as based on prevailing market interest rates. Usually, a fixed-rate obligation is preferable for a purchaser who plans to reside in the home for more than five years and who has a lower tolerance for risk. Alternatively, an adjustable-rate obligation is more suitable for a purchaser who expects to reside in the home for only several years and demonstrates a higher tolerance for assuming risk.

Here are the primary types of mortgages with several of their respective characteristics:

(a) Fixed-rate mortgage:
   - Interest rate repayment period and original loan balance remain fixed over the lifetime of the loan.

- Usually a 15–30-year loan.

(b) Biweekly mortgage:
  - Payment is every two weeks; 26 times per year.
  - Payment is half that of a monthly mortgage.
  - Advantage: shortens the life of the mortgage and decreases interest paid.

(c) Adjustable rate mortgage (ARM):
  - Interest rate and payment change with economic conditions and conditions in the contract.
  - Borrower bears the risk of interest rate changes.

(d) Balloon mortgage:
  - Fixed payments based on long-term rates but for a short (5–7-year) period.
  - Mortgage balance is due at the end of the period.

(e) Graduated payment mortgage:
  - Long-term loan.
  - Payments begin lower and increase to a fixed payment for the balance of the mortgage.

(f) Conventional mortgage:
  - Constitutes majority of nongovernment-backed obligations.
  - Requires, typically, either a 10% or 20% down payment; however, if only a 10% down payment, the purchaser is required to take out private mortgage insurance (PMI).

(g) VA/FHA mortgages:
  - Government-backed obligations; VA is for veterans only, whereas FHA mortgages are primarily offered only to lower-income individuals.
  - Features little to no down payment.

(h) Reverse mortgage:
  - Homeowner receives a loan for their home equity and receives payment.
  - Repayment to the lender is made at the sale of the home (or at the death of the borrower or borrowers).
  - Usually, only appropriate for senior or elderly homeowners with substantial equity in their homes that may be converted into retirement income.

Rattiner's Secrets: With historic low interest rates hovering around 3–3.5% fixed for the last few years (at the time of writing), I am a huge advocate for fixed-rate loans only. These rates are probably near the lowest of all time and sealing the client's fate to a low interest rate environment is a smart thing to do. Many of my clients swear to me that they will only be occupying their current house for several years and grandiose plans to move into something better are on the horizon. However, if that doesn't happen, affordability could be impacted if rates do go up. The economy will ultimately gain steam and things hopefully will start changing for the better. My thoughts are there is nowhere to go for rates but up. Having worked in the real estate industry in the late 1970s and early 1980s and seeing mortgage rates topple at 18.63% in 1981, there is nowhere to go but up!

HOME EQUITY LOAN AND LINE OF CREDIT

A home equity loan is a loan of a specific amount that is secured by the "equity" (difference between the fair market value of the home and the amount that is financed) in the home. A home equity line of credit is an agreement that the borrower can borrow up to a specified amount of money but will not be charged interest on any amount not borrowed. As stated earlier, this is a good backup plan to the emergency fund to be utilized once the 3–6 months of cash and cash equivalents are used up. The borrower can access the line of credit as often as they want and whenever the funds are needed. There is typically a minimum amount to pay each month, but the borrower is free to pay back more than that amount at any time.

Both types of financing arrangements are secured by the equity in the home. This means that if the borrower defaults on these loans, the lender(s) can foreclose on the home. Finally, the borrower can use the money obtained via either a home equity loan or line of credit in whatever manner they wish – the proceeds do not have to be expended on home-related improvements.

REFINANCING

Typically, when market interest rates decline, there may be an opportunity for the borrower to refinance their mortgage obligation at a lower overall interest rate, thus reducing the monthly payment due on the mortgage.

Rattiner's Secrets: Whether or not to engage in refinancing a mortgage is not an easy question to answer. A frequently cited rule of thumb is that if the market interest rate is now 1.5–2% lower than when the home was originally purchased and financed, it is beneficial to refinance. I don't agree with this assessment. I am often asked, "Since the current rate is less than my initial rate, should I refinance?" If the client plans on staying at the house for only a few years, I would pass on that because the saving is not worth the cost. The client needs to study the closing costs, and if points or original fees (prepaid interest) accompany the closing, then it usually is not worthwhile. Many times this prepaid interest can be negotiated away.

However, in all events, it only pays to refinance a mortgage when the borrower expects to remain in the home for a sufficient period of time to recoup the costs incurred in the refinancing. In addition, the borrower needs to be aware that the term of the mortgage obligation begins anew when the refinancing transaction is completed.

A good understanding of cash flow management tied into the client's budget can help put the client on the right path to attaining financial success in relation to their objectives.

CHAPTER 5

Dispensing Advice on Insurance

Once cash flow is determined to make objectives happen for the client so they can be on their way, the client needs to understand, evaluate, and gain a handle on the other financial planning disciplines. Some will be relevant while others will not. However, without question, the most important of these areas that affects all clients is being properly insured. It's the old joke. Why? Because my insurance agent told me it was!

In all seriousness, if insurance is not properly analyzed, exposures determined, and possible solutions disclosed, there is little to no chance of making a full recovery and accomplishing anything in the client's financial plan. Here's why. Many years ago, when I was a CPA working on taxes in New York City, I had a tax client visit me during tax season. He said, "Jeff, I have a significant issue I need help with. My house burned down this past year and I had no insurance. I owe a lot of people a lot of money, so I need you to help me get a refund." (Mind you, this was when casualty losses in general could be written off on the Form 1040.) I went through the numbers with him. I asked him what he paid for the house. He answered $19,000 (yes, a long time ago). I said, did you make any improvements to the house? He said yes, I put in $29,000, which made his adjusted basis $48,000. I asked him what the value of the house was before the fire and he stated $190,000. I then asked him what he sold it for and he said $92,000. Excluding personal effects, he had a gain on the loss of his house (capital gain rules were different back then). He had to cash out his retirement account, withdraw all of his investment accounts, pull the college savings plans from the kids, because the bottom line was, he and his family needed a place to live.

And that's the point. None of the other financial planning areas can be done properly without taking care of the basics. I have never had a client over the years tell me they have had too much insurance at the time of a claim. However, I have seen the opposite many times. And unfortunately, by that time, it's too late to make any adjustments or changes to the client's financial plan, which results in nothing being accomplished.

Risk Management and Personal Insurance Perspectives

Risk Management
Life Insurance
Disability Income Insurance (Individual)
Health Insurance
Long-Term Care Insurance (Individual)
Homeowners Insurance
Automobile Insurance
Personal Umbrella Liability Insurance
Directors and Officers (D&O) Liability

RISK MANAGEMENT

The risk management process incorporates the LIADPIM financial planning process from Chapter 3, generally, as part of the overall personal financial planning process. It is important to understand risk as it relates to insurance issues. Transferring risk is only one method of managing risk, although it is the most frequent method.

Rattiner's Secrets: I have a basic rule that I recite to my students and in my lectures about the purchase of insurance. "If you can't afford to write the check to cover an item/issue, or it will kill you to write that check, you need insurance!" For example, if your client ends up in the hospital for two months with a total bill of $500,000 (been there, done that), a safe bet is that the client will not be able to pay out of pocket to fully cover that expense, which is why health insurance would be necessary.

On the flipside, let's assume your client's 10-year-old car is totaled in an auto accident. The client is not injured, but the car loss per Kelley Blue Book value is $15,000. I say to the client, "I know you have $15,000 to cover the loss because I manage your investments, I know what you earn, I do your tax return," etc. And then I ask the million-dollar question: "How do you feel about writing a check to cover the $15,000 loss?" Pretty regularly, clients tell me that it would kill them to write that check. As a result, the client sees the significance and purpose of carrying collision and comprehensive insurance and can answer that question directly.

Now let me backtrack a little. Insurance (risk transfer) is only one way of dealing with client risk. Risk is a condition of the world, even if we are not aware of it. Risk can be briefly defined as the possibility of an unfavorable departure from a desired outcome that the client is clinging to, expecting, or hoping for. In other words, if something does not go according to plan, how can clients protect themselves? Risk management addresses the ways to deal with it.

There are other risk management options the client needs to be aware of to respond to risk. Once a risk is identified, it can be managed in one of the following ways:

Retention (a method of risk *financing*): This means that if the loss occurs, the client will absorb it. If we put leftovers in the refrigerator with the intention of eating them later, we run the risk of forgetting about them until it is too late and we will have to throw them out. Also called risk retention, self-insurance is the concept of insuring oneself or others (such as company employees) without transferring the risk to a third party. Sometimes, large companies may self-insure (for example, the medical needs of their employees) by establishing a separate fund for losses (known as an insurance reserve) and assuming the ability to predict future losses. Risk retention involves a client's son who recently got his license to drive. The client bought his son a 2012 Honda. He purchased liability insurance but no damage protection. The car gets totaled. The client assumed that risk.

Diversification (a method of risk *control*): This is closely related to risk avoidance and reduction. It is the process of spreading the risk over several or many potential possibilities for loss. It is most frequently observed in the context of investments, where a collection of assets (known as a portfolio) is spread over several investment categories or sectors and several stocks within those categories (see Chapter 6).

Sharing (a method of risk *financing*): This states that the client can absorb some but not all of the loss. A good example would be the use of a deductible. Client says, "Jeff, I can cover the first $100, $300, $500 deductible or whatever amount with an out-of-pocket capped at $3,000, but after that I need to turn that payment responsibility to someone who is in a better financial position than I am."

Reduction (a method of risk *control*): This is any attempt to lessen the chance that a loss will occur. With a car, you can protect the likelihood of a loss by prepping in advance. By installing a car alarm, the client minimizes the chance of the vehicle getting stolen, or by taking driver's education, the client minimizes the chance perhaps of getting into an auto accident; a homeowner who installs a burglar alarm, sprinkler system in the house or lives near a firehouse; a building owner who is tired of having his front window broken and items stolen so installs a protective grill and shatterproof glass.

Avoidance (a method of risk *control*): This means making changes or not engaging in the activity so the loss will not occur. If an individual is concerned that they will be severely injured while climbing a mountain, avoiding the climb will eliminate the possibility of that injury. It won't eliminate the possibility of getting hurt doing something else, but they won't get hurt climbing a mountain.

Transfer (a method of risk *financing*): This is the mechanism of insurance as discussed above. When a loss is big enough that we can't afford to retain it, we let someone else deal with the potential loss. For example, the client pays an insurance company a premium for a home in exchange for potential coverage worth hundreds of thousands of dollars.

There are four elements for a risk to be insurable (or permitting the risk to be transferred to a third person or entity, such as an insurance company). These elements are:

- There must be a sufficient number of large and similar (homogeneous) types of events to make the loss reasonably predictable and certain to occur.
- The losses must be definite and measurable.
- The losses must be fortuitous or accidental (not intentional).
- The losses must not be catastrophic to society.

The classic risk management process chart I have used for more than 30 years attempts to match the severity of the potential loss with the probability that the loss will occur. As a result, the following matrix may be used in practical application:

Severity with probability	High probability of loss	Low probability of loss
High severity of loss	*Avoid* the risk	*Transfer* the risk
Low severity of loss	*Reduce* the risk	*Retain* the risk

Finally, a few other pointers to consider. As distinguished from a risk, a peril is an event that causes a loss, such as fire, windstorm, theft, hail. A hazard is a condition or situation that either increases or creates the likelihood or chance that a loss will occur from a given peril. For example, building a house in a flood plain increases the chance that a loss from flood (the peril) will occur. The law of large numbers recognizes that as the more trials of a certain activity are observed, the greater the reliability is in predicting the outcome. Adverse selection says that individuals who are most likely to need insurance benefits are the ones most likely to buy it. Adverse selection happens when poorer-risk individuals are permitted to purchase insurance without paying adequate premiums for the risk assumed.

How much insurance is necessary?

Many times, the calculation for any type of insurance considered is not thorough. Working through the client's potential risk exposures is the surefire way to make sure coverage is adequate. The value of the asset, the additional liability exposure, both personally and professionally, the replacement of income to continue in the event of disability, the cost of practical health care now and in the future, the need to pay off debt such as a house or car, the financial situation that must continue for the family after death are all examples of aspects that should be taken into account.

Remember, when purchasing life insurance, the amount of coverage needed is more important than the type. My lineup is:

- Amount of coverage needed
- Resources available
- Product type

Purchasing what may be a better type of insurance but in a lesser amount really doesn't address the need.

> **Rattiner's Secrets:** In calculating the amount of life insurance necessary, I bring up this question during the data-gathering and goal-setting stage of the financial planning process. I would say to the client, "If you or your spouse were to die today, what would you want to continue in your absence?" A sampling of responses may include, "Jeff, I want enough money to pay for my children's education and enough money to give them while they are in college. I want money for my surviving spouse till he/she turns retirement age and from retirement age until death; money for an emergency fund; the ability to pay off all of the outstanding and perhaps anticipated debt; money to cover payments for estate taxes, for succession planning issues for our business, for child support, legacies, other obligations, and for many other significant issues which could arise." I then take the present value of each of these cash flows and total them up to determine the proper amount of life insurance needed now. Note that not all of these items are present today, but you need to figure out which exposures will be present at some point in the future. And the importance of monitoring the client's financial plan, including the amount of life insurance needed, is essential because things change. What may be an issue today may not be in the future, and vice versa.

LIFE INSURANCE

Life insurance is a unique and critical part of any financial plan. It is often compared to other products in an attempt to prove its superiority or inferiority. All of the comparisons only compare part of what life insurance is all about. More than anything, life insurance is the only product in existence that promises to deliver a specified amount of cash upon the death of the insured. It has other attributes, but it is this one attribute that makes it stand alone as part of the foundation of any viable financial plan.

Life insurance guarantees that time (dying too soon) is not a factor. All other alternatives require time combined with experienced investment advice and a cooperative economy to provide what life insurance provides from the day it is issued.

There are two primary types of life insurance: term insurance (also known as temporary insurance) and cash value insurance (also known as permanent insurance). Which one of these types of insurance is best for the client depends on the consideration of a number of factors:

- **Duration of the need:** If the need is short-term, term life insurance is likely best; if the need is longer-term, cash value insurance is preferable.
- **The amount of life insurance needed:** Either type of policy may be used in addressing this need, although term insurance provides the maximum benefit per unit of premium cost.
- **The amount of disposable income of the proposed policy owner:** If the client has little disposable income, term insurance is preferable.
- **The financial self-discipline of the policy owner:** Since cash value insurance requires fixed premiums for a longer period of time, the client must be disciplined enough to make the payments to ensure coverage.
- **The risk tolerance level of the policy owner:** If the owner demonstrates more risk tolerance, the client may wish to purchase a certain type of cash value policy known as a variable policy.
- **The attitude of the client with respect to life insurance:** If, for some reason, the policy owner exhibits a prejudice against life insurance as a viable financial product, he or she should likely purchase only a term policy, as it will provide for much shorter protection.

In practice, many clients will have a variety of short-term and long-term needs, thus a combination of term and cash value insurance is most appropriate.

Types of term insurance

Term insurance comes in a number of forms. Yearly or annually renewable term (YRT or ART) is a policy that typically has the lowest first-year premium, but it increases every year as the insured gets older. Some term forms have guaranteed level premiums (also known as level term) for up to 30-plus years. For competitive reasons, few companies actually guarantee premiums for more than 10 years. To do so requires substantially greater reserves, which force the premium to be much higher than for policies with only a 10-year guarantee. A small number of term policies sold are *decreasing term*. These are generally sold as mortgage policies. Most are designed to have straight-line reductions rather than mirror the decrease in a mortgage balance. These typically have a level premium. Finally, there is also *reentry term*, a policy where the insurance company may renew coverage at a lower rate than would otherwise apply, provided that, at the time of renewal, the insured furnishes evidence of continued insurability.

Types of cash value insurance policies

Cash value insurance also has a number of variations and hybrids since many companies put their own spin on them, but there are too many to mention here. There are traditional "whole life" forms and universal life forms. Either of these can be either fixed or variable. There are also many types of hybrid policies available. Our discussions will focus on the traditional types of policies. With fixed traditional forms of permanent insurance, there are participating and nonparticipating policies.

Participating policies pay dividends; nonparticipating policies do not. Among nonparticipating policies, there can be interest adjusted or excess interest forms. Since the mid-1980s, there have been very few traditional permanent, nonparticipating policies sold that do not have some method of crediting excess interest to them.

Whole life insurance

Whole life (WL) is the basic form of traditional permanent insurance. It features a guaranteed death benefit, a guaranteed premium, and a guaranteed cash value. These policies generally are designed to have premiums paid and benefits continue, many times to age 121, at which time the policy endows. It endows when the face amount of the policy and guaranteed cash value are the same.

Whole life insurance provides protection for the "whole" of one's life. That means for the entire lifetime of the insured. Whole life policies can take the form of a straight whole life policy and a limited pay life policy.

A straight whole life policy provides protection for the whole of life, with a level premium calculated on the assumption that it will be payable over the insured's entire lifetime. Variations of traditional whole life insurance include ordinary whole life, limited pay whole life, graded premium or modified whole life, and current assumption whole life (CAWL), a type of whole life where the interest rate credited to the policy owner fluctuates with the investment experience of the insurer. At one time the single premium whole life policy, where all future premiums are paid at once with a lump sum or at the time of initial issuance, was hugely popular. The single premium was for the amount a policy owner would pay to have the policy fully paid at issue date. This type of policy is rarely used today.

Limited pay whole life policies are a form of whole life insurance whose premiums are payable only for a limited number of years. Continuous protection is provided for the whole of one's life, but premiums are payable only for a limited period. These policies come in different endowment variations, such as a life paid up at 65 policy. This is essentially a whole life policy with premiums increasing so that they stop at age 65, but the policy is guaranteed to last until the age at endowment. The policy becomes a paid-up policy at the end of the premium paying period.

For either type of WL policy, the insured pays more money upfront than necessary to cover the costs, so when mortality costs become higher in the later years, there is sufficient money to dip into the policy and use those funds for the whole of one's life.

Rattiner's Secrets: One of the attributes of WL policies that clients like is that the investment risk of the policy is transferred to the insurance company rather than moving to the client, so if things do not go according to plan, the client will generally be protected with these types of policies. Many advisors today compare this to my earlier quote on the first page of this book, "your father's Oldsmobile," since WL has been around a long time and many products have come out since then. Because of the risk transfer mechanism and level higher premiums initially during the policy term that make funding easier as the client gets older, this is one of my preferential policy types.

Universal life (UL) policies tie a term policy with one whose investments are mainly in money market–type accounts. Flexibility becomes the key variable since the insured can either increase the premium or the death benefit within the existing policy, thus providing the insured with many options. In fact, if cash value is adequate to cover the expenses from the policy, in many types of universal life the insured does not have to put in premiums, thus leading to the term "vanishing pay" policy.

With UL insurance, there is no fixed premium and the premium is not tied to the face amount except in the first year. Premiums are paid into an accumulation fund. Each month the mortality charges, rider charges, and expenses are taken from the accumulation side of the policy. There are two death benefit options in universal life policies: Option A or 1 and Option B or 2. The Option A death benefit includes the cash accumulation fund. The mortality charges are based on the net amount at risk, the face amount of the policy minus the accumulation fund. With Option B, increasing death benefit, the death benefit is equal to the face amount plus the accumulation fund. This means that the monthly mortality charges are based on the face amount of the policy every year; thus, a greater accumulation fund is required to keep the policy in force.

The premium is credited to the policyholder's account minus any expense charges from which the insurer deducts mortality charges, which then allows the insurer to credit investment income based on the insurer's investment success.

> **Rattiner's Secrets:** Many clients like the flexibility of UL policies (although it was a better deal in the 1980s and 1990s when money market rates were higher) because if the client is strapped for cash and has issues regarding future premium payments, as long as there is a cash surrender value in the policy to cover the operating expenses and mortality costs of the policy, premiums can be minimized or even skipped. However, if the policy cannot support the lack of an annual premium, the policy could lapse, which may eliminate the insurance.

Variable life (VL) policies are a form of insurance that invests the policy-holder's contributions into a securities portfolio selected by the policyholder. Unlike whole life and universal life where the insurance companies select the investment mechanism, with variable life policies the insured selects from any number of investment types offered by the insurer. As a result, the owner's rate of return is dependent on the underlying investments selected by the insured. Therefore, these products, which combine insurance securities, also can only be sold by insurance advisors who hold an insurance license and a securities license (Series 6 or 7).

VL insurance policies have no guaranteed minimum return, with the actual return realized completely dependent on the return earned by the separate accounts (usually mutual funds) in which the accumulated funds are invested. If part of a universal policy (so-called variable universal life or VUL), the premium payments are also flexible (not fixed) so long as a minimum monthly mortality expense amount is satisfied. Since variable life insurance is considered to be a "security," as defined under current law, as well as a life insurance product, a financial planner who wishes to sell the product must have two licenses: a FINRA Series 6 securities license and a state insurance license.

There is risk associated with variable life policies. The primary risk or disadvantage is that the policies return less than a traditional life insurance policy while the advantages include the insured can earn a rate of return higher than investing in traditional insurance policies through the investment in securities.

Since variable life policies can be selected at the discretion of the insured, investing in the equity side of the market can allow for a better upside return potential and a better inflation hedge than with traditional insurance products.

As a potential hedge tool, when the insured takes on a higher level of risk by focusing mainly on investments in securities, the potential for greater cash values and increased death benefits provides more benefit than a traditional type of insurance product investment; however, if the investments don't turn out as well as initially thought, the cash value can drop below that of a traditional insurance product. With a VL policy only, in no instances can the death benefit be eliminated through poor investment performance because the insured always has a guaranteed minimum death benefit.

Both variable life and variable universal life policies require that the insurance company keep the client's cash value in an account separate from the company's general investment account. These separate account contributions are then invested in sub-accounts, with each being separately managed and tied to a specific investment objective. These sub-accounts provide for creditor protection. In tough times like the 2008 financial crises, clients who invested in these types of policies fared better. This sub-account is the primary difference between these types of products and traditional insurance products.

Rattiner's Secrets: Many clients like the VL (not VUL) policy essentially as a hedge. That means the VL policy has a guaranteed minimum death benefit where the similarities to WL exist and the same fixed premium is paid for the life of the policy. If the underlying investments tend to increase, that will increase the death benefit as well. If the client is aggressive with respect to the underlying investments, the worst-case scenario with a VL only is that a minimal amount of cash will be in the account but the guaranteed minimum death benefit (original amount contracted for) will still be met. However, this may make clients more aggressive than they need to be.

Nonforfeiture options

Permanent, cash-value type insurance policies have a reserve, a cash value that makes it possible for them to be permanent. Without such a reserve, the policies would be considered as term insurance. A policy owner may decide at some point in time that they no longer need the full amount of permanent insurance or can no longer pay the premium. When this happens, the client has a number of choices (see below). By law, when a policy owner no longer wants to pay for permanent insurance, all or a portion of the reserves must be returned to that owner. They are not required to forfeit these values, thus the name "nonforfeiture options."

There are three basic nonforfeiture options:

1. **Cash:** The full cash surrender value may be taken in a lump sum or applied to any of the settlement options (see below). The cash surrender value may be different than the actual reserves the company maintains to support the policy, especially in the early years. If the cash surrender value exceeds the premiums contributed, the difference could be subject to ordinary income tax.

2. **Reduced paid-up insurance:** This option permits the owner to maintain some insurance with no premiums due. The face amount of insurance is determined by the available cash value. The policy contains a table of guaranteed values which shows how much paid-up insurance would be provided at the end of each policy year. This is exclusive of dividend values that may increase the paid-up insurance. The reduced paid-up insurance has a cash value equal to the surrender value of the policy before the change.

3. **Extended term insurance:** This option takes the surrender value and applies it as a single premium to purchase the original face amount of insurance as a term policy for as long as it will last. An example might be that at the end of the 10th year of a policy, it can be surrendered for an extended term insurance policy for the same face amount that provides protection for the next 18 years and 72 days. If an owner stops paying premiums, as stated above, the policy generally pays the premium through an automatic premium loan. If that provision has not been provided for under the policy provisions, or if there is not enough money to pay the next premium, the default lapse option is extended term insurance. The presumption is that the insurance was purchased for protection against the financial hardships created by death, so keeping the most insurance in force for the longest period of time possible is the most logical choice for the policy owner.

Rattiner's Secrets: The reduced paid-up insurance option tends to work best for clients for a few reasons. It's tough to make a decision to give up all insurance. The client may decide after the children graduate college or some other milestone that they don't need as much life insurance as they initially did. As a result, the client can cancel the policy outright and receive the cash under option 1. However, if the client has a change of mind down the road and discovers they need more coverage, perhaps for other issues that arise at that time, many times health issues can get in the way, which may prohibit the client from purchasing insurance. In addition, even if the client qualifies to purchase insurance, as people get older, health issues may make underwriting conditions less favorable and more costly.

Long-term care rider

Similar to a nonforfeiture option, a long-term care rider is a hybrid type of policy that may be added to some life insurance policies for those clients who are concerned about losing the funds if they do not have a claim. (See more about long-term care later on.) By purchasing a life insurance policy with a long-term care rider, the insured will either receive a payout for long-term care or the beneficiary will receive the death benefit if the need for LTC never kicks in. Remember, using the life insurance policy for long-term care will reduce or eliminate the life insurance death benefit.

Settlement options

When a lump sum of money is available from a life insurance policy for any reason, such as death of the insured, termination of the policy, or maturity of the policy as an endowment, the money may be taken by the designated beneficiaries in several different ways. These are the ways the company "settles up with" (pays) the owner of the money.

The most common types of settlement options are:

1. **Cash:** This option is the most common distribution of death benefits, surrender values, and endowment maturity payments. It may not be preferable in all circumstances, but it is the most common choice of the insured or beneficiary.
2. **Specified amount of income:** This may be the best option to protect a beneficiary from spending the insurance proceeds much too quickly. The insurance company will use a current guaranteed annuity payout

schedule to determine how long the principal will last after the beneficiary chooses the monthly income to be received.

3. **Payments for a fixed period:** This option enables the future value of the proceeds to be calculated and paid in installments for a specified number of years. It is similar to the specified amount of income option, but instead the beneficiary states that the income is to be provided monthly for the next 10 years (or whatever period of time they desire). The insurance company then calculates how much each payment will be, again using current or guaranteed rates, whichever is higher.

4. **Interest only:** This should probably be the first option chosen by many beneficiaries. Here, the insurance company makes payments of the interest earned on the lump sum until one or more other settlement options are chosen. This permits all options under the insurance policy to remain available. The insurer holds the proceeds and pays interest to the beneficiary until such time as the beneficiary withdraws the principal.

5. **Life income options:** These options provide an income for the life of the beneficiary. It can be a "life only" choice, which provides the highest monthly income but ends at the death of the beneficiary, even it is only a few months after the benefits begin. Alternatively, the life income option can be a "life income with a period certain." This means that when the insured dies, if the period certain, such as 10 years, has not yet elapsed, payments will continue to their named beneficiary for the balance of that period.

6. **Joint and survivor life income options:** These are really another form of life income option but are based on two lives rather than one. With a joint and full survivor option, the benefit payment will be the lowest. However, the form also promises that the same payment will be made as long as either person lives. A joint and one-half survivor option will provide more income while both individuals are still alive but only half that amount to the survivor when the first payee dies.

DISABILITY INCOME INSURANCE (INDIVIDUAL)

The definition of disability is the most important rider on any disability income policy. There are three primary definitions of disability used in the underwriting of any individual disability income policy. These generally are:

1. Own occupation (own occ)/not working in any other occupation.
2. Hybrid/split definition/modified occupation.
3. Any occupation.

Finally, there is the Social Security definition of disability, commonly known as the inability to work in "any substantial gainful activity." This is the most restrictive and stringent definition; thus, qualifying to receive Social Security disability benefits is not easy.

Rattiner's Secrets: The issue most clients do not think about when deciding whether to purchase disability insurance is whether it is worth the cost. Some clients have told me that if they are really disabled, then the government will cover them under Social Security benefits. What they probably don't realize is that the payout for Social Security disability is limited, essentially to what the client's Social Security benefits would be. For example, if the client is making $500,000 per year and they say to you that they don't need disability insurance because the government will take care of them if they become severely disabled, you can point out while yes, that may be a true statement, the government is not going to support you at your current lifestyle. That number may be rounded down to somewhere around the $3,000 or so range, a far cry from what the client is used to!

The most generous definition is own occupation. This means that the insured is eligible if they cannot work in their occupation, or perform the specific duties of their occupation, at the time of the onset of the disability. It makes no difference if they are earning more money in a different occupation, as long as they are unable to work in their prior occupation. This very generous definition is often called "ego insurance." Next is own occupation and not working in any other occupation. This basically leaves it up to the insured. If they cannot work in the occupation they were in at the time of disability, and they choose not to work in another occupation, even if they could, benefits will be paid.

A hybrid or split definition provides own occ types of benefits generally for the first two years and reverts to any occupation benefits thereafter. Again, many clients probably don't realize it but this is generally most common. The next level is modified any occupation. This definition states that the insured cannot work in their occupation or any occupation for which they are suited by education, training, or experience. This means the insurance company cannot deny benefits if the person worked, for example, at a skilled job earning $25.00 per hour but is now only able to do nonskilled work at $8.00 per hour. Next is any occupation. This definition states that the insured will receive benefits if they cannot work and perform the duties in their own occupation or any other occupation. This is very restrictive, but not as much as the definition to receive Social Security disability income benefits. The Social Security definition states that the individual cannot work in "any substantial gainful activity" and that the disability is expected to last at least one year and/or end in death.

Beyond the basic definitions, some disability income policies provide different benefit levels for disabilities that are total, partial, and/or residual in nature. Total disability benefits provide for the full policy benefit. Partial benefits are typically paid at a fixed percentage of the basic policy amount if the insured is able to work but at a reduced level of income. Such a policy typically requires at least a 25% reduction in the policyholder's income. Partial benefits might be paid for as long as the policy benefit period, or for only a specified number of months. Residual benefits are based on the percentage of income lost following total disability or prior to a total disability. For example, if an insured has been totally disabled but can now return to work and earn only 40% of their prior income, the policy will pay 60% of the basic monthly benefit. This benefit typically lasts as long as the policy benefit period.

> **Rattiner's Secrets:** This is far and away the most important feature of a disability policy. The only one I ever recommend is the own occ definition. Yes, it's a rider and costs more, but it is well worth it. The example I use in my CPA lectures is, let's say you are an accountant and you can't account anymore. But you can teach accounting, sell accounting software, or even sell pencils on the street corner. If you can do a related job, you can work in that field and still receive your benefits. The issue I see is that most clients think they have that, and then unfortunately expectations are not managed because if disability strikes at a later age, they think they are going to receive benefits under this more favorable scenario only to find out more often than not that they don't.

Benefit period

The benefit period is the number of months or years that a policy will provide payments if the insured qualifies under the policy's definition of disability.

The greatest period that individuals can often obtain is until the insured attains age 65 (or qualifies for Medicare). Some companies have increased the age and more will continue to do so as people live longer and retire later.

Those who qualify for lesser benefit periods are generally limited to five years from the onset of the disability. In most cases, benefits for illness are the same as for injury, but some companies will offer different benefit periods in the same policy.

Premiums for disability insurance are based in part on morbidity rates for the benefit period. The morbidity rate is the probability of a person becoming disabled over a given time period.

Elimination period

The elimination period for a disability policy is equivalent to a deductible in other types of insurance coverage. Specifically, the elimination period is the number of days or months following the onset of a disability that must pass before any benefits will be paid. Essentially, it's the waiting period necessary to be satisfied before benefits begin.

The choice of elimination period has a direct effect on the premium of a policy. A longer elimination period reduces the premium because it reduces the potential number of disabilities that will be covered. Some policies have a presumptive disability provision. This provision states that if the insured suffers a loss of both feet, both hands, one of each, sight or hearing, or, in some cases, speech, then the insured is presumed to be disabled, even following a rehabilitative period, if the loss continues. Presumptive disability provisions may require the loss to be total and permanent or just as long as the loss persists. Still further, some policies require severance of the hands or feet while others require only the "loss of use of" the affected parts.

Benefit amount

The benefit amount is generally a fixed sum that is determined when the application for the policy is submitted. It is usually based on the applicant's income at the time. For example, the payment of a benefit equivalent to 50–60% of the insured's gross monthly pay is common. However, riders to the policy, discussed below, may modify this amount. Many policies also have a "relation to earnings clause" that permits the company to reduce the benefit if the insured has a reduced income for an extended period of time before the onset of disability. This is done to protect the insurance company from excessive claims and malingering when insureds suffer a loss of income because of a changing economy. Substantial nonpension assets at the time of application may also reduce or eliminate an individual's ability to obtain coverage.

Riders are attachments to the basic disability income policy that may provide additional benefits or modifications to the benefits. A guaranteed insurability rider permits the insured to increase their benefits at specified times in the years following the initial issuance of the policy. Unlike the similar rider used with life insurance, the insurance companies apply financial underwriting (but not health underwriting) at the time of application for the increase to determine whether the insured is eligible for the increased benefit. Cost of living (COL) riders automatically increase the benefits over time. There are two forms. The first increases the insured monthly amount every 2–5 years. Financial underwriting is also done at this same time. If the insured does not qualify for the increase, the policy stops increasing and the rider is dropped. This form is also called an additional insurance rider (AIR). The other approach is to increase the benefits once they begin. This is typically at a rate of 5–7% each year. The benefit increases in some cases are limited to doubling the initial benefit; in other cases they are limited to quintupling the initial benefit. Social insurance riders generally permit the insured to have an increased benefit that is paid unless and until social insurance of some sort, such as Social Security Disability Income, kicks in. At this point, the benefit amount under the policy is reduced by the amount of social insurance paid.

Practical examples:

1. Fred has a disability income (DI) policy with a 60-day elimination period that pays $2,500 per month. If he is totally disabled under the terms of his contract for six months, when will he get his first check and how much will it be? Fred's first check will arrive at the end of 90 days and will be for $2,500.

2. Katherine has a $3,000 per month DI policy with an additional insurance rider that automatically increases her benefit level by 5% every two years for 10 years, if she qualifies. When the third opportunity came up, the company did financial underwriting and found that she was eligible for a $100 per month increase. What was the result? Katherine will not be granted the increase and the rider will be terminated.

Continuation provisions

An important factor to consider before purchasing a disability income insurance policy is whether the policy may be renewed and under what terms. There are three basic options:

1. **Guaranteed renewable:** Under this provision, the right to renew the policy is guaranteed (regardless of the insured's health at the time), but the insurance company is permitted to increase the policy premiums if it does so for all insureds of the same underwriting class.
2. **Noncancellable:** With this provision, the insurance company guarantees the renewal of the disability income policy for a stated period without an increase in future premiums. For this reason, the premiums associated with a noncancellable policy are higher than those of a guaranteed renewable policy.
3. **Conditionally renewable:** A policy that is conditionally renewable may not be canceled by the insurance company during the policy term, but the company may refuse to renew the policy for a subsequent term if, for example, the insured's health declines. The policy premium here is less than either the guaranteed renewable or noncancellable policy since the insured does not have as much security that coverage will be continued.

Taxation of premiums and benefits

In an individual disability income policy, the insurance premiums are not deductible. However, since those premiums are nondeductible, any benefits paid from the policy are nontaxable to the insured upon receipt.

Note that the taxable result is the opposite for most group disability income policies. There, since the employer corporation is permitted a premium deduction as an "ordinary and necessary" business expense, the benefits payable are taxable to the insured employee.

Rattiner's Secrets: Unfortunately, there are those who write off disability premiums or reimburse themselves. A story I share in my lectures involves a business owner who would have his company reimburse himself on December 31 for the cost of the disability premium since he did

(continued)

(*continued*)

not file a claim for that current year. He started receiving disability benefits 12 years later. Fast forward about 20 years from the original policy issue date. He was audited on an unrelated issue and upon investigating the original audit issue, the auditor discovered that he was reimbursing himself on the cost of the disability premiums on the last day of the year, which again are not deductible. As a result, the audit was now extended to include the disability reimbursements. Because of this action, the reimbursements were disallowed, which resulted in higher annual incomes. The increased income led to the business owner paying more income tax, penalties, and underpayment penalties. Ouch!

HEALTH INSURANCE

Health insurance is an essential element of your client's financial security. If you go back to my rule of thumb example, it's pretty obvious, and should be purchased. Risk retention, as stated earlier, can be a possibility, but generally it is never a good one. The assumption is that this exposure is being well taken care of by you with your clients so only a basic level of information is devoted to this subject.

Health insurance can be provided on a group basis (through the employer) and on an individual-level, where policies provide for reimbursement for the insured's illness or injury. Group plans are generally better. Policies can be purchased through managed care plans (that emphasize cost control) and include health maintenance organizations (HMOs), preferred provider organizations (PPOs), and point of service plans. Tax-advantaged plans include health savings accounts (HSAs) and health reimbursement arrangements (HRAs). Major medical is a great setup but unfortunately more of a rarity. For those individuals who can't get coverage from other channels, the Affordable Care Act (ACA) provides hope. Medicare generally provides health insurance for people age 65 and older. To cover potential gaps in Medicare coverage, clients can purchase a Medigap policy.

HSAs are high-deductible plans and popular with clients. Generally, contributions made to an HSA may be made by the employer or by the client, or both. If made by the employer, contributions are excluded from the client's income. If made by the client directly, HSAs are generally deductible from income. Distributions from HSAs are not includable in gross income if they are used exclusively to pay qualified medical expenses.

Premiums can be paid on either a pre-tax or a post-tax basis. Premiums are tax-deductible. For self-employed persons, it can be written off as a separate above-the-line deduction. For employees, it gets lumped together with other medical expenses as an itemized deduction and in aggregate must exceed 10% of adjusted gross income (AGI) to be deductible. Benefits are generally exempt from income tax.

If your client works for a company of 20 or more employees and quits or gets fired, they could apply for COBRA (Consolidated Omnibus Budget Reconciliation Act), which is federal legislation that certain employers use to extend existing health insurance coverage to newly departed employees. This means that if you quit, or get fired, as long as you don't get fired for gross misconduct, COBRA can extend coverage for up to 18 months for an individual, 29 months if disabled, and up to 36 months in death or divorce situations at group rates. The misperception with COBRA is that clients think it is expensive. While there is some truth to that, the reality is the maximum premium that can be charged to the client is 102% of the applicable premium. Coverage may not be conditioned upon evidence of insurability. All who qualify can apply and receive coverage. It appears expensive because the company no longer has to subsidize some of the health insurance premium.

> **Rattiner's Secrets:** I generally coach my clients to take COBRA, if applicable, and if they do not have an immediate job prospect. With COBRA, the client knows what they are getting. They have already experienced it. They know their doctors participate in the existing plan and can better prepare for what's in store. Companies have 14 days to ask the employee whether they would like to participate and employees have 60 days to respond. An employee can go to the doctor during the 60 days and then elect to take COBRA. If the client is going to take another job right away, it probably makes sense to go to that plan, but care should be taken to compare the two. I like to draw a side-by-side comparison chart to highlight the pros and cons for each particular plan of coverage.

LONG-TERM CARE INSURANCE (INDIVIDUAL)

The basic provisions of any long-term care insurance policy include a specified monthly benefit and the definition of when the individual is eligible for benefits. Generally, eligibility is measured as the lack of the ability of the insured to perform a specified number of activities of daily living

(ADLs). Typically, the requirement is that the individual needs "substantial assistance" with two of either five or six.

ADLs

The Health Insurance Portability and Accountability Act of 1996 (HIPAA) lists six ADLs: dressing, transferring, toileting, eating, bathing, and/or maintaining continence. These are the ADLs that must be used for an individual to be eligible for benefits under the policy. Additionally, an individual who has "cognitive impairment," which is the loss of brain function (such as Alzheimer's disease), must be a benefit trigger to activate the LTC policy.

If the LTC policy is tax-qualified under the provisions of HIPAA, premiums paid by the policy owner are deductible as medical expenses on Schedule A, IRS Form 1040 (in other words, the taxpayer must itemize their deductions to claim the deduction for long-term care insurance premiums). However, the amount of the deduction that may be claimed is limited to a dollar amount based on the individual's age (not adjusted gross income as is the case with most other medical deductions) and is indexed annually. The older the client is, the bigger the maximum allowable deduction.

Services covered

LTC insurance often does more than pay for those confined to long-term care facilities. It may provide for in-home care, assisted living, as well as day care–type facilities for seniors who need assistance or supervision. (Indeed, most individuals do not purchase an LTC policy to provide payment for assisted living or any custodial care coverage but because they want to stay at home in their senior years and thus are most interested in the home health care coverage.) Some policies also provide respite care for primary caregivers.

There are seven basic types of coverage afforded by the standard LTC policies. They are as follows:

1. **Skilled nursing care:** This is the highest level of medical care available and is provided by most nursing homes on a daily basis (often in a separate part of the facility). Note that Medicare may pay for a limited number of days here, but only when there is skilled nursing care being provided and the patient prognosis is for improvement.
2. **Intermediate nursing care:** This is similar to skilled nursing care, except that care is provided on an occasional rather than a daily basis.

3. **Home health care:** Care is provided at home, typically by a licensed nurse or nurse practitioner.

4. **Custodial care:** This is traditional nursing home care and does not have to be ordered or supervised by a physician.

5. **Assisted living:** This provides support services for individuals who need some (but limited) help with the activities of daily living.

6. **Adult day care:** This care is provided for individuals who need assistance at home but whose spouse or other caregiving family members must work outside the home.

7. **Hospice care:** This is care for the terminally ill and may take place at the patient's home or at a hospice care center.

Benefit period

Most LTC policies are underwritten using a defined-period approach where the benefit is paid for a defined amount of time (for example, three years) following an elimination period (see below). As might be anticipated, the longer the benefit period, the higher the monthly period. Currently, the average stay in a nursing home is only 2.28 years; however, the average is 270 days for residents who have been discharged. Accordingly, many individuals will reside in a nursing home or assisted living facility much longer than that. As a result, you may be well advised to purchase for your client a five-year benefit period or, perhaps, a lifetime benefit period. Of course, as stated, an LTC insurance policy with a lifetime benefit period will be much more expensive than those limiting the period over which benefits are paid.

Elimination period

Like a disability income insurance policy, LTC policies also include an elimination period before any benefits are payable. Usually, this elimination period is structured to match the emergency fund amount (discussed in Chapter 4) held by the insured, for example, three months or 90 days. The period can be longer, of course. If the insured elects a longer elimination period, the monthly policy premium will be lower, but, alternatively, additional months of LTC expense must be self-funded by the policy owner (usually, also the insured).

Those with relatively low income and few assets would be well advised to not purchase LTC insurance at all and expect that, if need be, the government Medicaid program will provide assistance with payment of LTC expenses.

Those of moderate income and with assets they want to pass on to their heirs should likely have LTC insurance (and with as short an elimination period as affordable). Finally, those who are well off may choose to retain the risk of LTC, using assets and income to pay LTC costs (a self-funded approach).

Rattiner's Secrets: Probably the hardest issue in this type of planning is to get family members all together and in agreement on how to act in the best interests of their relatives. I have run through these issues countless times with clients and have seen many families go their separate ways as a result. My general rules of thumb include advising clients with under $100,000 of net worth or over $2 million that they probably don't need LTC policies. In the former case, the client can probably qualify for Medicaid and alleviate this expense. In the latter, they can self-insure. The ones in between those numbers are the more likely group who will need these benefits.

If you believe your client needs to purchase an LTC policy and they don't want to for whatever reason, have them a sign a waiver. Many clients think if they don't use it, it's a waste of money and could impede them in other issues. There are refund options that could be purchased but are more expensive. Here is what I learned from a student in one of my Fast Track classes.

He was involved in a lawsuit on this very issue from the children of a client. The children, whom he had never met, expected a huge inheritance, but were seemingly stunned when the parents had to go into nursing homes, thereby wiping out all of what supposedly was going to their offspring. The children hired an attorney who took the case on contingency, so the children had nothing to lose. The student went back to the company where he was associated and found the financial plan he wrote on this client (which was saved on microfiche – I'm dating myself). He went to the section dealing with LTC and found that indeed he had recommended this and the client had rejected it flat out – they said they did not want it and both of them signed waivers absolving the planner of any responsibility or liability. Once that was determined, the lawsuit was settled in his favor, eight years after it started. During the process, he was protected through the company and covered through E&O insurance. He had no real outlay of funds, but when it was all said and done, the added and unnecessary stress took a toll on him.

Rattiner's Secrets: Here is where today's issues come in. I have had many family members approach me insisting that they are going to use their planned inheritance to change the world (sort of). But with the client who has net worth over $2 million, who is adamant about not spending the money on LTC policies and figures to use what they have accumulated to pay the costs for themselves, and the beneficiaries are staking their claims to this future inheritance (which they really have no right to) and which may not be there when everything is all said and done, the result is a huge disagreement over the best way to approach this difficult situation and keep everyone happy.

What I do *only* if the clients are totally willing to make this information public and available to their heirs is the following. I get them all together, ideally in a live meeting at my Scottsdale or Denver office. (If this is not possible with people living all over the country or they are just not available, we get them to "link in" using Skype, Zoom, Adobe, or a similar video meeting site.) I then explain the situation about the client's (grandparents, parents, or whoever) reluctance to spend *their* money on long-term care policies and their wish to fund these potential costs themselves while everyone else is waiting for the inheritance. Let's put some numbers on this example to follow along. The grandparents have $10 million and there are five heirs (two children and three grandchildren). I have LTC policies run for them and let's say the policies cost $10,000 in total per year. (Disclaimer: I don't sell any products or receive any commissions.) I then proceed to use my whiteboards, as always, to diagram the situation. I make a recommendation that each of the five heirs contribute $2,000 to pay for the LTC policies, essentially to hedge their bets, to be assured of perhaps receiving at least some or all of the grandparents' moneys, plus whatever the sum may grow to.

Let's overstate and assume that the grandparents live another 20 years. In a worst-case scenario, they are each on the hook for $40,000 and if things work out as planned, they each stand to gain $2 million income tax free (excluding any potential inheritance taxes and assuming the grandparents are under the federal estate tax limits). I'm a numbers guy and think this is a no brainer. And if there are one or more heirs who cannot afford to do this upfront, I ask for someone, if possible, to front them the premiums and they would then receive it back before the assets are

(continued)

(*continued*)

divided. I then go around the room individually and have everyone state their piece. There is also another individual in the room, assisting with the process, taking copious notes. It is also video recorded so if someone forgets about this meeting in 10 years or whenever, we can go to the video-tape! In my experience, this usually gets people to act, but more importantly, everyone knows where each family member stands on the issue so this helps avoid disagreements later on.

HOMEOWNERS INSURANCE

Most financial planners do not work in the property and casualty area, which includes homeowners (HO), automobile (auto), and excess liability (umbrella) insurance. As a result, these key critical exposures can often be very misunderstood.

Every financial plan should include a summary page of all insurance, including homeowners or renters insurance. Unlicensed planners should not give advice about the adequacy of the specific policies and are well advised to encourage their clients to evaluate their coverage with a qualified agent. Developing a working relationship with a good property and casualty insurance agent may give a planner the expertise they need to include recommendations, proposed by the agent, in a client's plan. Understanding the different forms of insurance will also tell the planner whether the right form is being used, or at least what was recommended, which may give them information about the client which they previously did not have. For example, the homeowner may say their home is worth $500,000 but it may be insured for only $200,000 with an HO8 form. This may indicate that it is an old home with a lot of labor-intensive interior finishing and architecture, which is not necessarily insurable at full value.

Homeowner policies are generally valued at replacement cost, not fair market value. Real property consists of land and buildings, such as an individual's home or personal residence. Note that the cost of land is never insured under any form of homeowners insurance. There are a number of forms of insurance that apply to this real property. The two basic types of coverage are for losses to the property and for liability arising out of the ownership of the property. The liability coverage is the same for all forms.

Policy coverages

HO policies can be broken down into two sections, I and II.

Section I Coverages

Coverage A: This includes the dwelling building and anything that is permanently affixed or attached to the main structure/building itself. The land itself is not covered. All covered amounts under coverages B, C, and D are dependent on coverage A. Recommended amounts are listed below. Based on where the property is located, if property is purchased, it will have an effect as to what amount should be carried under coverage A. We remove the cost of the land, but depending on where you live in the country, that could be a huge chunk, like in California, New York, New Jersey, etc., or it can be more standard, as in smaller metropolitan areas.

    Coverage B: This includes other structures and insures any structures separated from the dwelling or connected only by clear space, such as a wall or fence. Examples include a detached garage or a detached fence, separated by clear space.

    Coverage C: This includes personal property owned or used by the client anywhere in the world. Also called contents coverage, this includes your possessions with certain assets covered at reduced amounts. If the client wants additional coverage, then an endorsement, also called a rider and personal property floater, will be warranted up to the appraised value, which covers the asset in full vs. the reduced amount built into the policy. For some of those assets, an appraisal will probably be necessary.

    Coverage D: This includes loss-of-use coverage for additional living expenses incurred if the dwelling becomes uninhabitable due to damage by an insured peril. These are costs above and beyond the client's typical monthly housing expenses. For example, if the client's house burns down, this would cover the temporary housing costs until the house is back in move-in condition.

Section II Coverages

Coverage E: This is personal liability designed to protect the insured from claims brought up by noninsured for bodily injury and property damage claims. A key point is that this amount should tie into the underlying deductible from the umbrella policy (see below). Homeowners policies' liability limits also serve as the basis for any additional personal liability insurance coverage. Such coverage generally covers the cost of defending the individual against potential liability as well as any damages assessed as long as the liability was covered.

Coverage F: This covers medical payments to others for noninsureds injured on the insured's property.

Homeowner policy types

There are many policy types that you should be familiar with. Here's a quick summary. Remember, this coverage is for all owner-occupied residences, primary or secondary properties, and not rental properties. Separate dwelling policies (DP) can be had on those. If your client is a homeowner, the type of policy you would recommend is either both an HO3 policy (replacement cost on the dwelling) and an HO15 policy (replacement cost on the contents) together, or in some states where these benefits are combined, an HO5 policy. If the client is renting, then an HO4 policy is warranted. If the client owns a condominium, then an HO6 policy is warranted. If the client owns an older house, an HO8 is probably where they will be. But the key takeaway here is that coverage on the dwelling may be limited to actual cash value (ACV) = RC − DEP (depreciation). For a house that is 50-plus years old, that could have a big impact. To acquire a more up-to-date policy, the client can update a structural component, say the electric, plumbing, or heating, that could elevate the home into the HO3 category.

The HO15 rider that can be attached to the homeowner's HO3 policy changes coverage for personal property from broad form to open perils. (Sometimes HO3 and HO15 are combined in certain states as an HO5 policy.) Open perils means that everything is covered unless it is specifically listed as an exclusion in the policy. This means that loss and damage are covered. This is great for some losses. However, certain high-value items such as jewelry, silverware, cameras, fine art and antiques, and furs still may not be adequately covered. First, there is an overall limit to the amount of coverage for personal property. Individuals with high-value personal property may rapidly exceed this amount. Second, the basic coverage for personal property limits the amount of liability the insurance company accepts for certain types of property. To adequately cover these high-value items, additional coverage is recommended. This can be obtained in two basic ways: (1) through a personal articles floater (PAF) or personal property endorsement (PPE), an addendum to the basic policy that lists the specific property insured, and its insured value; or (2) through inland marine coverage, which accomplishes the same thing. This is called "scheduled coverage" because there is a schedule, or list, of the property covered and its value attached to the policy. Losses are then reimbursed based on the insured value, not on an actual cash value basis.

Rattiner's Secrets: The better policies have Section I limits to coverages in the following higher amounts based on coverage A:

Coverage B is 30% of coverage A.
Coverage C is 70% of coverage A.
Coverage D is 50% of coverage A.

There are several homeowner companies where potential claims may be reported by an agent directly to the company (before it is filed). Since the client's homeowner policy covers that person for noncommercial purposes, be careful if you rent your house outright or are working with any services, because by definition, that rental probably no longer falls under personal usage. Just double check with the company in advance. Also if the client has renters occupying their property, make sure they tell the renters to purchase an HO4 policy. I have seen situations where renters hold a party, something tragic happens, and as a result, the homeowner's names are attached to a lawsuit of which they had no prior knowledge.

Practical examples:

1. Marlene was playing with her children when one of them bumped a table and knocked over a valuable vase she inherited from her grandparents. What form of insurance would provide coverage for this type of loss? Marlene's vase would be covered with the HO15 rider on her HO3 policy. Without the rider, accidental destruction by the owner is not a named peril, and it is not an exclusion under the HO15 rider.

2. Bill was teaching his daughter how to hit a tennis ball. They were using the garage for a target. She decided to see how hard she could hit the ball and swung with all of her energy. Unfortunately, the racket left her hand and sailed into the neighbor's car, leaving a rather nasty dent. Is this loss covered under Bill's homeowners policy? If so, which coverage? Bill's coverage E, personal liability, would pay for the damage to the neighbor's car.

3. Derek and Daphne were newlyweds renting their first town home. A friend of theirs mentioned that they should get renters insurance to protect their valuables. They considered all of their furniture to be "early attic" hand-me-downs from family, and all of their clothes could probably be replaced at the local thrift store for less than $100. Even their computer, TV, and small kitchen appliances weren't worth much. They wondered why they should consider spending even a few dollars a month on insurance. What coverage as part of the renter's form of homeowners insurance is always important? The personal liability insurance as well as the medical payments to others part of the renter's HO4 policy is very important in case someone is injured while visiting them.

4. Andy wanted to buy a fixer-upper house. He found a great house in an older part of town that was in reasonable condition but needed updating. If the same house had been in a better neighborhood, it would have sold for over $450,000. Because of the neighborhood, he got it for $150,000. He was able to insure it for $130,000 when he bought it. Three years later, there was new wiring, new plumbing, lots of paint stripping to show the 6-in cross-cut cove boards and door frames. Andy called his agent because he knew that it would cost over $400,000 to rebuild this house from the ground up. He also knew that even with the house updated, the most he could sell it for was likely $200,000. He didn't know what to do. His agent told him that he could get $200,000 of coverage with a special policy that would allow him to replace the building if it was destroyed, but with a functional replacement. What policy is he talking about and what coverage does it generally provide? The policy is an HO8 modified form. It only insures against 10 perils for the structure and would provide functional replacement. This means they would pay to have a house built, but with current building methods and materials rather than the labor-intensive methods using rare or unavailable materials as used in the original home.

Terminology

Here are some important terms used in the application of property, casualty, and liability insurance coverage:

- **Replacement cost coverage:** When a loss occurs, the loss is covered to the amount it will cost to replace or repair the lost or damaged property. It doesn't matter if the property is 20 years old, if a like item can be purchased, or if an appraisal determines the property's current fair market value, that is, the amount that is covered if replacement cost coverage applies. As a result, replacement cost coverage does not take into account any physical depreciation of the property.

- **Actual cash value (ACV):** This is the depreciated value of an item. For example, if the same item was covered under this form of insurance rather than the replacement cost form, the 20-year-old item might be fully depreciated and nothing will be paid if there is a loss. ACV is computed as replacement cost less physical depreciation.
- **Coinsurance:** For property claims, coinsurance is generally a measurement of coverage. If a structure is not covered for at least 80% of its fair market value, then replacement cost coverage is not available for partial losses.
- **Deductibles:** For property insurance, this is an easy concept. When there is a loss, the insured must pay the deductible before any coinsurance coverage applies.

How much coverage does a homeowner need?

This is a direct correlation with the amount of insurance that should be carried and the replacement cost to be adequately covered. A good example would be if my house has a replacement cost of $1 million and I have $100,000 of homeowner coverage and the house burns down to the ground. Would I be entitled to reap the full $1 million? The answer is obvious, which explains why clients need to be totally comfortable with the amount of coverage on the property. Let's look at the following hypothetical calculation.

Calculation for benefits paid from partial coverage paid from a loss

The calculation when the coinsurance requirement is not met for property insurance is a bit complex. When a building is not insured up to the coinsurance limit, usually 80% of the property's replacement cost, only partial losses are paid to the insured party, equal to the greater of the actual cash value or application of the following formula:

$$\left[\left(\frac{\text{Amount of coverage}}{80\% \text{ of replacement cost}} \right) \times \text{amount of loss} \right] - \text{deductible}$$

In no instance will a partial loss be covered in an amount in excess of the specified limits of policy.

Practical example: Jared's home would cost $190,000 to rebuild if destroyed. Insurance on the home is currently $125,000 with a $500 deductible. A kitchen fire causes $25,000 in damage. How much will the insurance company pay on this claim? The amount of insurance carried is $125,000 / 80% of replacement cost required, $152,000 = .82. Then .82 × $25,000 amount of loss = $20,500. Finally, $20,500 − $500 deductible = $20,000 to be paid by the insurance company. (Note: Jared must pay the remaining $5,000 of the $25,000 loss. This would have been avoided if Jared had maintained insurance of at least $152,000 or 80% of the replacement cost of $190,000.)

AUTOMOBILE INSURANCE

The personal auto policy (PAP) is the form used by the majority of drivers. If a driver has recreational vehicles, the same policy with a special endorsement is used. Different forms of insurance are used if the vehicle is not owned by an individual vs. an individual and/or a member of their household who owns the vehicle. Policies owned by unrelated individuals or business entities require the use of different forms of insurance, such as a business automobile policy (BAP).

Insurance is a personal contract. All family members of driving age should be listed on the policy. The liability follows the vehicle. For example, if you are driving the car and get into an accident, you are covered. If your spouse, your child, or even the neighbor with your permission is driving your car, your policy covers it. If you drive the neighbor's car, the neighbor's policy would be primary. Yours could provide secondary coverage, if need be.

Coverages

The six basic parts of the PAP are:

1. Part A, Liability coverage – usually split limits in US.
2. Part B, Medical payments coverage – for insureds.
3. Part C, Uninsured motorist coverage.
4. Part D, Coverage to damage to your auto.
5. Part E, Duties after an accident – you have to do your part.
6. Part F, General provision.

Part A liability coverage is the norm in the United States and is required when auto insurance is necessary to prove that the driver has the wherewithal to pay for any damage created as a result of an accident. It can be written as a split limit liability, such as $100,000/300,000/50,000, which means: $100,000 coverage for each person injured in an accident with a maximum of $300,000 coverage for all injured parties and up to $50,000 for property damage. It could also be written as a single limit $300,000. The minimum amount of split or single limit liability coverages that must be carried by the insured is often specified by the state in which the insured resides.

Part B medical payments coverage extends to people getting into or out of the car and when insured individuals are injured by a vehicle while being pedestrians or riding a bicycle. This clause typically interrelates with the subrogation clause of health insurance.

Part C allows a driver to purchase underinsured or uninsured motorist coverage. Underinsured means that the driver has too little coverage, perhaps whatever the state requirements are, and uninsured means the driver has no coverage at all. Part C brings the driver's coverage up to the amount of their Part A coverage. These benefits are available when a driver with no insurance or inadequate insurance causes injuries to an insured, or damage to an insured's vehicle. In some states, this coverage is available only if the insured chooses not to insure their own vehicle against damage. In those states, otherwise known as "no-fault states," the individual's collision coverage will pay for the damages, less their deductible.

Part D coverage insures against damage to the insured's auto in two parts: (1) collision, and (2) other than collision, also known as "comprehensive coverage." Collision coverage pays for damage if you hit something. Other than collision coverage pays if anything else happens to your auto unless it is excluded. Exclusions should be carefully reviewed. Remember that the exclusion of coverage for certain property that may be in the auto is only an exclusion from the auto policy coverage. These same items are often covered under the homeowner's policy.

After a loss resulting from an automobile accident, the insured is expected to:

1. Cooperate with the insurer in settling the claim.
2. Send the insurer notices or legal papers related to the claim.
3. Submit to a physical exam at the insurer's request if it is relevant to the claim.
4. Permit the insurer to gather medical reports and any other relevant records.
5. Submit proof of loss when required by the insurer.

Since recreational vehicles are popular but still not owned by the majority of the population, coverage is available only as supplemental coverage attached to the PAP. Such coverage is available to cover go-carts, minibikes, ATVs, motor homes, snowmobiles. For classic/antique autos, stated amount damage coverage is available as supplemental coverage with the PAP. Though not a "valued basis" policy, there is a specified amount of coverage that represents the maximum the company will pay for damage to or loss of such vehicles.

Practical examples:

1. Stu was waiting at a light in his new Corvette and his car was rear-ended by an insured 20-year-old driver. After filing the police report, Stu took his car to get an estimate from the other driver's insurance company. Unfortunately, the at-fault driver had the minimum required insurance for his state, which covered only $10,000 worth of damage. Because of the angle of the impact, not only did the entire body of Stu's car have to be replaced but the frame was bent and the damage considerably exceeded $10,000. Under what circumstances can Stu obtain payment for the balance of the damage? Stu can attempt to get the rest of the money from the 20-year-old driver. However, chances are that the other driver doesn't have adequate assets to cover it. This 20-year-old is an underinsured driver. If Stu is in a no-fault state, his collision coverage will cover the balance of the damage, and if he is not in a no-fault state, he will be covered if he had uninsured and underinsured motorist coverage.

2. Carley bought a snowmobile to keep at her condo near one of the major ski areas in Colorado. The dealer told her it was covered by her regular auto policy. Is the dealer right? Carley's dealer might be right. The snowmobile can be covered under a PAP, assuming that is what she has, but only by an endorsement adding that specific coverage for an additional premium.

Rattiner's Secrets: After an auto accident, make sure a police report is filed, regardless of the amount of damage. It may be a hassle for the local police to come out if the accident is under a certain dollar amount, but here is the reason why it should be. Many years ago, I had a tax client driving from south suburban Denver north into downtown Denver on a Monday morning for work. Traffic made everyone slow down and unfortunately she was hit by the car behind her and that car was hit by the car behind that individual. The police came and a report was filed. Three years from the date of the accident, my client received notice that she was being sued for an accident she created. We talked about it and then assumed it was for this accident that left virtually no marks. What we found out is that the person filing a motor vehicle lawsuit has three years from the date of the accident to do so due to the statute of limitations rules in Colorado. This was done on the last possible day under Colorado law. Then we found out that the driver of the second car which hit her said they incurred more than $1 million of medical issues. The second car tried to sue the third car, but since they had no insurance, nothing could be claimed. The second car had only minimal liability coverage and did not have anything above the required auto coverage. Since this medical expense was owed, the second car went after my client. When it was all said and done, my client was acquitted, thankfully, because of the police report. Had a police report not been filed, who knows? It's one person's word against the other.

Rattiner's Secrets: If clients are employed by a ride-sharing company, have them make sure that their existing personal automobile coverage will be satisfactory if they get into an accident on the job. Perhaps the company has its own liability policy as well, but it could be uncomfortable if an unfortunate situation occurs where the client was not properly protected by their personal auto policy because the accident was related to business purposes.

PERSONAL UMBRELLA LIABILITY INSURANCE

The personal umbrella policy provides broad liability protection over basic personal liability coverage found under coverage E of the homeowners policy and Part A of the automobile policy. This policy provides high levels of liability protection; $1 million is typically the lowest amount, for a relatively low cost. Clients can purchase higher limits where there essentially is a quantity discount for additional amounts purchased. There are, however, substantial limits on the umbrella coverage, such as the deductible found within the policy. This deductible should equal the underlying policy liability limits of coverage E and Part A. Defense costs are, as with the underlying coverage, provided *in addition to* the limits of the coverage.

Rattiner's Secrets: The minimum way to ensure that the client has sufficient liability protection and coverage is to make sure that the policy covers the net worth and then some. A client with a $5 million net worth and $1 million umbrella policy is not going to cut it. In addition, I tell the client it is probably a good idea to go above and beyond this limit if they have children in the house who are of driving age. I have heard too many stories where a child, not deliberately, is involved in an auto accident with significant repercussions. First, if the child is age 16 or 17 and still a minor, and they are driving the parent's car, the parent may be held ultimately responsible. Second, if someone borrows the car or is involved in an issue where they are an extension of the insured and something disastrous happens, again, liability issues arise. I have seen situations where the liability has been extended forward! Even for my clients with less than $5 million of net worth, that's the number I like to use for this type of protection. The client may say, "Jeff, I don't need that much coverage." If I ran the numbers and said the additional amount of coverage would cost you $600, I go back to my rule of thumb mentioned earlier in this chapter. That will hit home!

Rattiner's Secrets: It is very important to have the liability coverage set up properly. First, I make sure the client uses one company, if possible, to cover all their property and casualty (P&C) exposures, including homeowners, automobile, and excess personal liability coverage. There should be a discount to the client for having all of these coverages housed under one company – it can be as large as 20% off the premium. Second, even more importantly, this will ensure that there are no gaps in coverage. That means where one policy's liability limits are reached (from either the homeowners or automobile policy), the next one (umbrella) begins so there are no gaps in coverage. Essentially where one policy ends, the other starts for complete coverage.

Professional liability

In addition to the typical commercial liabilities that businesses may incur, there are certain specific forms of liability that arise from individuals doing their jobs. With certain jobs, any mistakes are the responsibility of the professional owner and owners and not the business entity. These situations may result in liability issues for planners that may arise because of the specialized nature of the work done by these individuals or because of their particular position and fiduciary responsibility.

Physicians, accountants, financial planners, dentists, etc. are always responsible for their actions. In other words, malpractice cannot be "organized away" by virtue of the business entity, such as a regular corporation. These professions demand that even in the face of employer pressure, professionals are obligated to work for the benefit of their clients/patients. Failure to exercise the degree of skill expected or to practice due care in the provision of these services opens professionals to professional liability claims. There are two types of injury that can be inflicted by professionals: physical (including emotional) damage and fiscal (financial) damage. If the general type of injury a professional can inflict is physical, the policy they obtain for protection is known as malpractice insurance. If the injury is financial in nature, the policy is referred to as errors and omissions insurance. However, these are not all-inclusive descriptions since malpractice insurance also typically protects a physician, hospital, etc. against breaches of patient confidentiality, invasion of privacy, and libel or slander claims. Many of us have E&O insurance from our employer, broker/dealer, RIA, or independently. Better safe than sorry!

DIRECTORS AND OFFICERS (D&O) LIABILITY

The board of directors of a corporation is there to oversee the corporate activities for the benefit of shareholders. Officers of corporations are hired by the board to profitably run the business, again for the benefit of shareholders. When a business is run in such a manner as to harm the interests of the shareholders, the board and officers may be held responsible. Therefore, the business usually purchases a special policy, known as directors and officers (D&O) liability insurance, to protect those individuals from personal liability. Without this, some businesses would not be able to recruit individuals for those positions. Note that many charitable organizations with unpaid, volunteer boards want well-qualified individuals in those positions and many individuals will not serve without directors and officers coverage.

Rattiner's Secrets: This is such an overlooked area that I have to relay an unfortunate story. I had a student in one of my Fast Track classes a number of years ago who volunteered as a treasurer on her church Board. Long story short, one of the Board members absconded with a significant amount of church money. Since procedures were not followed properly, all of the Board members ended up being responsible and had to pay a certain share of the loss. As a result, the student had to sell her house to cover her share.

As a result, when clients mention to me they plan on volunteering somewhere, I say, great ... but ... make sure the nonprofit has a D&O policy for your protection, just in case.

As you can see, there are multiple areas for the planner to understand and evaluate and to determine recommendations for the client. Having your client's insurance house in order before working in any of the other financial planning disciplines is most critical.

CHAPTER 6

Dispensing Advice on Investing

There are many issues that run through both planners' and clients' minds today concerning investing. The 2020s will not be like any decade we have seen previously. Part of that reasoning is that the world has changed so much that things are not on automatic pilot in the way that we had become accustomed to. There is too much impatience and people use shorter barometers for measurement than before. Further, at the beginning of this decade, with COVID playing a major disruptive role, and other future uncertainties, people are concerned about investment markets changing too rapidly. Unfortunately, people tend to be reactive rather than proactive. This chapter is not going to focus on investment types; there are plenty of great books and super class curriculums covering that. The concepts explained here will include the term investor more so than the client. This chapter will focus on those issues you need to have a handle on to counsel your clients through the investment planning process.

The problem with today's world is everyone acts a little too quickly, and based on social media news and other reports they may have heard, they wish to change their approaches even more rapidly instead of sticking with an appropriate strategy and making modifications where planned and where necessary.

So, if there is so much uncertainty in the world of investing, the question becomes, what do you do when a strategy performs poorly? We have generally had success in this arena for many years, especially during this last major and longest bull market, which unfortunately ended abruptly. "The basic mistake clients make is when it comes time to judge performance, three years is a long time and 10 years is an eternity," says Larry Swedroe, Chief Research Officer, Buckingham Strategic Wealth, St. Louis, MO.

"Don't run away from risk, and diversify as much as possible. There is much added value through passive investing which still would enable higher prices when adding value," says Swedroe. He also quoted Nassim Nicholas Taleb from his book *Fooled by Randomness*: "A strategy should be judged in terms of its quality and prudence before, not after, its outcome is known." That supports the short time frame that clients use today. So how long is enough to determine whether strategy works? Per Buckingham Strategic Wealth: "To have confidence, a strategy must have evidence of premium and persistence over long periods of time and across economic regimes; pervasiveness across sectors, countries, geographic regions and even asset classes; robustness to various definitions; implementability surviving transaction costs; and intuitive risk- or behavioral-based explanations."

Swedroe says, "The bigger firms are moving assets into a commodity-like setup, thereby pushing down fees ... if you don't integrate into an asset management platform, you're a dead man walking." He adds, "Advisors must be scale based and have access to products that others don't have. Also be broad based and anticipate total market, US markets, emerging markets for very long periods. Spend money on tech and need to be on top of cybersecurity and compliance." Swedroe thinks the industry will bifurcate like two barbells consisting of major nationals and a few others, and niche shops.

Dispensing Advice on Investing

1. Investment Risk
2. Other Issues that May Impact Investment Decisions
3. Investor Returns
4. Risk-Adjusted Performance Measures
5. Investment Policy Statements
6. Asset Allocation and Portfolio Diversification
7. Practical Approaches
8. Tax Efficiency

We need to have a handle on the level of risk the client is willing to assume. It is paramount to everything else we do for the client. We have covered this during the data gathering and interactive goal and objective setting session of the financial planning process (Chapter 3). As we have learned from the financial planning process, each client is different. Therefore, there is not a one-size-fits-all mentality or approach. Before any investing is recommended, we have to make sure our clients understand the risk in getting there. Let's take a look at the risk that your clients need to understand before setting up their investment portfolios.

INVESTMENT RISK

This should be the starting point for any client conversation in this area. Investment risk is the uncertainty that an investment's actual, or realized, return will not equal its expected return. In turn, "expected return" is defined as the return that the investor demands or expects to make. It is computed by multiplying each of the investment's possible annual returns by the probability that these returns will occur and then summing up the results. (Note: It can also be computed using the capital asset pricing model and/or dividend discount models as discussed later.)

Investment risk may also be thought of as total risk, which consists of two particular kinds: systematic and unsystematic risk. Another name for total risk is standard deviation (this will be discussed later). Since unsystematic risk can be diversified away, the only kind of risk for which the investor is rewarded with an expected return is systematic (or nondiversifiable) risk.

Systematic risk

Systematic risk is that risk associated with the entire market rather than being unique to an individual company. As a result, all securities tend to move together in a systematic manner in response to these risks. In my classes I use the acronym PRIME, standing for the first letter of each type of risk: purchasing power risk, reinvestment rate risk, interest rate risk, market risk, and exchange rate risk. Systematic risk cannot be eliminated through diversification because it affects the entire market – it may only be effectively managed. Beta is used to measure the amount of systematic risk that the investor has assumed. However, beta, as we will see later, is an accurate measure of systematic risk only if calculated for a diversified portfolio.

In addition, not all "betas are created equal" since the computation of beta may vary slightly from one investment reference service to the next.

Systematic risk consists of five different types of risk, as follows:

1. **Purchasing power risk:** The risk that inflation will erode the real value of the investor's assets. As prices for goods increase, the purchasing power of assets will decrease. The objective, therefore, is to have earnings in excess of inflation, so that the real value of the assets is not eroded. Inflation is the main cause of purchasing power risk. Bonds held to maturity are likely to suffer from purchasing power risk because the maturity value will remain the same.

2. **Reinvestment rate risk:** That part of interest rate risk resulting from uncertainty about the rate at which future interest coupons can be reinvested and earn current rates of return. This also can be thought of as the risk of an income decline due to a drop in interest rates. For example, if a bond promises a return of, say, 8%, assuming that the issuer does not default, will its actual rate of return equal 8%? Callable bonds are most impacted by reinvestment rate risk, although the price of mortgage-backed securities (such as a collateralized mortgage obligation (CMO)) also is influenced by this risk. It is also high on short-term maturity bonds. This is because the *shorter* the maturity of the bond, the *fewer* the years when the relatively high old interest rate will be earned, and the *sooner* the funds will have to be reinvested at the new low rate. Reinvestment rate risk also greatly impacts mortgage-backed securities, such as real estate mortgage investment conduits (REMICs). When market interest rates decline, borrowers tend to refinance mortgages, which in turn leads to an early payoff of the principal obligation and the need for reinvestment of terminated funds backing the REMIC. The investor is thus confronted with the need to reinvest their original REMIC investment in a lower interest rate environment.

3. **Interest rate risk:** The risk that changes in interest rates will affect the value of securities. There is a tendency for an inverse relationship to exist between the value of fixed investments and changes in interest rates (i.e., as interest rates increase, the value of bonds declines, and vice versa). Rising interest rates will also generally have a negative effect on stocks. Reasons for this include the increased discount rate (required rate of return) for valuation of cash flows, increased

borrowing costs, and increased yields on alternative investments. Bonds are most impacted by interest rate risk. The duration of a bond is a measure of the bond's interest rate sensitivity.

How much interest rate risk a bond has depends on how sensitive its price is to interest rate changes. In turn, this sensitivity depends on two factors:

- the bond's term to maturity
- the bond's coupon rate

These factors are succinctly captured in the concept of bond duration (to be discussed later). However, generally:

- The *longer* the bond's term to maturity, the *greater* its interest rate risk (in other words, there is a direct relationship).
- The *lower* the bond's coupon rate, the *greater* its interest rate risk (an inverse relationship).
- The *lower* the bond's yield to maturity, the *greater* its interest rate risk (an inverse relationship).

The duration of a bond with coupons is always less than its maturity date. (Note: A zero coupon bond's duration is always equal to the bond's maturity date.)

4. **Market risk:** The tendency for stocks to move with the market. When the market is increasing, most stocks will have a tendency to increase in value; conversely, most stocks will tend to fall with declines in the market. Often, a move in the market will be preceded by some change in the economic environment. Fluctuations in market prices of assets are caused by unanticipated world events (e.g., 9/11) and the reaction of investors to actual and anticipated events in the economic, social, and political world. The investor cannot reduce this market risk of loss by increasing the number of companies whose common stocks are in his portfolio because the market prices of equities tend to rise or fall together.

5. **Exchange rate risk:** The variability in returns on securities caused by currency fluctuations. An exchange rate specifies the number of units of a given currency that can be purchased with one unit of another currency (for example, Japanese yen for U.S. dollars). The inherent volatility of exchange rates under the current "floating" system (not tied to the gold standard) prevalent in international trade and investments *increases* the uncertainty of investor cash flows.

For example, a U.S. investor who buys a German stock denominated in euros must ultimately convert the returns from this stock back to dollars. If the exchange rate has subsequently moved against the investor, losses from these exchange rate movements can partially or totally negate the original return.

As a result, an investor in foreign securities may see a realized profit turn into a recognized loss due to changing currency exchange rates. This is known as exchange rate risk and impacts any investments made in other countries where the return is not denominated in U.S. dollars.

Unsystematic risk

An unsystematic (or nonmarket) risk is one that affects only a single asset or small group of assets. Because such risk is unique to an individual company or industry, unsystematic risk may be diversified away, minimized, and even eliminated by not investing (or investing only marginally) in company stocks that exhibit unsystematic risk.

Four common types of unsystematic risk are business, financial, regulatory (also known as political), and default risk. Each is discussed in more detail below.

1. **Business risk:** Business risk is the economic or operating risk associated with how the company earns its income and of the company's stock if the company uses no debt in its capital structure. More generally, business risk may be thought of as the amount of investment risk inherent in company operations. A corollary risk to business risk in some firms is financial risk.

2. **Financial risk:** Financial risk is the loss possibility due to leverage from the additional risk placed on the common stockholders of a company as a result of its decision to use debt (bonds) as part of its capital structure. If a company issues any bonds, then, in effect, it is partitioning the investors into two groups and concentrating its business risk on only one group: the common stockholders. The additional risk that the stockholders of a leveraged company assume, in excess of the risk assumed if the company used no debt in its capital structure, is the company's financial risk.

3. **Regulatory/political risk:** Regulatory or political risk is the possibility of expropriation and the unanticipated restriction of an investor's cash flows by a foreign government. It is greatest in foreign countries

that are unstable politically (or may become so in the future). Since such risk is greatest with international investment, to avoid political risk investors should not invest in stocks of companies operating in unstable countries.

4. **Default/credit risk:** Default risk is the loss possibility arising from a borrower's failure to pay interest and principal on a timely basis. The borrower can be a government, company, or individual. This is a concern for clients who hold corporate or municipal bonds in their portfolio. Federally government-backed bonds have the lowest risk and the lowest interest rate return among bond issuers while corporate bonds generally have the highest interest rates but have the highest default rates. Bonds with a lower chance of default are called investment grade while bonds with a higher likelihood of default are generally listed as junk bonds.

Rattiner's Secrets: I have had many clients who would have liked to invest with me or with me assisting them, but they had reiterated that they did not want to assume any risk. I told them, "Not happening!" What I tried to clarify for them is that we can maneuver certain types of risk from the equation. That means they are going to have to accept the systematic risk associated with investing, but depending on the approach and investments, we can probably minimize, diversify, or even eliminate the unsystematic risk.

Standard deviation

Standard deviation is an absolute measure of the variability of the actual investment returns around the average or mean of those returns (otherwise referred to as the "expected return" of the investment). There is a direct relationship between standard deviation and risk. Often, standard deviation is used as a measurement of the risk that is assumed by an investor with respect to any asset (or portfolio), also known as total risk.

Assuming a normal probability distribution, standard deviation may be used to predict the expected return of an investment based on historical performance of the asset or portfolio. For example, the expected return of an investment should occur within a range of one standard deviation from the mean 68% of the time, assuming that the series of historical returns forms a normal probability distribution curve.

Dispersions around the standard deviation and the bell-shaped curve are:

- approximately 68% of outcomes fall within ±1 S.D. of the mean
- approximately 95% of outcomes fall within ±2 S.D. of the mean
- approximately 99% of outcomes fall within ±3 S.D. of the mean

Beta (or "beta coefficient" as it is sometimes known) is a relative measure of an asset's or portfolio's systematic risk. Thus, it is best used as a measure of risk for a diversified portfolio or a portfolio that has no unsystematic (or diversifiable) risk. Alternatively, standard deviation is best used as a risk measurement for all assets, including a nondiversified portfolio. (However, remember that an investor is rewarded – in terms of expected return – only for assuming systematic risk since a portfolio should be diversified as a matter of good investment practice.)

Specifically, beta measures the volatility of a particular security's rate of return or price relative to the volatility of the market as a whole. Therefore, since the overall market has a beta of 1.0, a stock or portfolio exhibiting a beta of 1.2 is 20% more risky than the market. Alternatively, a stock or portfolio with a beta of 0.8 is 20% less risky than the market.

Betas can also be negative. For example, the risk characteristics (and expected returns) of gold stocks frequently exhibit negative betas. (This means that their risk is relatively independent of the broader financial markets.) An asset with a negative beta may assist greatly in protecting the investor from a significant decline in the value of their portfolio in a down (or "bear") market.

Finally, the concept of a stock or portfolio's beta forms the basis for the capital asset pricing model (CAPM) from which an investor may determine an appropriate required rate of return before making an investment decision.

Covariance

Covariance is included as a significant component in the standard deviation of a portfolio formula. Specifically, covariance measures the extent to which two variables (the expected returns on investment assets) move together (positively) or opposite to one another (negatively). Thus, covariance may best be described as the relationship between or among stocks that includes not only the individual stock's variability but also its impact on and interaction with other portfolio securities.

Semi-variance

Unlike standard deviation that measures the risk of all expected returns, semi-variance measures only those series of historical returns that are below the mean or average return.

Thus, for a relatively risk-averse investor, semi-variance is a better measure (than standard deviation) of the total risk that is assumed in making any investment.

OTHER ISSUES THAT MAY IMPACT INVESTMENT DECISIONS
Tax risk

Tax risk is the uncertainty associated with a country's tax laws that potentially affect the rate of return that may be generated by an investment. This could become more of a concern based on where the country is now. Thus, it is really a subcomponent of political or regulatory risk.

All investment alternatives should be analyzed on an after-tax basis so that the returns from tax-exempt investments are comparable to taxable investments. The specific computation that compares the yield on a tax-exempt investment to that of a taxable investment is the taxable equivalent yield (TEY) computation (as discussed later).

Investment manager risk

Investment manager risk is the risk that a portfolio's performance will be negatively impacted with a change in investment managers. It is really a subcomponent of market risk, although it can be minimized by simply not investing in a particular mutual fund or other professionally managed asset. The risk is highest with mutual fund families, which do not generally communicate staffing or money manager changes ahead of time to investors (or potential investors). Some fund families try to eliminate this type of risk when they list the fund manager as a team approach.

Investment manager risk may be evaluated by constant research regarding mutual funds (and mutual fund families), but is otherwise terribly difficult to manage if you do not know the professional intentions of a particular fund manager.

Liquidity and marketability

Clients with limited investments or those saving for a particular personal or business expenditure, such as a down payment on a home, are often concerned about the liquidity of their investments. They want to minimize delays and significant transaction costs if they decide to convert their investments to cash in the near future.

Marketability and liquidity are often confused. The speed and ease with which a security may be bought and sold determines a security's *marketability*. An actively traded stock that has a large number of shares outstanding is highly marketable but is generally not liquid.

Alternatively, *liquid* assets are those which can be readily converted into cash without significant loss to principal. Such assets include short-term government securities, money market funds, and savings accounts.

You should try to understand your clients' feelings about liquidity. Some clients need a great deal of liquidity to feel comfortable about their investment program. Others look at too much liquidity as costing them money. Illiquid investments typically provide a higher rate of return than liquid investments, so the investor has to consider this trade-off as well in their investment planning.

Planners' recommendations about liquidity, other than establishing a reasonable emergency fund, are based on (1) the client's lifecycle position, (2) the client's near-term financial goals, (3) the rate of return required by the client to meet financial goals, (4) the client's wishes, and (5) the client's health.

As stated in Chapter 3, one of the first considerations in preparing a financial plan for a client is the need for an emergency fund. This fund should consist of liquid assets to be easily accessible in the event of an emergency. If a client does not have an emergency fund, or has not previously made arrangements to access cash in the case of an emergency (such as a line of credit), then investments that have the potential for large price fluctuations, such as common stock, should be a smaller portion of the overall portfolio. Likewise, investments that do not have efficient markets, such as real estate, should also be limited in the investment portfolio.

The following investments are ranked in descending order of liquidity:

1. Savings accounts
2. Treasury bills
3. Certificates of deposit
4. High-grade common stocks
5. High-grade corporate bonds

6. High-grade tax-exempt bonds
7. High-grade preferred stock
8. Speculative corporate stock
9. Puts and calls
10. Futures contracts
11. Speculative corporate bonds
12. Speculative tax-exempt bonds
13. Real estate
14. Collectibles and physical assets
15. Limited partnership interest

Risk tolerance

We have all heard the saying that our clients are risk averse. I don't agree with that statement at all. Clients are "loss averse." Clients would say, "Jeff, find an investment that will earn 10% but I don't want to lose any of my money." "No worries, Mr. and Mrs. Client. We can invest somewhere in Fantasyland!" Most advisors use a risk tolerance questionnaire to help assess the client's risk. That can be obtained from the broker/dealer, RIA, or many other places. Many times, it also ties into the E&O questionnaire.

Time horizon

When the client needs funds to satisfy their life's ambitions is important. Different objectives come into focus during the many stages of life. As a result, proper investments and allocations are necessary to insure the monies will be there when they need to be. In other words, retirement accounts for younger people should probably be more aggressive and as clients get older they tend to get more conservative, but I tell them not too conservative. For example, even an 80-year-old client may need to have at least some of their portfolio in equities in order to best keep pace with inflation. With clients living longer, running out of money is a real concern.

Diversification

Designing a portfolio to include proper diversification encompassing many of the above potential issues is important. (Please see strategic asset allocation below.)

Appropriate benchmarks

In evaluating the performance of any investment or portfolio manager, specific performance criteria and objectives should be identified in the investment policy statement – see below. The criteria should include, as a minimum, the index and the investment style (for example, value or growth) against which the manager's performance will be compared, as well as expectations for performance net and gross of fees. When performance criteria are signed off by the manager at the start of the engagement, there is less tendency for controversy between the investor and the manager if the manager has to be replaced subsequently.

A critical part of the performance criteria is establishing an appropriate "benchmark" for purposes of comparison. For example, if the investor and investment manager agree on a portfolio of primarily large-cap stocks, an index like the Dow Jones Industrial Average of 30 stocks or the Standard & Poor's index of 500 stocks should be used to evaluate portfolio performance. Similarly, if small-cap stocks are the focus of the portfolio allocation, an index like the Russell 2000 index of smaller stocks should be used. If international stocks make up a major portion of the portfolio, an index of international stocks, like the EAFE index, should be employed.

Further, in evaluating portfolio performance, and as mentioned earlier, a time-weighted return measurement (such as geometric average) should be used to fairly evaluate the portfolio manager's performance.

INVESTOR RETURNS
Expected return

The expected return is the anticipated growth, earnings, or income generated from an investment. It is the return that is expected to occur for the amount of risk undertaken in making a particular investment. It is normally computed simply by summing the total of all possible returns multiplied by the probability of those returns. However, if we know the amount of the next year's dividend on the stock (D_1), we can divide that by the stock's current market price (P) and then add the anticipated growth rate of those dividends (g). The formula to derive the expected return in this manner is:

$$E(r) = \frac{D_1}{P} + g$$

Practical example: The next year's dividend on KRF stock is $2.50 per share. If the current market price of the stock is $45.00 and the anticipated growth rate of the dividends is 5%, the expected return of KRF stock is 10.56% ($2.50 divided by $45.00 plus .05 growth rate).

Realized or actual return

The realized return is simply the return that is actually earned from an investment. It includes any interest or dividends collected plus any price appreciation less any price depreciation.

Total return

The total return on an investment is the sum of:

- the capital appreciation/depreciation on the underlying investment, and
- any income generated from the investment.

Note that in the case of a stock, the income generated from the investment is in the form of taxable dividends and in the case of the bond, the income generated is in the form of taxable interest. However, if the dividends paid from a stock are "qualifying dividends," they are eligible for a preferential income tax rate (either 15% or 5%, depending on the taxpayer's marginal income tax bracket).

Taxable equivalent yield (TEY)

Some bonds, like municipal bonds, return federally tax-free income (and, in some cases, state tax-free income as well). As a result, investor/taxpayers (TPs) require a method of computing the tax-free yield on municipal bonds with those of taxable issues, such as corporate bonds. The TEY formula provides for this comparison and is computed as follows:

$$TEY = \frac{\text{tax-exempt bond's nominal yield}}{(1 - \text{TP's marginal income tax bracket})}$$

Practical example: Larry owns a municipal bond, trading at par, with a 6% coupon rate. He is in the 33% marginal income tax bracket. He is also considering the purchase of a corporate bond yielding 8%. Which bond should Larry buy? He should buy the municipal bond since, using the TEY formula, that bond will actually yield Larry 8.96% (.06 divided by .67), whereas the corporate bond is yielding only 8%.

You should note that the after-tax rate of return formula is the reciprocal of the TEY formula and is computed as $r_{after-tax} = r_{nominal}$ times $(1 - TP's$ marginal income tax bracket). Hence, in the above example, Larry would be receiving an after-tax return on the corporate bond of only 5.36% (.08 ×.67).

Correlation coefficient (R)

The correlation coefficient measures how the returns of two assets are related and ranges in value from −1.0 to +1.0.

If $R = +1 \Rightarrow$ the two securities are perfectly positively correlated; the two securities move together exactly and there is no reduction of portfolio risk.

If $R = -1 \Rightarrow$ the two securities are perfectly negatively correlated; the two securities move exactly opposite each other; risk is eliminated; the portfolio standard deviation = 0.

If $R = 0 \Rightarrow$ there is no correlation between the price changes of these securities; that is, they move completely independently of one another; portfolio risk is unaffected.

Practically, the correlation coefficient standardizes (places all values between a −1.0 and a + 1.0) the covariance between two assets. Covariance measures the extent to which two variables (such as the returns on two assets) move together. However, you should note that because of the direct relationship between the correlation coefficient and the covariance between two assets, if the covariance is negative, so will be the correlation coefficient (and vice versa).

Coefficient of determination (R^2)

The coefficient of determination, or R^2, is the square of the correlation coefficient, referred to here as "R" (but note ρ also refers to the correlation coefficient) and measures the proportion of the variation in one variable explained by the movement of the other variables. Specifically, the two variables used in the concept are the movement of the portfolio in relation to the overall market.

Practical example: If the correlation coefficient of two securities is 0.81, then the coefficient of determination for these two securities is 0.81 × 0.81 = 0.656, or 65.6%. This means that 65.6% of the variation in the return of security A may be explained in the return of security B. The remaining 34.4% of the variation in security A is due to other factors.

R^2 may also be used in comparing the movement of one stock to the market as a whole and the extent to which a portfolio is diversified. For example, an R^2 of .70 or more reflects a relatively well-diversified portfolio since the market has a correlation coefficient of 1.0.

> **Rattiner's Secrets:** I once had a client who came to see me to analyze his investment portfolio. After I saw his investment portfolio, consisting of a single "growth and income" mutual fund, I reiterated the importance of diversifying away from that particular mutual fund. I explained the concept of risk/return and gave some examples. The individual said "Understood" and said he would make the necessary adjustments and visit with me the following week. When he came back to the office, I asked him if he had diversified from his mutual fund as we had discussed, and he said "Yes." I then asked what he was now invested in. He said, "Jeff, I like the original mutual fund and decided to keep 20% of my portfolio in it." Then he proceeded to rattle off another four "growth and income" mutual funds, insisting that he was following orders to diversify from the original fund!

Use of R^2 in portfolio evaluation

There are common measures of portfolio evaluation combining the coefficient of determination (R^2) in conjunction with these ratios (the Jensen, Treynor, and Sharpe ratios – all discussed below) to select the most appropriate portfolio for an investor. The Jensen (alpha) and Treynor evaluation methods use the portfolio's beta coefficient as the relevant risk measure; therefore, since beta is a measurement of only systematic risk, Jensen and Treynor assume a diversified portfolio. Thus, the use of Jensen and Treynor is indicated only where the portfolio has an R^2 of .70 or more (a high relative amount of diversification relative to the market). Moreover, if this is the case, the highest index number of either or both of Jensen or Treynor should be used to select the most appropriate portfolio to implement.

Conversely, the Sharpe method of portfolio evaluation uses the portfolio's standard deviation as the relevant risk measure; therefore, since standard deviation is a measurement of total risk, Sharpe assumes a nondiversified portfolio. Thus, the use of the Sharpe method is indicated for any portfolio where the R^2 is less than .70 (a low relative amount of diversification relative to the market). Like Jensen and Treynor, if the Sharpe index is called for, the portfolio with the highest index number should be used to select the most appropriate portfolio.

RISK-ADJUSTED PERFORMANCE MEASURES

Risk-adjusted performance measures represent the process by which the performance of a portfolio is evaluated by combining risk and return into one single calculation.

Minimum required rate of return

This is the return that is required (on a risk-adjusted basis) by the investor to induce the purchase of the investment. In other words, this is what the investor needs to earn to determine whether a return is acceptable or to evaluate which of the returns from different investments is preferable based on the degree of risk that must be taken into account.

> **Rattiner's Secrets:** This is an important rate of return because it incorporates risk and spells out what the client needs to earn to "do the deal." What that means is if the client set up certain objectives during the planning process to earn, let's say, 8%, and when the portfolio is put together the return comes in at 5%, those investments will not enable the client to reach that particular objective(s), so the client does not do the deal. Translation is that you and the client will have to reevaluate the situation with different investments at a similar risk tolerance level for the client to make it happen.

Different investments will have different required returns. For instance, an investor will require a higher return for common stock than for T-bills because he has undertaken more risk with the equity investment.

The required rate of return is also used as a discount rate for valuation purposes. It is the rate at which the future value of a stream of cash flows will be discounted back to a present value for purposes of evaluating the "intrinsic" or true value.

The formula for required rate of return is the same as the capital asset pricing model:

$$\text{Required return} = \text{CAPM} = r_f + \beta(r_m - r_f)$$

Capital asset pricing model (CAPM)

There are numerous assumptions that underlie the application of the CAPM:

- All investors have uniform expectations about the risk-return relationship of risky assets.
- All investors have the same one-period time horizon.
- Investors can borrow and lend at a specific risk-free rate of return (r_f).
- Transaction cost = 0.
- Taxes = 0.
- Inflation = 0.
- Since there are many investors, no one investor can affect stock prices with their buy/sell decisions.
- Capital markets are in equilibrium – stock prices are at levels such that there is no incentive for speculative trading.

A macro model of CAPM is represented by the capital market line (CML). This line shows the risk-return trade-off for all combinations of risk-free and risky portfolios. The slope of the CML reflects how much more return can be achieved with a given increase in risk (or how much more risk must be accepted in order to achieve a given increase in expected return). The portfolio that an investor actually selects is depicted at the point of tangency of the CML with their utility (indifference) curve, which shows their preference for return vs. risk for a given level of satisfaction.

A micro level of CAPM is represented by the security market line (SML). Here, the slope of the line reflects the risk-return trade-off applicable to individual securities.

The major difference between the CML and the SML is that the risk undertaken with and shown by the CML is measured by standard deviation (total risk), whereas the risk associated with the SML is measured by beta (systematic risk). Also, from the use of the SML, we can derive the formula for the CAPM as follows:

$$\textbf{Required return} = \textbf{k} = \textbf{rf} + \beta(\textbf{r}_m - \textbf{r}_f)$$

where

$$
\begin{aligned}
r_f &= \text{risk-free return} \\
(r_m - r_f) &= \text{market risk premium of the stock} \\
\beta &= \text{beta of the stock}
\end{aligned}
$$

CML: a macro view of the CAPM:

specifies the relationship between risk and return on all possible portfolios

assumes a completely diversified portfolio at point Y

total risk is measured by the portfolio's standard deviation, σ

$$\text{The formula for the CML is : } r_p = r_r + \sigma_p \left\{ \frac{r_m - r_f}{\sigma_m} \right\}$$

where

$\begin{aligned}
r_p &= \text{required return of the portfolio} \\
r_f &= \text{risk-free return} \\
r_m &= \text{return on the market} \\
(r_m - r_f) &= \text{market risk premium of the portfolio (r_m that exceeds r_f)} \\
\sigma_p &= \text{standard deviation of the portfolio} \\
\sigma_m &= \text{standard deviation of the market}
\end{aligned}$

SML: a micro-view of the CAPM:

- Specifies the risk-return relationship of efficient portfolios *and* individual securities.
- SML relationship is similar to the CML, except that risk is measured by β (beta).
- The equation for the SML is the equation that is generally thought of as the CAPM.
- The SML, like the CML, can be used to compare actual returns to expected returns on a risk-adjusted basis.

$$\textbf{Required return} = \mathbf{k} = \mathbf{r_f + \beta(r_m - r_f)}$$

where

$\begin{aligned}
r_f &= \text{risk-free return} \\
(r_m - r_f) &= \text{risk premium of the stock or portfolio} \\
\beta &= \text{beta of the stock or portfolio}
\end{aligned}$

Sharpe ratio

The Sharpe ratio is a quantifiable portfolio performance tool that measures the risk premium of a portfolio per unit of total risk as measured by the portfolio's standard deviation. Specifically, attributes of and the most appropriate use of the index are as follows.

Sharpe Performance Index (S_i)

- Relative measure of the risk-adjusted performance of a portfolio based on total risk (= systematic + nonsystematic risk).
- Standard deviation (σ) is used as the measure for total risk.
- Since Sharpe uses standard deviation, it implies that the portfolio is not widely diversified. Therefore, it is most appropriately used when evaluating the performance of a smaller, "thinly diversified" or nondiversified portfolio. Using standard deviation as the risk measurement removes market influence from the analysis, therefore allowing comparisons of nondiversified portfolios and those tracking different benchmarks.
- Since it is a relative measure, the Sharpe index must be used to compare alternative investments or portfolios. Note: When comparing, "bigger is better." Generally speaking, a ratio of 1.00 represents "good" compensation or reward per unit of total risk, a ratio of 2.00 earns a "very good" rating, and 3.00 or better is "outstanding compensation."
- The formula for the index is:

$$S_i = \frac{r_p - r_f}{\sigma_p}$$

where

r_p = portfolio rate of return
r_f = risk-free rate of return
σ_p = standard deviation of the returns from the portfolio

- If the portfolio is fully diversified (all nonsystematic risk has been eliminated), then the Sharpe index should yield similar results for a comparison of several investments as the Treynor index.

Practical example: Assume that portfolio A had a return of 19% over the evaluation period and a standard deviation of returns of 6%. Also assume that the risk-free rate of return (as measured by the 90-day Treasury bill rate) is 5%. Therefore, the Sharpe index is 2.33 (19% less 5% divided by 6%), or "good" compensation for the amount of total risk reflected in the portfolio.

Treynor ratio

The Treynor ratio is a measure of portfolio performance that measures the risk premium of a portfolio per unit of nondiversifiable (systematic) risk, which is measured by the portfolio's beta. Specifically, attributes of and the most appropriate use of the index are as follows.

Treynor Performance Index (T_i)

- Relative measure of the risk-adjusted performance of a portfolio is based on the market risk, i.e., the systematic risk, so therefore use with diversified portfolios.
- Risk is measured by the beta coefficient (β). Therefore, it implies that the portfolio is diversified. Note that the Treynor ratio's reliance on beta also implies that unsystematic risk may be eliminated by diversification. For that reason, the ratio has only limited utility in evaluating nondiversified portfolios, or in comparisons of portfolios with different benchmarks.
- If the portfolio is fully diversified (all nonsystematic risk has been eliminated), then both indices (Sharpe and Treynor) should yield the same results because diversification will eliminate all unsystematic risk from the portfolio.
- Since it is also a relative measure, the Treynor index must be used to compare alternative investments or portfolios. Like the Sharpe index measurement, the higher the ratio, the better a portfolio's performance. However, the best use of the Treynor index is to compare the ratio against the Treynor index of the market as a whole, the ultimate diversified portfolio.
- The formula for the index is:

$$T_i = \frac{r_p - r_f}{\beta_p}$$

where

r_p = portfolio rate of return
r_f = risk-free rate of return
β_p = measure of market or systematic risk.

Practical example: Assume that the same portfolio return (19%) and risk-free rate (5%) as in the Sharpe example apply here. However, the beta of the portfolio is .80. Therefore, the Treynor ratio is .1750. If the portfolio's Treynor number is higher than that of the overall market, the portfolio manager has outperformed the market.

Jensen ratio (aka "alpha")

The Jensen ratio (alpha) is a measure of portfolio performance that uses the portfolio's beta and CAPM to calculate its excess return, which may be positive, zero, or negative. Specifically, the attributes of and most appropriate use of the index are as follows.

Jensen Performance Index (α, alpha)

- Alpha, α, is an absolute measure of performance and measures how well the managed portfolio performed relative to an unmanaged portfolio of equal risk. The formula for the index is:

$$\alpha_p = r_p - [\, r_f + (r_m - r_f)\beta_p\,]$$

where

α_p = the return that can be earned above or below an unmanaged portfolio with identical market risk
β_p = measure of market or systematic risk
r_m = return on the market
r_f = risk-free return
r_p = return on the portfolio

- From the above relationship you can see that the Jensen Performance Index determines how much the actual or realized return of the portfolio differs from its required return, as specified by the CAPM. The index specifically measures a portfolio's over- or underperformance in relation to the portfolio's expected return.
- Like Treynor's ratio, alpha measures portfolio performance in comparison to the market. Since the metric takes only systematic risk into account, portfolio comparisons are fair only if the investments within the portfolio have the same market exposure.
- Since beta is the measure of risk, it is implied that the portfolio is diversified. The value of alpha indicates superior or inferior performance; thus, you are looking for the biggest positive number.

> **Rattiner's Secrets:** Assume that your client's all-equity portfolio has an actual realized return of 17%, the realized return of the S&P 500 index for the same evaluation period is 18%, and the risk-free rate is 6%. The beta of the portfolio is .75. Therefore, the alpha of the portfolio is 2%, computed as follows: 17% − [6% + {(18% −6%) × .75}] = 17% −15% = 2%. This means that the portfolio manager has added value, outperforming the portfolio's expected/required return by 2%.

INVESTMENT POLICY STATEMENTS

An investment policy statement (IPS) is a key component for any investment plan. An IPS is a written document that establishes the foundation for how the investor's preferences, objectives, and constraints will be reflected in the client's asset allocation. This also includes the selection of investment assets within each allocation category by defining the broad parameters and boundaries for managing and rebalancing the client's portfolio. The IPS can specify what a going rate of inflation will be, its impact on risk-adjusted returns, determine specificity for what types of securities to invest or not invest in, and provide other guidelines. The IPS describes how funds will be invested, the target date for achievement of each investment goal, and the associated amount of tolerable risk. Determining the objectives for risk and return must be done simultaneously due to their interrelatedness.

Originating from retirement plans in the 1970s, they have expanded into individual and after-tax accounts. An IPS details the foundation upon which investment decisions are made, which is why they are an absolute necessity. They remove the subjectivity from the investment equation. The document establishes portfolio goals, clarifies investment guidelines, and identifies investment parameters and monitoring benchmarks. Hence, an IPS is essentially a business plan or blueprint for investing portfolio assets.

While typically thought of in conjunction with the portfolios of qualified retirement plans, charitable institutions, or trusts – situations where a fiduciary directs investment activities – an IPS is a critical factor in managing the investments of any portfolio. For fiduciary-directed portfolios, the IPS provides a benchmark to determine whether the fiduciary is making prudent investment decisions and ensures a continuity of investment strategies for a portfolio managed by an investment committee. In addition, the IPS may be used to satisfy the guidelines of the Employee Retirement Income Security Act (ERISA), if applicable, for qualified retirement plans.

Rattiner's Secrets: For individual investors, an IPS helps to ensure the logical implementation of established investment strategies. Because sound investment decisions are an integral part of your client's financial planning strategies, an IPS is often a key factor in successful planning for retirement, education, or any other goal. And because investors typically save and invest for a number of different goals, I have my clients develop a separate IPS for each set of objectives.

Each year more and more planners are profitably providing general and specific investment advice to their clients, and many find an IPS extremely helpful because it:

- summarizes in a written document the investor's goals, risk tolerance, preferences, time horizon, and other investment constraints
- clarifies the risk/return trade-off to investors and documents that this important concept has been discussed in connection with the investor's expectation of return on the investment portfolio
- creates a structure for making investment decisions and managing the investor's portfolio
- establishes a standard of agreed-upon goals and other criteria upon which investment performance can be measured

In addition, the use of an IPS may reduce professional liability exposure by documenting that prudent procedures were followed in making investment decisions and in enabling the financial planner to offer a discrete value-added service to clients who wish to implement investment planning strategies with other advisors.

The following is an example of the major parts of, and considerations, in designing an IPS.

DESIGNING AN INVESTMENT POLICY STATEMENT
- Purpose & Background
- Statement of Objectives
- Guidelines & Investment Policy (Client Investment Parameters)

Risk Tolerance	Liquidity	Asset Class Preferences
Time Horizon	Marketability	Expected Returns
Diversification	Income Tax Consequences	

- Securities Guidelines
- Selection of Money Managers
- Control Procedures
    Duties & Responsibilities of Investment Committee
    Duties & Responsibilities of Money Managers
    Monitoring of Money Managers

ASSET ALLOCATION AND PORTFOLIO DIVERSIFICATION

Asset allocation refers to the process of apportioning assets available for investment among various investment classes. These investment classes include the following investment types:

(a) Money market securities.
(b) Fixed-income securities.
(c) Common stock.
(d) International investments.
(e) Real estate.
(f) Collectibles (generally small or nonexistent).

More simply, most asset allocation is done by using only three categories of assets:

1. Cash and/or cash equivalents.
2. Stocks (equities).
3. Bonds and/or fixed income (debt obligations).

The objective in building an asset allocation model is to determine what investment categories will be used and the appropriate percentages for each asset class. The asset allocation model may encompass any one of many different strategies, but each should be built with the following considerations:

- The client's level of risk tolerance.
- The client's level of sophistication with regard to investment alternatives.
- The required rate of return necessary to meet the objectives of the client.
- The financial position and tax situation of the client.

Brinson-Hood-Beebower (BHB) published a paper in the *Financial Analysts Journal* in 1983 entitled "Determinants of Portfolio Performance" in which the authors set out to answer: "What determines portfolio performance?" This study helped change the way investing is done today. For their study, the authors used the SEI large plan universe database and studied 40 quarters of data (1974–1983). The final database used for their study included 91 plans ranging in size from $700 million to $3 billion in assets. The plan assets were separated into three categories: cash, bonds, and common stock.

The 8.5% of assets that did not fall into these categories (i.e., real estate, venture capital, and private placements) were allocated among the three main asset classes.

The authors concluded that there were three factors that would impact portfolio performance:

- **Security selection:** The active selection of a specific security.
- **Market timing:** The active decision to underweight or overweight a specific asset class.
- **Investment policy:** Since investment policy is not an option but instead is mandated by the client, this "asset allocation" decision included what asset classes to weight in accordance with the investment policy developed.

After doing the analysis, the authors concluded that over 93% of the variation in portfolio returns was attributable to the asset allocation decision. A repeat of the study analyzed 82 pension plans in 1991 and yielded similar results.

> **Rattiner's Secrets:** Years ago, I had many clients who were adamant about me telling them when they should get in and get out of the market on a regular basis. In fact, most would say, "If you can't tell me that, then there's no reason to work with you." I then proceeded to tell those individuals, "If I knew how to do that, no offense, but I'd be working on my own account and not for you!"

Strategic asset allocation

Strategic asset allocation is a strategy wherein assets are combined in a manner designed to produce superior results with minimum risk. The allocation is based on a client's long-term financial goals, risk tolerance, and lifecycle. For example, a client who is in the asset accumulation stage of life (generally, under age 45) should be able to tolerate more risk than a retiree client.

In strategic asset allocation, the allocation remains constant once put in place until a major life-changing event occurs. As a result, the type of allocation relies very little on changing market conditions and/or changing investor sentiment. Rebalancing is done every so often (usually annually) to bring the portfolio back in line with initial asset allocations. In addition, correlations between assets are used heavily in determining the optimal asset mix. Be aware that most investment policy statements incorporate strategic asset allocation into the risk/reward agreement between client and portfolio manager.

Rebalancing

Portfolio rebalancing as used in conjunction with strategic asset allocation should not be confused with rebalancing resulting from market timing or changing market conditions. Rebalancing done as a result of changing market conditions tends to occur much more frequently than rebalancing done only to bring about portfolio compliance with a pre-established asset allocation.

PRACTICAL APPROACHES
Modern Portfolio Theory (MPT)

MPT looks at portfolio performance based upon a combination of its assets' risk and return to help provide a framework for the investor to understand the relationship between the two. The objective is for optimal asset allocation. The set of portfolios serving as the foundation for MPT is the efficient frontier. All possible portfolios below the efficient frontier line are attainable. As a result, they do not maximize return for the risk level assumed. This risk can be classified as unsystematic risk because the investor is earning less than possible, as shown below.

- For a given level of expected return, there is no other portfolio characterized by lower risk.
- For a given level of risk, there is no portfolio with a higher expected return.
- The rational investor will choose the highest expected return with the lowest risk.

Efficient Market Hypothesis (EMH)

This theory suggests that investors are unable to outperform the market on a consistent basis. The market's efficiency in valuing securities is very quick and accurate and does not permit investors to find undervalued stocks on a consistent basis. In other words, under this hypothesis, an investor cannot consistently outperform the market, but will tend to earn a return that is consistent with the market and the amount of risk borne by the investor. Any excess returns are temporary and will regress to the mean. The basic tenet of this theory is that current stock prices reflect all available information for a company and that the prices rapidly adjust to any new information.

Behavioral finance

Behavioral finance uses psychology-based theories to explain investor behavior, particularly that behavior not appearing rational (or that is irrational) at first blush. This looks at how social, cognitive, and emotional factors impact investment decisions with the realization that there are boundaries on how rational a person can be. This approach is a major departure from modern portfolio theory and the efficient market hypothesis, which assumes that all investors are rational and will always invest accordingly. Many of the advisors I interviewed in Chapters 1 and 2 took to the expansion of this area for the 2020s.

There have been several major contributions to investment theory by academics studying and teaching behavioral finance. Among these are:

- Investors usually fear losses much more than they value gains. As a result, they will often choose the smaller of two potential gains if it avoids a sure loss. In the context of behavioral finance, this finding is known as "prospect theory."
- Investors tend to look for information that supports their previously established decision, even if that decision was imprudent. This is also known as "confirmation bias" and may explain why investors are so slow to sell an underperforming stock (if they sell it at all).
- Investor decisions are often affected by how the problem or opportunity is framed. For example, if an investor is told enough times that a particular stock or mutual fund is a good investment, they will tend to invest money even though past performance has shown it is not a good investment.

Strategies for concentrated portfolios

A concentrated portfolio is one that includes a majority percentage of one type of stock, usually employer stock. It is a common problem that many small business owners and/or corporate executives face. Most of my small business owner clients have more than 90% of their net worth in their small business. Of course, the major challenge is that the portfolio is not well-diversified and, thus, is subject to considerable unsystematic risk.

There are, however, several strategies that may be implemented to manage a concentrated portfolio. Among the most prominent are:

- **Sell all or a portion of the stock over time:** Normally, this will be difficult for an executive or owner to do, but it is simple and should at least be considered.
- **Gift all or a portion of the stock over time:** This is similar to the sale alternative, but no income tax consequences result to the executive or owner. There may, however, be a gift tax imposed if the stock is of significant value and/or is not gifted to the executive's spouse, where an unlimited gift tax marital deduction applies.
- **Use a charitable remainder trust (CRT):** When a CRT is established and the concentrated stock is transferred to the trust, a charitable income tax deduction is created for the donor, which in turn may be used to offset any ordinary, compensation income of the executive. In addition, since it is a tax-exempt entity, the CRT can sell the stock without any income tax liability.
- **Use an exchange fund:** Some financial institutions sponsor exchange funds (not to be confused with an exchange-traded fund) that permit investors with concentrated portfolios of publicly traded stock to contribute the stock to the fund. In exchange, the executive receives a proportional interest in the fund and diversifies their portfolio without a taxable event occurring.

Bond duration

Bond duration is a measure of bond price volatility and captures both price and reinvestment risks. It is also used to indicate how a bond will react to different interest rate environments. Specifically, duration has the following characteristics:

- It is defined as the weighted average time it takes to receive all payments (interest and principal) from the bond on a present value basis.

- It is used to compare interest rate risk among bonds with different coupons and different maturities, i.e., to determine the bond's price sensitivity to interest rate changes.
- Recall that bond prices are inversely related to the interest rate. Therefore, for any given change in interest rates, a bond's price will change (inversely) approximately equal to the interest rate change multiplied by the bond's duration. If, for example, the interest rate increases 1% (e.g., 8% to 9%) for a bond with a 12-year duration, the bond's price will decrease by about 12% (i.e., 1% × 12).
- Finally, duration provides for a technique that immunizes a bond from loss of principal due to interest rate changes. At the point when the bond's duration equals the time frame of a predetermined cash flow, the bond is said to be immunized (protected) against any adverse effects from changes in interest rates (i.e., interest rate risk, reinvestment risk).

For every 1% movement of interest rates, the bond price will fluctuate by the amount of duration in the opposite direction.

- There is an inverse relationship between the coupon rate of a bond and its duration. Therefore, the lower the coupon rate, the greater the bond's duration (and the more its interest rate sensitivity).
- There is an inverse relationship between the yield to maturity (YTM) of a bond and its duration. Therefore, the smaller the YTM, the greater the bond's duration.
- There is a direct relationship between the maturity date of a bond and its duration. Therefore, the longer the maturity date, the greater the bond's duration.

Capitalized earnings

Capitalized earnings are earnings that get added to the cost basis of an investment for tax purposes. However, the "intrinsic" (or proper) value of an investment may be computed by discounting back the amount of those earnings to a present value at an appropriate required rate of return, such as the YTM on a bond. If this intrinsic value is greater than or equal to the market price of the investment, then you would likely buy the investment. In other words, that investment is currently undervalued by the market. Alternatively, if this intrinsic value is less than the investment's market price, all other considerations equal, you would not buy the investment, or, perhaps, sell it short. In other words, in that case, the investment is currently overvalued by the market.

Fundamental analysis

Security analysts who practice fundamental analysis believe that at any time, there is an intrinsic value for the overall market and individual securities and that these values depend on underlying company and economic factors. Therefore, a fundamental analyst would attempt to determine the intrinsic value of an investment by examining the variables that determine value, such as the prospects for a company's future earnings, cash flows, market interest rates, and other risk variables. As such, this type of analyst looks closely at company ratios in comparison to its peers, as well as using such models as the dividend growth model and CAPM.

There are two forms or types of analysis practiced by fundamental analysts: top-down analysis and bottom-up analysis.

Top-down analysis: Top-down fundamental analysts begin with researching the overall economy and current conditions within the secondary market. (This is the "top" of the top-down strategy.) They then proceed by selecting an industry or industry sector (such as energy or technology) that they believe will generate superior performance over the upcoming time frame. Finally, they screen a database of securities to determine within the selected industry to recommend acceptable individual companies and their stock.

Thus, in order of the steps taken, top-down analysts move from:

- the economy or overall market, to
- the relevant industry, to
- the individual company or stock.

Most fundamental analysts today practice top-down analysis.

Bottom-up analysis: Bottom-up fundamental analysis reverses the steps used by the top-down analyst. In other words, bottom-up analysts begin with an examination of the company fundamentals (typically, like the top-down analyst, by using ratio analysis) and then consider the financial prospects for the industry in which the company operates. Finally, they analyze the prospects for the overall economy.

Thus, in order of the steps taken, bottom-up analysts move from:

- the individual company or stock, to
- the relevant industry, to
- the economy or overall market.

Bottom-up analysts are sometimes known as "stock pickers" since that is where they begin their use of fundamental analysis techniques.

Probability analysis/Monte Carlo simulation

The use of probability distributions in measuring investment risk has already been discussed. However, the analysis of those probability distributions, known as probability analysis, may also be used in estimating investment return. Currently, a type of that analysis, Monte Carlo simulation, is rapidly becoming the standard in evaluating the chance of an actual return given the occurrence of certain independent conditions or factors.

In a Monte Carlo simulation, the computer begins by picking a random of each variable, such as the chance of a possible return in a worst-case, base-case, and best-case scenario. Then, thousands of those variables are used to determine the probability of an actual return being achieved. In effect, Monte Carlo simulation marries probability distributions with scenario analysis, but on a much larger scale than may be performed with a simple spreadsheet.

Passive investing/indexing

If passive (vs. active) investing is being practiced, investors are typically not attempting to beat the market. Rather, they are looking to immunize their portfolios in an effort to lock in specified rates of return they deem acceptable, given the risks involved. These strategies do not generate significant transaction costs. For bonds, passive investment strategies are characterized by a lack of input regarding investor expectations of interest rates and/or bond price changes. A practice of investing only in index mutual funds is probably the most passive strategy.

A passive asset allocation begins by setting specific percentages for each asset class. The investor then attempts to maintain these percentages over time. Given market volatility, and to achieve this goal, the portfolio usually requires rebalancing every six months or so.

For example, an investor may decide to have a portfolio consisting of 50% equities and 50% fixed-income securities. Over time, the ratio of common stock and fixed-income securities will deviate from the original asset allocation because of gains, losses, and income. Therefore, to maintain the original asset allocation, assets from one class will have to be sold and reinvested in the other asset class. This process is often called "rebalancing" and will be discussed again in the next topic. Rebalancing will cause transaction costs and taxes to be incurred, however.

Buy and hold

In a "buy and hold" strategy, investors do not look for active trading to achieve attractive returns. Instead, they hold on to their securities to minimize transaction costs since they do not believe that active management adds any returns to their portfolios.

A buy and hold strategy, a form of passive investing, typically begins with a set percentage of assets in each class. However, over time this ratio will change as the value of each asset class changes. A major benefit of this strategy is that transaction costs and taxes are minimized.

Another major advantage of the buy and hold strategy is that the investor is not out of the market during an upturn in prices or during its most profitable trading days.

Dollar cost averaging

Dollar cost averaging is a formula plan for timing investment transactions in which a fixed dollar amount is invested in a security (like a mutual fund) at fixed intervals. Thus, the strategy may be said to be the process of purchasing securities over a period of time by periodically investing a predetermined amount at regular intervals.

The goal of dollar cost averaging is to reduce the effects of price fluctuations. When the market is rising, additional shares will benefit from the price increases. When the market is declining, the additional shares will be purchased at lower prices and will yield more shares per dollar investment. Therefore, when the market reverses course and begins increasing in value, the investor will own more shares and share in a greater dollar amount of appreciation.

Dividend reinvestment plans (DRIPs)

Dividend reinvestment plans are plans in which shareholders have cash dividends automatically reinvested in additional shares of the firm's common stock. Dividends are basically returns from an investment. Hence, investors must choose either to consume (spend) the dividend payment or to invest it in the same investment or some other investment. The term "dividend reinvestment" generally refers to dividends being invested back into the investment from which they were earned.

Practical example: Assume a stock, currently selling for $30 per share, pays a dividend of $2.00 at the end of each year and will appreciate over time at a compound rate of 10%. The following table illustrates the results of consuming or reinvesting the dividends after 10 years.

Consuming Dividends	Reinvesting Dividends
PV = $30.00	PV = $30.00
n or N = 10 years	n or N = 10 years
I or I/YR = 10%	I or I/YR = 10%
PMT = $0.00	PMT = $2.00
FV = $77.81	FV = $109.69

Thus, reinvesting the dividends will result in a 41% larger asset at the end of a 10-year period.

Dividends that are reinvested are treated the same for tax purposes as a dividend received in the form of cash. That is, they are taxable as ordinary income to the payee. These dividends, like other dividends, are reported to the IRS on Form 1099-Div.

TAX EFFICIENCY

In order for any portfolio to be constructed as optimally as possible, income tax implications have to be considered. Whereas most of these implications will be discussed in greater detail in Chapter 7, certain factors are relevant here.

Remember, investing needs to make sense. Always substance over form! Long-term buy and hold wins the race. Trying to time the market and outperform through quick trades generally does not work.

Rattiner's Secrets: I had a tax client many years ago who received a huge inheritance from her mother's passing. While working on her tax return, I noticed she had 83 short-term trades on her return during the calendar year generating a profit of $300 for the year. I mentioned to her that I thought her investment counselor was taking unfair advantage of her. She said to me, "How dare you say that. My boyfriend is my broker!" Oh well, another client I lost!

Turnover: Turnover measures the level of buying and selling of investments held within a portfolio or mutual fund. Whereas with an individually managed portfolio or individual securities turnover can be managed effectively through the timing of sales by the owner, this is not possible with mutual funds. Therefore, when investigating the purchase of mutual funds, the investor should inquire with respect about the "turnover ratio" experienced by the fund, which in turn will determine the pass-through tax impact to the investor of mutual fund sales.

Timing of capital gains and losses: A major tax benefit of investing in securities is that the investor gets to determine when they will recognize a taxable event. Moreover, once incurring this taxable event via the sale of the security, a disposition of a capital asset takes place, entitling the investor to a possible preferential capital gain tax rate.

Specifically, assuming the investor has owned the security for more than one year (and sells the security for a profit), they are entitled to report any gain as a long-term capital gain, affording them a maximum tax rate of no more than 20% (plus 3.8%). In addition, if a capital loss is incurred on sale, the investor can offset any gains by these losses and, if such losses are in excess of gains, may offset their regular or ordinary taxable income up to an amount not exceeding $3,000 in any one year.

Rattiner's Secrets: I still get many clients who are more concerned about the tax issues rather than the underlying investments. I always reiterate, "substance over form." The first question I ask when considering an investment concerns the specifics. I need to see if it's good value and makes sense. The second question, or byproduct, is what the tax ramifications are. Too many people get lost on the tax angle. Not that I enjoy paying taxes, but if the client receives a substantial tax hit from an investment(s), that must mean the client is making plenty of money having picked the right investment(s).

Accordingly, the offsetting of gains with losses speaks to an important tax management technique: if possible, the investor should sell any security in which they have a loss in the same year in which they also have a gain from the sale of the security. In that manner, the taxable impact of any gain may be minimized, and the losses can be fully used up to the extent of the total of recognized gains.

Wash sale rule

The wash sale rule prohibits the selling of any shares at a loss and then buying back those same or "substantially identical" shares within 30 days of the sale and deducting such loss for income tax purposes.

> **Rattiner's Secrets:** This should not be a concern for your clients. Generally, the application of the rule may be easily avoided by merely waiting until after 30 days before purchasing back the shares. However, you should note that the rule also applies to purchases of replacement stock within the 30 days before the sale, so it is actually a 60-day prohibited period during which the loss may not be deducted. I try to have all of my clients meet with me routinely for tax planning sometime in October, so even if this comes up, they have more than enough time to avoid the wash sale rule for that year's tax return, if need be.

Qualified dividends

There is usually not much problem in determining that a dividend payable from a stock or mutual fund is indeed a tax "qualified" dividend and qualifies for the favorable maximum 20% tax rate. Nonetheless, the investor should be careful about investing in foreign stocks or any stock where the issuing company headquarters is outside the 50 states or a possession of the United States, like Puerto Rico. If this is the case, the dividend will be considered to be "nonqualified" and taxed as ordinary income at higher marginal rates.

Tax-free income

Finally, as most investors are well aware, municipal bonds generate federally tax-free income. As such, and particularly if the investor is in a higher marginal income tax bracket, an investment in municipal bonds or a municipal bond fund may prove to be highly tax efficient.

As you can see, there are many ways for you to help build your clients' investment portfolios. The key takeaway is making sure they understand the process of investing from a risk-return analysis standpoint. There are so many ways to proceed and so many biases, the client needs to feel comfortable in the approach they are ultimately going to take. I'll leave you with two great quotes:

"People can build their own portfolios for free. We are paid to manage their money through the process of financial planning," says Intelligent Capitalworks' Vince Rossi.

"Individual decisions can be badly thought through and yet be successful, or exceedingly well thought through but be unsuccessful, because the recognized possibility of failure in fact occurs. But over time, more thoughtful decision making can be encouraged by evaluating decisions on how well they were made rather than on outcome," says Robert Rubin, former Co-chairman of Goldman Sachs.

CHAPTER 7

Dispensing Advice on Income Tax

> **Rattiner's Secrets:** A common question I get from clients is "What can I do tax-wise to minimize my tax liability?" Sometimes the lines are not that clear for our clients. I have had many clients over the years who want to make their sole purpose for investing to avoid paying income tax. As I mentioned in the last chapter, if the client is paying income tax on an investment, chances are that person has made some money on that investment, which would be a good place to be!
>
> Whether you work in the tax area or not, you always must deal with erring on the side of extreme caution. Certainly, if you don't provide tax advice, reach out to an affiliate or to your client's personal CPA. I proceed to answer clients with "We have to make sure we practice tax avoidance vs. tax evasion." I'm generally asked, "What's the difference, Jeff?" I say, "20 years!"

In all seriousness, tax avoidance is the arranging of financial affairs to minimize tax liability working within the law while tax evasion involves the reduction of taxes through illegal means. There are plenty of ways to work within the system legitimately to minimize the tax liability paid. We'll cover that throughout. Also, the term *taxpayer* will be used more often than *client* in this chapter. Lastly, this is not an income tax textbook. There are plenty of good ones around. This chapter covers the practical applications for how you can help your clients in this area.

Planner Income Tax Issues for Client Discussion

Filing Status Issues
Seven Steps to Calculating Income Tax Liability
Business Entities
Section 179 Deduction
Tax Planning Strategies
Like-Kind Exchanges
Income Recognition

Since we are all required to file Form 1040 (individual tax return) if the income thresholds warrant it, a good place to start is with selecting the appropriate filing status.

FILING STATUS ISSUES

The specific amounts of gross income that must be generated before an individual is required to file an income tax return depend on the individual's filing status. However, in all cases, this floor amount is equal to the standard deduction (for the applicable filing status). For example, a single individual/ married couple is not required to file an income tax return so long as their income does not exceed the standard deduction for that year, which is an indexed number. There are no personal exemptions allowed through 12/31/25.

Tax implications of marriage

While tax implications should not be the likely reason for (or for not) getting married, they should be considered. The most important of these tax implications is the filing status that should be chosen.

Filing status is determined on the last day of the tax year (December 31). I have seen people purposely get married or divorced on the last day of the calendar year. Generally, married filing jointly (M/J) is beneficial. However, the so-called "marriage penalty," while greatly minimized, may still kick in when both spouses are working and their combined income moves the taxpayer unintentionally into a higher tax bracket. When M/J is less expensive is when one spouse is the main breadwinner. Essentially, you are dividing that money over two individuals (M/J), so the overall tax liability is less.

As an alternative to married filing jointly, married individuals may file separate returns. However, this is rarely advantageous unless one spouse wishes to avoid the joint-and-several tax liability that is inherent in married filing jointly status (as discussed above) or if one spouse has substantial medical expenses. By filing separately, the base adjusted gross income (AGI) threshold to exceed is lower, thereby making the amount to be written off higher.

There are five types of filing status that an individual may use in figuring and reporting their federal income tax liability:

1. **Single (S):** Generally, this is any unmarried, legally separated, or divorced individual who does not qualify for any other filing status. The most notable exception to this status is a married individual who lives apart from their spouse, as of the last day of the calendar year, and maintains a household for a dependent child (or children). If this is the case, the taxpayer may file using "head of household" tax status.

2. **Head of household (H/H):** This is an unmarried (or, in some cases, married) individual who has lived apart from their spouse for the last six months who maintains a household for a dependent child or children as of the last day of the calendar year. Accordingly, the taxpayer may use a favorable set of income tax rates and brackets that falls between single and married filing jointly.

3. **Married filing jointly (MFJ):** A husband and wife may file a joint income tax return, even though one spouse has no income or deductions, so long as they are not legally separated or divorced as of the last day of the calendar year. The advantage of this filing status is a very favorable set of income tax rates and brackets. The disadvantage of the status is that the husband and wife now assume "joint and several liability" for the reporting of income and payment of the tax, meaning that if one spouse does not pay the tax (for example, is absent from the home), the other spouse is liable for that payment. Note that it may be possible for the other spouse to claim "innocent spouse" relief under the tax law, although it is very difficult to qualify for such relief under current law (as previously stated). A surviving spouse may also

file using MFJ status for the year in which the death of their spouse has occurred.

4. **Married filing separately (MFS):** A husband and wife may also file separate tax returns, although at the expense of sometimes punitive tax brackets and tax rates. When filing separate returns, each spouse reports only their own income and applicable deductions and tax credits. Typically, MFS status is used only by married individuals in the process of divorcing and who do not wish to assume joint and several liability for the tax reporting of their soon-to-be ex-spouse (as stated above).

5. **Qualifying widow(er) with dependent child status:** A taxpayer with a dependent child whose spouse has died during the current year and for up to two years thereafter may take advantage of this filing status. For example, an individual with a dependent child whose spouse has died during the year 2021 may file as a qualifying widow(er) for taxable years 2022 and 2023 with dependent children. However, this is only the case where the surviving spouse remains unmarried for taxable years 2021 and 2022. It needs to be emphasized here that qualifying widow(er) status entitles the surviving spouse only to joint income tax rates; the status does not authorize them to file a joint tax return.

Rattiner's Secrets: Funny story. Many, many years ago, during a discussion on filing status, I had a student in one of my Fast Track classes tell me how she filed her tax return. She said, "Jeff, I have been married the last 23 years...happily... but I have been filing married filing separately." As a fellow New Yorker, of course I said "Why?" And she proceeded to tell me that she had no idea what her husband did for a living or what he earned! I said, "Really?" She said they made $30,000 a year but that couldn't be right. They had live-in help, many expenses, and their real estate taxes alone in Westchester County, NY, were over that. Looking at my own vulnerability, I said, "Please don't say anymore and I'll give you all 'A's!"

Well, that last sentence is a little bit of an exaggeration, but here's the point from all of this. When you sign a tax return jointly, you are both jointly and severally liable. That means even if one spouse makes all of the income and the other spouse does other relevant but unpaid work, and the paid spouse does something wrong, deliberately or not, then the unpaid spouse can be liable for 100% or more of the tax liability, including penalties and interest. Some clients ask me if the innocent spouse rule protects them. My response is that in all the years I have done this and asked this question during my CPA presentations, I can probably count on one hand how many CPAs' clients actually were able to use that strategy to their advantage. I also have this discussion with clients who think they may be getting a divorce (see Chapter 10), when speaking with both of them together, or if a prospect visits my office and tells me their situation. Lesson here: Better safe than sorry!

SEVEN STEPS TO CALCULATING INCOME TAX LIABILITY

The individual tax return (Form 1040) has many steps and we'll cover the first seven. By the way, the estate tax return (Form 706) is a similar setup for the first seven steps, but more on that in Chapter 9.

Seven steps to calculating income tax liability (brackets based on filing status):

Step 1 – Total gross income (broadly conceived).

Step 2 – Subtract your above-the-line deductions from gross income to find AGI.

Step 3 – Determine itemized deductions to find out if they exceed the standard deduction amount. Deduct the greater of total itemized deductions or the standard deduction.

Step 4 – Subtract your total itemized deductions or the standard deduction amount to determine your taxable income.

Step 5 – Find your tax from either the tax tables or tax schedules.

Step 6 – Subtract tax credits, if any, from taxes determined in Step 7.

Step 7 – Amount equals income tax liability.

Step 1: Gross income

For federal income tax purposes, gross income is defined as all income from "whatever source derived except those items that are otherwise specifically excluded (by the Internal Revenue Code)." See IRC Section 61(a). This includes not only legal income but also illegal income (which is how Al Capone was caught and pleaded guilty to tax evasion on June 16, 1931). Implicit in the definition is the assumption that any economic benefit received by the taxpayer (for example, as the result of an employee benefit) is taxable, unless there is a specific exception. Thus, here are some commonly included items of gross income for any taxpayer:

- Alimony
- Award for special services
- Bonus paid for prior year's service
- Commission on sales
- Dividends or interest income received
- Forgiveness of debt (other than bankruptcy)
- Gambling income
- Honorariums
- Income earned on gifts or inheritance
- Jury fees
- Pension (and retirement) income
- Prizes
- Rents and royalties
- Salaries
- Scholarship to nondegree candidates for room, board, and incidentals
- Self-employment ("Schedule C") income
- Wages
- Tips and gratuities
- Unemployment compensation

Alternatively, items excluded in the Code include some type of charitable, social, or even political purpose, or essentially for the greater good. Here's a partial list of some items of excluded income (or economic benefit received) by IRC statute:

- Accident and health benefits received
- Forgiveness of debt in bankruptcy
- Military combat pay
- Gifts
- Gain from sale of personal residence (limited)

- Inheritances
- Interest from municipal bonds used for public purposes
- Life insurance death proceeds
- Scholarship to degree candidates for tuition, fees, and books
- Social Security benefits (partial)
- Bargain purchases by employees (qualified employee discount)
- Child support payments received
- Christmas gift of nominal value
- Compensation for damages to personal rights
- Awards (unsolicited) in recognition of scientific achievement
- Lodging and meals furnished for the convenience of the employer
- Educational assistance payments provided by employer (limited)
- Miscellaneous fringe benefits, such as employee discounts and working conditions benefits

Step 2: Adjustments to income: above-the-line deductions

Once gross income is determined by the taxpayer or by their tax preparer, the next step in the federal income tax formula is to compute the taxpayer's adjusted gross income. To do this, certain deductions are permitted, commonly referred to as "above-the-line" deductions, with the "line" being the amount of the taxpayer's adjusted gross income.

Here is a list of the major deductions that may be taken above-the-line and without the necessity of itemizing the taxpayer's total deductions:

- Ordinary and necessary business (Schedule C) expenses
- Capital losses
- Alimony paid to taxpayer's ex-spouse – for divorce decrees dated before January 1, 2019
- Moving expenses repealed beginning in 2018, except for members of the military
- Interest on education loans/student loan interest deduction – subject to phaseout
- Tuition and fees deduction (extended through end of 2020 by President's December 2010 Tax Act)
- Deductible traditional IRA contributions
- Payments to Keogh plans, Simplified Employee Pension Plans (SEPs), and Savings Incentive Match Plan for Employees (SIMPLEs)

- Self-employed health insurance deduction (deductible up to 100% of premiums paid)
- Employee contributions to health savings accounts (HSAs)
- Deduction for one-half of self-employment tax paid

This takes the taxpayer to AGI.

Steps 3 and 4: Determine the higher of the standard deduction or itemized deductions

The taxpayer would take the higher of the standard deduction or itemized deductions as the below-the-line deduction. With the standard deduction, no receipts are necessary, and the taxpayer would take the allowable amount in that year based on filing status (discussed above). With itemized deductions, the taxpayer would need receipts exceeding the standard deduction amount to receive any benefit. Taxfoundation.org estimates that about 86.3% of households take the standard deduction rather than itemizing their deductions.

For example, allowable itemized deductions on Schedule A of IRS Form 1040 consist of medical expenses, taxes, interest, charitable contributions, and casualty losses with certain limitations, and include the following:

- Medical expenses must exceed 10% (2020 and beyond through 12/31/25) of AGI.
- Taxes consist of real estate, personal property, state, and local. The state and local taxes (SALT) deduction is capped at $10,000.
- Interest includes a primary and secondary residence with maximum indebtedness of $750,000. Investment interest expense (IIE) is deductible only to the extent of net investment interest income (III).
- Charitable contributions are deductible up to 60% of AGI, with the balance carried forward for up to five years.
- Casualty losses are deductible above a $100 floor and in excess of 10% of AGI, and only if the site was declared a presidential disaster area.

> **Rattiner's Secrets:** Since so few taxpayers itemize on their Form 1040 because of the increased standard deduction, what is more commonplace now is for your clients to bunch their itemized deductions every few years so they can max them out in a particular year while taking advantage

of the standard deduction in those other years. For example, if taking an itemized deduction wouldn't work out numbers-wise for the client until the end of the third year, that client would make all their charitable contributions deliberately during that year (which may mean that these donations are purposely held back and utilized during that time period) in order to include them all. Clients should compare the two each year. It's easy to do. My tax software program automatically does that.

But here's the catch that many people don't realize. If you itemize and the numbers equal the standard deduction, you don't capture any additional tax benefit. If you donate property in a particular year and the sum of all itemized deductions for that year is less than the standard deduction, it won't benefit the client at all on the tax return. Sure, it's nice to donate whenever possible, but financially it won't benefit the client. That's a decision the client needs to think through. Furthermore, there could be some ramifications involving state refunds, if applicable, where the client has to recognize the state refund income received in the current year (if applicable) in the following year's Form 1040 tax return if the client itemizes.

Essentially, the standard deduction amounts are a free pass. No receipts. Nothing to prove. The client is entitled to that stated amount designated for that year. As a cash basis taxpayer (more on that later), the expenses such as medical or taxes are deductible when the client writes the check, so there may be opportunities to try to lump those expenses together all in that particular year. As mentioned in Chapter 6, during your end-of-year review with your clients, hopefully in October, determine what approach may be better off worked out for the client for the remainder of the current year. Based on the above, that could mean making charitable contributions every third year.

Step 5: Tax liability is calculated, credits are a way of reducing that liability

Rattiner's Secrets: As ridiculous as this sounds, for those clients preparing their own tax returns, make sure the client is working from the proper tax table! I have seen clients who end up doing their tax return by hand incorrectly use the wrong tables. As stated above, if you look at the taxable income and calculate their tax liability from each table,

(continued)

> (*continued*)
>
> certain tables have higher or lower tax liabilities than others. As a side note, I always try to encourage my clients to do their taxes through a software program. There are several investment companies that even provide free annual tax software for their clients.

Step 6: Tax credits

One of the best planning opportunities to work with your clients is in the accessibility of tax credits. Unlike income tax deductions that provide only an offset against the taxable income of the taxpayer equal to the taxpayer's marginal tax rate, income tax credits are a dollar-for-dollar reduction of income tax liability due by the taxpayer. Thus, as a general rule, such credits are very advantageous, particularly to lower-income or middle-income taxpayers.

Credits can be either refundable or nonrefundable in nature. A nonrefundable credit is one that cannot reduce a taxpayer's income tax liability below zero; in other words, if the taxpayer has no taxable income, they cannot receive a check from the government for the credit amount difference. In contrast, a refundable credit is one where the taxpayer's income tax liability can be reduced to below zero, meaning that a check from the government for the amount of the refund will be forthcoming. The most notable form of refundable income tax credit is the earned income credit for taxpayers earning under the poverty level.

The most important types of tax credits are:

- child and dependent care credit
- child tax credit (note: a portion of this credit may be refundable, but will not be discussed here)
- American opportunity tax credit
- lifetime learning credit
- credit for the elderly or the permanently and totally disabled
- adoption credit
- foreign tax credit

Child and dependent care credit. This is allowed in a two-parent household if both parents are working or in a one-parent household if the single parent is working. Essentially, it is like the cost of doing business (going to work) since the parent(s) may not be able to work if there is no one to watch the child(ren). If the child is under age 13 and is a dependent, the maximum dollar credit is $600 for one dependent and 1,200 for two or more dependents. There is no phaseout of the credit due to income limitations.

To determine the credit:

- Take the lesser of actual expenses or $3,000 if one dependent and $6,000 if two or more.
- Take the percentage applied toward above dollar amounts based upon AGI.
- 35% credit applies if the taxpayer's AGI is under $15,000 with a 1% reduction for each $2,000 increase of AGI up to $43,000, when it caps at 20%.

Child tax credit. A maximum tax credit of up to $2,000 is provided for each qualifying child. Even better is the ability to receive a refundable portion of the credit (up to $1,400) if the taxpayer's taxable income is under the AGI limits. However, there is a phaseout which could affect high-income taxpayers. A qualifying child is defined as an individual under the age of 17 (determined at the close of the calendar year in which the taxpayer's taxable year begins) for whom the taxpayer may claim a dependency exemption. A qualifying child includes a child or a descendent of a child, a stepchild, or an eligible foster child. Another temporary $500 is available for other qualifying dependents. The phaseout has been increased to begin at $400,000.

American opportunity tax credit. This is a maximum credit of $2,500 (a 100% nonrefundable credit on the first $2,000 and a 25% credit on the next $2,000) for qualified tuition and expenses (but not room, board, or textbooks) incurred by the taxpayer, the taxpayer's spouse, or a dependent during all years of post-secondary education, during which the student attends school at least half-time. In addition, you should note that the American opportunity tax credit is computed per student and is limited only to that education leading to a recognized undergraduate degree. The credit is subject to phaseout.

Lifetime learning credit. A nonrefundable credit of up to $2,000 is available. The credit is equal to 20% of qualified tuition expenses up to $10,000. Although the lifetime learning credit is generally similar to the American opportunity tax credit, with respect to limitations (AGI) and definitions, there are a number of differences. The lifetime learning credit is:

- available annually for an unlimited number of years (not just two years as in the case of the American opportunity tax credit)

- available for expenses related to acquiring or improving job skills, such as continuing professional education through qualifying institutions (not just in a degree program as in the case of the American opportunity tax credit)
- available for undergraduate, graduate, or professional degree expenses (not just undergraduate school as in the case of the American opportunity tax credit)
- subject to phaseout

Election of a specific credit for one student does not preclude the use of a different credit for another eligible student.

Credit for the elderly or the permanently and totally disabled. The credit is available to a taxpayer who is:

- age 65 or older, or
- under age 65, retired, and permanently and totally disabled. (Also, the individual must currently be receiving disability income from a public agency or a private employer's policy.)

The maximum amount of credit is 15% of $5,000 for all filers except those married filing jointly, where it is $7,500, and those married filing separately, where it is $3,750.

Adoption credit. An individual is allowed an income tax credit for qualified adoption expenses up to an annual amount indexed (which is also allowed to be carried over for up to five years). The credit begins to be phased out if a taxpayer's AGI exceeds certain annual indexed thresholds. Qualified adoption expenses are for reasonable and necessary adoption fees, court costs, attorney fees, and other related expenses. The full credit is permitted to anyone who adopts a special-needs child, even if the couple has under the permissible credit amount to expend for adoption expenses.

Foreign tax credit. The foreign tax credit is a method of avoiding double taxation for American expatriates. Hence, a tax credit is granted for taxes paid or accrued to a foreign country or U.S. possession. However, a taxpayer may not take advantage of both the foreign tax credit and foreign earned income exclusion that is also permitted under U.S. tax law. Thus, if the tax in the foreign country is more than the U.S. tax (typically the case), the taxpayer is generally better off by electing to take the foreign tax credit instead of the foreign earned income exclusion.

Step 7: Comparing amounts paid in through estimated payments or federal withholding tax against tax liability will determine gains and losses

> **Rattiner's Secrets:** I hear from clients often that they don't want to over-withhold their tax liability and would prefer to break even or perhaps owe a little at the end of the year because they don't want the government to hold their hard-earned money interest free. While I understand that premise, it does not work in many client scenarios. That's because there are some clients who do not do a good job saving! In other words, let's assume the client was entitled to a $6,000 refund for the year. The client says to me, "Jeff, I'll change my withholdings to take home an extra $500 per month" to break even at year-end. My experience has shown that at the end of the period, the client has little to show for it. For that type of client, I would say, "Why don't you take that lump sum when you receive your refund and perhaps use it to follow through on one of the objectives we have identified during the planning process?" This could include putting it into an investment account, such as an IRA, Section 529 plan, annuity, or perhaps use for a vacation, or to fix up the house, purchase another car, or perhaps for gifting, funding something else, and a ton of other possibilities.

BUSINESS ENTITIES

What type of business entity makes sense for you, or for your clients? The following discussion includes sole proprietorships, partnerships, limited liability companies, limited liability partnerships, S corporations, and C corporations.

Section 199A deduction for qualified business income

Since January 1, 2018, Section 199A of the Internal Revenue Code provides many taxpayers a beneficial deduction for qualified business income resulting from a qualified trade or business operated directly or through a pass-through entity.

Eligible taxpayers may be entitled to a deduction of up to 20% of qualified business income (QBI) from a domestic business operated with income generated as a sole proprietorship (individual) or through a partnership, S corporation, trust, REIT dividends, and estate.

QBI is the net amount of qualified items of income, gain, deduction, and loss from any qualified trade or business. The only counted items must be linked to the taxable income of a U.S. trade or business. Capital gains and losses, certain dividends, and interest income are excluded. The deduction is available, regardless of whether the client itemizes their deductions on Schedule A or takes the standard deduction. The taxable income limits (depending upon filing status) are adjusted for inflation each year. These are difficult calculations. The use of software or seeking professional help is highly recommended.

Sole proprietorship

This is an unincorporated business where an individual is engaged in a business without the benefit of associates or a corporate charter and is responsible for all aspects (i.e., operations, income, and debts) of the entity.

Advantages:

- Simplest.
- No formal legal requirements.
- Lack of regulation.
- No separate tax return; income and expenses reported on Sch. C, IRS Form 1040.
- Accounting procedures are simple.
- Management structure is straightforward.
- Flexibility of management.
- No identity apart from the owner – title held by the owner.
- Sues and is sued in owner's name.
- Formation is never a taxable event – no tax on dissolution.
- Owner entitled to contribute to Keogh on their behalf as well as that of any employees.
- Losses are favorable, that is, may be taken in entirety to offset ordinary income.
- Premiums for health insurance on sole proprietor are 100% deductible (above-the-line).

- Allows portion of business profits to be paid out as salary with deduction as business expenses to family member (so long as valid business purpose).

Disadvantages:

- Lack of distinction between the affairs of the sole proprietorship and its owner.
- Unlimited liability.
- Difficult to borrow or raise money.
- Lacks continuity of business life. (Business operations generally cease upon owner's death.)
- Disability severely impacts the business continuity.
- Difficult to transfer ownership.
- Profits are subject to self-employment tax.

Partnership

This is an association of two or more persons to carry on a business as co-owners for profit. The general partnership is a conduit and is not a separate taxpaying entity. Income and losses flow through individually to the general partners through a K-1. The association may include general and/or limited partners; however, if a limited partnership is formed, there must be at least one general partner. The general partner has all the skin in the game, which means unlimited liability. A limited partner, for all intents and purposes, is like an investor and if things go south, that person's liability is generally limited to their investment.

Rattiner's Secrets: I knew of a client who was a 1% general partner (GP) in a business with the other individual acting as 99% GP. Long story short, the 99% GP was engaged in illegal activity which ultimately brought down the business of 20 years and created significant liability, over which he committed suicide. Unfortunately, it made the 1% GP liable for 100% of the acts of the partnership. It's fine to be in business with others; however, the use of a general partnership would be at the bottom of my list.

Advantages:

- Provides for conduit taxation (partnership entity of two or more individuals files only an informational tax return, IRS Form 1065).
- Taxed at individual's ordinary rates.
- No recognized income upon formation, except:
  - if formed with a service partner
  - if partner's individual liability is decreased because partnership assumes that debt
  - if formed with appreciated portfolio securities
- Certain elections can be made at partnership level or at the partner level.
- Income tax treatment on liquidation is generally considered an advantage.
- Easily organized (no legal requirement of written partnership agreement, although strongly advisable).
- At-risk rules for deducting losses up to each partner's basis, which includes all loans both by partner and by partnership itself (not possible for S corporation).

Disadvantages:

- Unlimited personal liability of the general partners can get to personal assets after the assets of the partnership.
- Partnership's liability may be satisfied directly from one or more of the partner's personal assets.
- Lack of continuity in the life of a partnership.
- Might be subject to management deadlock.
- All income is taxed at the highest marginal rate of the partners.

Limited partnership

This type of entity is formed with both general partners and limited partners, but unlike general partners, limited partners are passive investors in the partnership who are financially liable only up to their investment. They cannot participate in management decisions, essentially being treated the same as shareholders.

Rattiner's Secrets: I have seen several cases where creditors try to prove where the limited partner acted in the day-to-day running of the business, thus trying to make that individual a general partner. Remember, then, as a general partner that individual could be held responsible for all of the partnership debt.

Advantages:

- Pass-through of losses from tax-advantaged investments.
- Well suited for investors who wish to invest in a business, but who desire to protect the rest of their financial resources.
- Offers the entrepreneur the advantage of locking any financial partners out of the management of the venture.
- Permits the limited partner to invest without being subject to personal liability.
- Allows special allocations of income and expenses.

Disadvantages:

- More formality (must have written agreement).
- Application must be filed with the state.
- There can be no limited partners providing only service to the partnership.
- Limited partners may not have control of the day-to-day management.
- Limited partners could lose the limited liability if the partnership fails to file required certificates or files a false certificate.

Limited liability company (LLC)

This type of entity provides limited liability to owner-members and is certainly one of the preferred business methods of choice.

Advantages:

- Combines the limited liability of corporations with partnership treatment for federal income tax purposes (conduit) without having to comply with S corporation eligibility requirements.

- Like a corporation but unlike a general partnership since it is a statutory entity and must be formed under a specific state law.
- LLCs generally have the following features:
  1. Limited to all owners or "members."
  2. Limited life such as 30 years or a period stated in the operating agreement.
  3. Dissolution upon the death, retirement, or resignation of a member unless remaining members elect by majority to continue.
  4. Majority approval required to transfer management or management rights.
  5. Operating agreement determines management structure.

Limited liability partnership (LLP)

This is a general partnership that provides limited liability protection to partners. Liability for professional malpractice of the general partnership or of the other partners is limited to the partnership assets. However, the partners are liable for their own malpractice, and/or for any debts of the firm.

Advantages:

- Similar to a general partnership and taxed as a partnership.
- Partial liability protection for claims against partners arising from obligations of the partnership but the liability shield does not protect partners due to their individual actions.
- At-risk rules for deducting losses include loans made by partners and indebtedness by LLP.

S corporation

This entity, set up by election with the IRS and the state, is a conduit that provides limited liability to owners and is generally taxed at an individual level.

Advantages:

- Conduct parallel to partnerships.
- Items of income, deduction, and credit from the S corporation retain their original character when they are passed through to the individual shareholders.

- Purpose is to provide the protection afforded by the corporate form without the disadvantages of corporate taxation.
- Noted for pass-through of operating losses.
- If S corporation has no basis, it can deduct losses if the owner lends money or contributes capital.
- Versus partnerships:
  - Shareholders are allowed to elect directors, etc.
  - Not subject to potentially being reclassified as an association.

Disadvantages:

- No more than 100 shareholders.
- May not have more than a single class of stock.
- Income deductions and credits must be allocated directly in proportion to the shareholders' interest in the corporation.
- Losses may be deducted only to the extent that shareholders have sufficient adjusted basis in their stock. (Does not include loans by S corp itself, only by shareholders.)
- Finally, there is also a tax on "built-in gains" imposed at the S corporation entity level on S corporations that dispose of assets that appreciated in value during years when the corporation was a C corporation. The recognition period is the 10-year period beginning on the first day on which the corporation is an S corporation or acquires C corporation assets in a carryover basis transaction. Again, if the corporation has always been an S corporation, it escapes the penalty.

Requirements for a valid S corporation election:

- Must be a domestic corporation.
- No more than 100 shareholders.
- Must file Articles of Incorporation with the state.
- Only one class of stock permitted (no preferred stock).
- Shareholders must be U.S. citizens or residents.

Revocation of S status:

- Simple majority of stockholders can elect to revoke.
- Failure to meet requirements for S status.

- Excess "net passive income" if previously C corporation with earnings and profits.
- Any qualifying (other than service) corporation that had terminated its S status within five years prior to 8/22/96 may reelect S corporation status without consent of Secretary of Treasury.

Rattiner's Secrets: Put those kids to work! Many times I ask the client business owner if there are any job responsibilities they can employ their children to undertake. Again, it has to be a legitimate job that the child is capable of performing. For example, using the definitive 2020 amount for the single standard deduction for illustrative purposes:

Wage for the child	$18,400
IRA contribution	$6,000
AGI	$12,400
Standard deduction	$12,400 (2020)
Taxable income	$0

If you multiply that amount by the number of children who could be employed, the numbers can look real good! There must be real payments for real work done and providing the appropriate year-end tax form (w-2 or 1099 Misc.) to the child. There are many good reasons for employing this strategy. One, the child enjoys it because they feel they are contributing to the family household. I have heard many children tell me they like being an active part of the family business. Second, the child (while not enthusiastic, I'm sure) is contributing to their own "play fund" by making IRA contributions for that rainy day – perhaps when they retire, even though they are too young to appreciate it now; perhaps to help create a wonderful living environment, if they wanted to purchase a house, or make another major purchase. Even though there would be tax consequences, they gain access to valuable funds.

The next thing I would encourage the child to do is set up a college fund, either on their own or, more preferably, by gifting the $12,400 from above (which is under the $15,000 annual gift tax exclusion) to a parent and then having that parent set up a Section 529 plan (see Chapter 10) and have those funds grow tax-deferred for the child. I tell the client, "Inform your child that they can attend whatever university they are capable of gaining admission to. Essentially, some or all of the college funding is there for this option." This is a huge benefit. If the child does not go to college or perhaps receives a scholarship, the child would still gain access to their money at some point.

Third, clients say to me, "Jeff, what should I have my child do work-wise?" Remember, it has to be something the child is capable of providing. And the child does not have to go to the office to fulfill those responsibilities – they can work from home. I've had clients converse with me about clerical responsibilities. A better avenue and an overlooked area where children are probably better than many adults is in the area of technology. Children learn these skill sets at a very young age. As a result, have the child help the business owner client on marketing issues. For example, the child can help with keeping track of direct marketing campaigns, drip marketing, or similar types of services. The client would produce a "weekly client letter," for instance, and hand it over to the child to follow up. The child can mail merge and send to clients electronically and keep track of the responses, if necessary. This allows the child to help with your business owner client's constant communication with their clients. They can also do things through various types of social media to expand your reach and brand into areas the business owner client may not have considered previously, or where the business owner client did not have the proper expertise – and probably at a fraction of the cost.

Pay the child a reasonable wage. Take the $18,400 from above (or any amount the client would feel comfortable paying) and divide by the number of hours the child will work to arrive at a reasonable hourly wage. Technology employees do fairly well (the client can look up hourly wages based on where the business is located to help determine what a reasonable hourly wage would be). I used $18,400 deliberately to essentially wipe out any current income tax liability on wages based on today's numbers. Even if the client were able to pay more, and have the child work more hours, subtracting the $18,400 would still create a low taxable income. Paying less would essentially accomplish the same thing with less money funded in the child's IRA.

C corporation

C corporations provide limited liability to the owners and pay income tax at the entity level at a rate of 21%. These corporations, which are owned by the shareholders and run through an elected board of directors, calculate their taxable income, pay taxes, and can distribute the remaining earnings as dividends to the owners. They must pay estimated tax in any year they owe more than $500 in tax. The dividends are not deductible by the corporation but are taxable as income to the shareholders (although, under current law, they may receive favorable income tax treatment as a "qualified dividend"). Thus, a C corporation is subject to double taxation.

Advantages:

- Corporation is considered a separate entity for tax purposes.
- Business owner's liability is limited to the owner's capital contribution.
- Perpetual life.
- Stock makes the transfer of ownership simple.
- Can divide ownership interests into smaller portions.
- Transfer of a share of stock has no effect on the conduct of business.
- Separation of management from ownership.
- By choosing their state of incorporation, corporations can control their degree of regulation.
- Progressivity of tax rates creates income-splitting advantage.

Section 1244 stock (small business stock election)

Stock qualifies for special income tax treatment under IRC Section 1244 if it is stock in a domestic corporation (C or S corporation) and is issued in exchange for money or property (not services). For Sec. 1244 to apply, the issuing corporation must not have received more than $1 million in exchange for its stock (at the time of corporate formation) and must have 50% of its receipts from business operations.

If an investor holds Section 1244 stock, they may take up to an annual $50,000 ordinary loss deduction when they sell such stock at a loss or if the stock becomes worthless. This amount increases to $100,000 annual loss for couples married filing jointly.

> **Rattiner's Secrets**: I like this provision for the client who decides to open up a small business and wants to attract investors. Ideally, there will be profit, taxed at capital gains like always. But for the business owner who is looking to attract investors who are concerned about investing in a small

business, since most of them go under, the business owner states that the stock from the small business has been issued under Section 1244, which provides for favorable loss rules, if necessary. Stock issues under these guidelines have the ability to take $50,000/$100,000 annual ordinary loss, which if need be can provide greater relief to investors of the new business owner client. To sum up, the effect is to provide an exception to the rule that stock sold at loss creates a capital loss that in turn may only offset $3,000 of ordinary income in any one taxable year. Section 1244 stock maintains its character as a capital asset for capital gain purposes, meaning that gains from such stock when sold are still eligible for the preferential long-term capital gains rates.

Advantages:

- Unlike capital losses deductible annually up to $3,000, investors could receive preferential treatment and possibly deduct up to $100,000 (M/J) or $50,000 (all else) annually, which leads to greater ability to raise capital for small business types.
- Income is treated as capital gains.

Disadvantages:

- Very formal in nature.
- Copious paperwork.
- Must have corporate charter, articles, bylaws, special meetings.
- Usually more expensive to run – legal, accounting, state franchise fee.
- Limited in corporate affairs to act specifically (state statutes, bylaws, etc.).
- Minority shareholders can oppress the majority.
- Potential for taxation upon liquidation.
- Potential for classification as a personal service corporation (a flat 21% tax rate (35% before 2018) with no progressivity of tax rates). A personal service corporation (PSC) performs health, law, engineering, architecture, accounting, and actuarial science, engaged in the performing arts or consulting.
- A C corporation may also be subject to an accumulated earnings tax and/or personal holding tax; both imposed a flat 15% tax penalty beginning in tax year 2008. Since a C corporation might be inclined

not to distribute dividends to avoid the double tax, an accumulated earnings tax is levied on any accumulated earnings not distributed to shareholders and not needed in the reasonable course of business (although up to $250,000 may be accumulated for "reasonable business needs" – $150,000 for PSCs – as decided by the IRS). A personal holding company (PHC) is a corporation owned by five or fewer individuals and creates most of its income from investment or passive activities.

Personal capital gains and losses

A capital gain or loss is the difference between the basis and the amount the seller gets when they sell an asset. Capital gains have a maximum tax rate on net capital gain of 20%. A 25% or 28% tax can also apply to certain types of net capital gains. Capital losses can be written off up to $3,000 on the sale of investment property and not on personal property on Form 1040. Excess amounts can be carried forward. Short-term capital gains, property held 12 months or less, are essentially treated as ordinary income. Long-term capital gains are from property held for more than 12 months.

> **Rattiner's Secrets:** All of the entities outlined above provide for cash flow by passing through any income and/or losses to the owner, partner, shareholder, or member (in the case of the LLC), with the exception of the C corporation whereby income and losses are reported (and taxable) at the entity level. However, the deductibility of losses in the case of the limited partnership and limited partner may be extremely limited because of the "passive loss rules," to be discussed subsequently.
>
> Because of the flow-through of losses, it is generally advantageous for start-up businesses to be formed as any of the flow-through types of entities (that is, other than as a regular or C corporation). Nonetheless, to limit the personal liability of the owners, forming the business initially as either an LLC or an S corporation is likely most preferable.

Basis

The calculation of any assets depends upon how the asset was acquired by the owner. In most cases, original basis begins with the initial cost of a purchased asset, plus expenses of sale, such as sales tax paid, installation costs, freight charges, and any commission or fees incurred in acquiring the assets.

A few other basis descriptions are worth noting. For gifted assets, the donor's basis is increased by gift tax paid by the donor. For inherited assets, the fair market value is determined on the date of death or the alternate valuation date, which is six months afterwards (more on this topic in Chapter 9). For improvements to tangible assets, the cost of improvements (vs. repairs) is added to basis. If a client is assuming debt in an asset purchase, any debt assumed by the buyer in the purchase will be added to the price of the original basis. If the asset is converted from personal usage to business usage, then the cost or fair market value (FMV) at the time of conversion is used, whichever is lower. This ensures that individuals do not purposely convert a personal asset into a business asset to generate an immediate built-in loss which can then be written off.

The adjusted basis (AB) of property is usually calculated as cost plus the expenses of sale (original basis) discussed above, less tax factors, such as depreciation (cost recovery deduction), Section 179 expense deduction or amortization. Knowing the AB is critical in the computation of gain or loss. Specifically, the amount realized on sale or conversion of any asset is reduced by the taxpayer's adjusted basis in that asset to reach the taxable amount of gain or loss, with the character of that gain or loss determined by whether the asset sold consisted of a capital or noncapital (ordinary income) asset.

SECTION 179 DEDUCTION

A separate deduction is provided for taxpayers in the initial year of purchase who elect to treat the cost of qualifying tangible personal property, also known as "Section 179 property" after the same IRC section. This means the client can treat it as an expense rather than as a capital expenditure (and, hence, depreciable or amortizable over the life of the asset). In other words, the election to treat qualifying property as Section 179 property permits the taxpayer to write off the cost of such property (up to a specified amount adjusted annually for inflation) dollar for dollar without reference to the Modified Accelerated Cost Recovery System (MACRS). This creates a huge benefit since the capitalized cost (basis) of assets purchased is generally written off annually as depreciation over their useful life as defined by using the appropriate MACRS table.

Rattiner's Secrets: I often get a question from a client who wishes to utilize this strategy for an expensive item used exclusively or mainly on a personal basis. To qualify for the election, the property must be used more

(continued)

(*continued*)

than 50% for business in the first year that it is placed in service (with only the business percentage eligible for the election). This strategy enables the client to capture a significant write-off in year one vs. depreciating it based on the life expectancy table. If the property is sold before then, the excess must be recaptured.

A key limitation in using the Section 179 election is that the expense deduction cannot exceed the taxable income from the trade or business. In other words, Section 179 cannot be used if it creates a loss for the taxpayer. Any expense deduction that would be disallowed by this limitation is then carried forward to the next taxable year or years when the taxpayer/business has any taxable income. Section 179 cannot be used for rental properties and is capped for trucks and light trucks (those with gross vehicle weight of 6,000 pounds or greater).

Rattiner's Secrets: There are plenty of vehicle lists (light trucks and trucks) online that have vehicles with a gross vehicle weight of 6,000 pounds or more. Vehicles are produced to conform with these rules deliberately for this reason. Maximum write-off for the vehicle is $25,000 under Section 179. If the vehicle costs more, the balance can be depreciated over the following five years. Again, Section 179 purchases can be made at any time during the year, including December 31. Remember, the vehicle does not have to be new – it has to be new to you! Also, financing is irrelevant. You can purchase it outright or take a 100% loan, it doesn't matter. It has to be owned and not leased by you. The salesperson at the car dealership will be very familiar with that list and this strategy.

The most common type of property for which the Section 179 election is made is computers and computer installation. But among the other types of property that may be "expensed" under the section are office equipment, automobiles and trucks used in the business, and off-the-shelf computer software.

What amount of qualifying property may actually be expensed or written off by the taxpayer in the year of the property's acquisition? For the taxable year of 2020, the aggregate cost of property that a taxpayer may elect to treat as a Section 179 expense cannot exceed $1,040,000. However, the

$1,040,000 limitation is reduced dollar for dollar by the amount Section 179 property placed in service during the 2020 taxable year exceeds $2,590,000. This means your company can deduct the full cost of qualifying equipment, up to $1,040,000, from your 2020 taxes. This deduction is good until you reach $2,590,000 in purchases for the year.

Rattiner's Secrets: To me, the Section 179 election is the most underused and best-kept secret for the business owner. During my fourth-quarter meeting with the business owner client, I try to project approximately what the client's business will earn during the year. I say to the client, "To help reduce this year's income and thus tax liability, and again don't do things for tax purposes, what assets or things are you thinking about acquiring next year that, if it makes sense, we can push up to this year? Anything from new computers, network, furniture, or whatever else that may be essential for the future growth of the business." The benefit of using the Section 179 approach is that the client can buy everything literally on the last day of the year (12/31/2x) and obtain a full write-off for the year as if it were purchased on the first day of the year (1/1/2x). With depreciation, the amount deductible is limited to writing off only a portion of the entire purchase (with limitations based on asset life) in the year of purchase. The client would generally take a half-year of depreciation for an asset (mid-year or half-year convention), unless if 40% or more of the assets are purchased in the last quarter (mid-quarter convention). With real estate, depreciation is based on the month purchased. There is no Section 179 election for real estate. With proper planning, the client can really maximize the current year's deductions.

TAX PLANNING STRATEGIES
Accelerated deductions

Here are some possible ways to accelerate deductions into the current year, thus potentially reducing income tax liability:

1. Early payment of state income or property taxes (capped at $10,000).
2. Early payment of mortgage interest (probably will not work more than once because the client will always be one payment in advance).
3. Year-end charitable contributions. (However, as discussed above, if the client doesn't itemize, a write-off will not happen.)

4. Payment of year-end business expenses. (As a cash basis taxpayer, the client can control when expenses are paid – discussed later in the chapter.)

5. Year-end purchase of assets (Section 179).

6. Review of possible asset acquisitions (similar to Section 179, but does not qualify).

7. Payment of education expenses. (Section 529 contributions will not reduce the client's federal tax liability, but depending on the state can help reduce state tax liability.)

Deferral of income

Here are some methods of deferring income. You should note that there are also methods of avoiding income, such as purchasing municipal bonds generating tax-free interest. In some cases, deferral techniques can turn into avoidance techniques – for example, by purchasing a nonqualified annuity and then dying before beginning distributions – but for the most part, all of these techniques defer or delay the taxable receipt of income to sometime in the future.

1. Tax-advantaged retirement savings (see Chapter 8).

2. Deferred sales (cash basis taxpayer).

3. Deferred billing (cash basis taxpayer).

4. Delayed bonus payment (if employer pushes into the following year. Commonly done).

5. Stock options (exercise in the future).

6. Deferred compensation (see Chapter 8).

7. Installment sales (see below).

8. Exchange of like-kind assets (see below).

9. Annuities (can possibly reduce income tax liability).

Rattiner's Secrets: The above two strategies are the general rule. However, it may not be advisable to proceed with these strategies. One example is if tax rates increase. If that is the case, deferring the client's income to the following year will result in more of that income being taxed at a higher percentage (rate). The same is true for accelerating deductions.

Spending those funds in the current year will result in a smaller offset percentage-wise against income while waiting to the following year will provide more tax benefit.

LIKE-KIND EXCHANGES

Before beginning the details of this topic, you should be aware that a so-called "like-kind exchange" (or Section 1031 exchange under the IRC section of the same number) is actually only one of three common types of nontaxable exchanges. Other common nontaxable exchanges are a Section 1033 exchange, dealing with the involuntary conversion of property, and a Section 1035 exchange, involving life insurance and/or annuity contracts.

Notably, there used to be another nontaxable exchange section (Section 1034) that applied to the "trading up" of a personal residence; however, that section has been repealed in favor of a specified amount of excluded gain (see below), depending on the taxpayer's filing status (sometimes known as the "Section 121 exclusion" of the tax code).

Rattiner's Secrets: Textbook examples have A and B trading properties with one another. In the real world, like-kind exchanges could involve many individuals. A could be trading with B, who is trading with C, etc. The only concern for the client is that the property has to be used for business purposes by your client. Personal property does not qualify under 1031. Also, how the other individual who is part of the trade with your client used that property previously is irrelevant.

Section 1031

Section 1031 like-kind exchanges only involve real estate transactions today. If qualifying like-kind property is exchanged, the transferor must file IRS Form 8824 in the year of the exchange. On the form, the taxpayer must describe the property given up and the property received.

Additionally, a deferred like-kind exchange is permitted under the law. Here, qualifying replacement property received must be identified within 45 days after the date on which the original property is transferred and exchanged within 180 days after the date on which the original property is transferred.

The property must be like-kind – but does not have to be identical. For example, an apartment building exchanged for farm property or an office building exchanged for a shopping center could be like-kind in nature (realty for realty).

The income tax rules and consequences associated with like-kind exchanges are:

- Gain realized on the transaction is equal to the difference between FMV of property acquired and adjusted basis of property transferred along with any relief of indebtedness, receipt of cash, and unlike or nonqualifying property received.
- Gain recognized can never exceed the amount of gain realized and is always the lesser of the gain realized or any boot received (see below).
- No losses can be recognized by either party as a result of the transaction.
- No gain is recognized unless one party receives cash, is relieved of a mortgage, or receives unlike or nonqualifying property.
- The "substituted basis" of either party equals the FMV of property acquired less the difference between any gain realized vs. any gain recognized.

Liabilities. When a taxpayer transferor gives up property that is subject to a liability, and the taxpayer transferee assumes the liability, then the taxpayer is treated as having received cash in the transaction equal to the amount of the liability being transferred. If the taxpayer has liability that is assumed and in turn assumes a liability on the replacement property, the liabilities are netted together to calculate the cash received or paid.

Practical example: Mr. Hamilton exchanged investment land with Ms. Thomas, receiving land with an FMV of $260,000. In addition, the land transferred by Mr. Hamilton was subject to a mortgage of $120,000 that Ms. Thomas assumed as part of the transaction. Therefore, in computing the amount realized by Mr. Hamilton, the FMV of the property received ($260,000) must be added to the liabilities assumed by Ms. Thomas ($120,000) for a total amount realized of $380,000.

Boot. In reality, it is very difficult for two parties to identify equivalent-value property to exchange. Therefore, typically, one or both parties, to make the exchange equal in value, transfer cash or other property. This cash or other nonqualifying property, including debt relief or liabilities assumed, is known in income tax law as "boot." Whereas the receipt of boot does not disqualify the entire transaction for nontaxable exchange treatment, it does result in:

- the recognition (taxability) of gain if there is a realized (economic) gain), or
- the precluding of a recognized loss if there is a realized loss.

Where there is boot received, the actual amount of recognized gain is equal to the lesser of the realized gain or the boot received. Hence, a realized gain on transactions involving boot may be recognized, but only to the extent of the boot received.

Section 1033. This code section is defined as a destruction or loss of the property through casualty, theft, or condemnation action pursuant to government powers of eminent domain, as well as the resulting compensation from such destruction or condemnation. For example, if your client's property is destroyed by an earthquake, fire, or hurricane, the client can postpone any gain from the insurance proceeds if they meet the following conditions.

For most property, the taxpayer has until the end of the second year to replace the property. For business property, it is until the end of the third year. That's because tax returns have reporting periods through December 31.

Section 1035. In short, the following are the main tax-deferred exchanges under this code section:

- life insurance for life insurance
- life insurance for annuities
- annuities for annuities

You cannot do annuities for life insurance.

Sale of personal residence

Prior to the enactment of IRC Section 121, providing for an exclusion of taxable gain, the sale of a personal residence was part of the nontaxable exchange provisions (specifically, IRC Section 1034 mentioned above). Those provisions provided for nontaxability of any gain so long as the taxpayer bought a more expensive home than the home that they sold. Since May 1997, this is no longer the rule.

Rather now, Section 121 permits an exclusion of up to $250,000 in taxable gain ($500,000 for married couples filing jointly) to any taxpayer who satisfies two basic tests. These are known as the "ownership" and "use" tests, respectively, and specifically read:

- **Ownership test:** The home must have been owned and used as a principal residence for at least two of the five years preceding the date of sale. Note that the two-year period may be one of aggregation, meaning that the years do not have to be consecutive so long as a total of two years (730 days) is met. In addition, the five-year period may be suspended for up to 10 years for taxpayer absences due to service in the military.

- **Use test:** Either spouse can meet the two years of ownership test but both must satisfy the two years of use test. As a result, this restriction may limit the use of the exclusion for couples who have divorced or are in the process of divorcing before the two years of use test has been met.

Unforeseen circumstances. The exclusion may not be used more than once within a two-year period. However, if the taxpayer fails to meet either the ownership or the use test because of a change in (1) employment, (2) health, or other "unforeseen circumstances," such as a divorce (as determined by the IRS), the taxpayer may be entitled to a partial exclusion based on the shorter of the taxpayer's use or ownership.

Practical example: Louise has owned her home for a period of 18 months prior to her relocation because of employment. However, she has lived in the home only for a period of a year since she resided elsewhere while the home was being built. Assuming Louise has a taxable gain of $50,000 at the time she sells her home, she can exclude $25,000 of the gain ($50,000 divided by two for her 12 out of 24 months of use). She cannot exclude the greater amount of $37,500 ($50,000 divided by .75, or 20 out of 24 months of use) since the partial exclusion amount is based on the shorter of the taxpayer's use or ownership.

The basic computation to determine the recognized taxable gain (or realized loss) on the sale of a personal residence is as follows:

Selling price
Less adjusted basis and selling expenses
Less reduction in tax basis due to excluded debt forgiveness income
Equals gain or loss realized
Less Section 121 gain exclusion
Equals recognized taxable gain

Finally, in accordance with previous law, losses on the sale of a personal residence are unrecognized and not deductible even if the taxpayer satisfies the ownership and use tests.

Vacation homes

There are restrictions included in the tax law that are designed to prevent taxpayers from using vacation or second homes to generate deductible rental losses. The tax consequences of vacation home use depend on the relative time that the home is used for personal use vs. the period of time for which it is rented. There are three categories of use with different tax consequences:

1. **Primarily personal use:** If the property is rented for less than 15 days per calendar year, it is treated as a personal residence and, accordingly, all rental income generated during this time is excluded from the taxpayer's gross income.

Rattiner's Secrets: Many times clients will rent out their house if a special occasion comes up in town and the client can leave and avoid the hoopla while making tax-free money if the house is rented out for 14 days or less. I remember when the Pope came to Denver in the 1990s and many people bailed to the mountains and rented out their home. Or sometimes there could be an annual event, like a car or horse race, or something that fits this time frame.

---

2. **Primarily rental use:** If the property is rented for at least 15 days per calendar year and is not used for personal use more than the greater of 14 days per year or 10% of the rental days, it is classified as primarily rental use. This treatment may permit a deduction of rental losses up to $25,000 per year (see below under "active participation").
3. **Mixed use:** If the property is rented for at least 15 days a year and it is also used for personal use more than the greater of 14 days per year or 10% of the rental days, rental expenses may be deducted only to the extent of rental income during the calendar year. Thus, there is no possibility of rental losses.

INCOME RECOGNITION

There are many ways to recognize and record income. Income can be recognized by clients under either a cash or an accrual basis method.

Cash vs. accrual basis taxpayer

Your client may elect to be taxed as a cash basis taxpayer, an accrual basis taxpayer, or a hybrid of the two. A cash basis taxpayer must include as income any amounts that are "constructively received" during the year, which means when the amount is available to the taxpayer. Essentially that means when the client receives the cash. Expenses would be recognized when paid (when the client wrote the check). An accrual basis taxpayer picks up income where earned (that work has already been done) and expenses were incurred (went to the office supply store and gave the credit card). An exception to this is regarding inventory, which must always be picked up under the accrual method. Any changes in methods must be approved by the IRS.

Active income

Active income is earned income that comes from the client's w-2 (wages), salaries, tips, 1099 (self-employed), other employee compensation, and even alimony (pre-1/1/19). That is because these are generated from the efforts of the taxpayer. The key takeaway is that if the client subtracts active expenses to net an active loss, that loss is deductible in full. Certain situations may generate active losses (from passive activities, below).

Passive income

Passive income representing passive activities is governed by "at-risk rules," which allow a taxpayer a deduction for losses only to the extent that the tax-payer is actually at risk for the amount lost.

A client can deduct losses only from business, rental, or other activity to the extent of basis. For real estate activities with active participation, up to $25,000 of losses from such activities may be used to offset other nonpassive income. Under the active participation standard exception (explained below), this exception begins to be phased out for taxpayers whose modified adjusted gross income (MAGI) is over $100,000. The allowance is reduced 50 cents for every dollar of MAGI over $100,000 and is fully phased out for married taxpayers in excess of $150,000. An exception exists for taxpayers who essentially work full time in the real estate business. If that individual performs more than 750 hours of service during the taxable year in that property trade or business, and that participation represents more than one-half of the total hours of service provided by that client for active businesses during the year, then the rental activities for that taxpayer are not automatically treated as passive activities. If the client is an employee, they would need to be a 5% owner of the business to count toward the 750-hour requirement. Lastly, the client would still need to meet the material participation requirements test (explained below).

Passive activities are those activities that involve the conduct of a trade or business in which the taxpayer does not "materially participate." Examples of passive activities include rental activities. Many clients assume that if they manage properties, fix them, secure the tenants, etc., it would not be considered passive and thus fully deductible. That is incorrect. With a possible exception under active participation (see below), it is always treated as inherently passive. Another example is limited partners because they generally are not considered to have materially participated in the partnership unless an exception applies.

Losses that exceed the amount at risk will be suspended and carried forward indefinitely to future years to offset future income from passive activities. Passive losses can be used to offset passive income but not active income (such as salaries and wages) and/or portfolio income (such as dividends and interest).

The taxpayer's participation determines whether the activity is treated as a passive activity or a nonpassive activity. To be a nonpassive activity, the taxpayer must materially participate in the activity.

Material participation. Generally, to be considered as materially participating in an activity (and thus not subject to the passive loss rules), a taxpayer must satisfy any one of the following tests:

- They participate more than 500 hours per year in the activity.
- Their participation constitutes substantially all of the participation in the activity.
- They participate for more than 100 hours per year in the activity and this participation is not less than the participation of any other individual. They satisfy a facts and circumstances test that requires them to show that they participated on a regular, continuous, and substantial basis for more than 100 hours during the tax year.
- The activity is a "significant participation activity" (separately defined in the Treasury Regulations) and their participation in significant participation activities exceeds 500 hours per year.

- They materially participated in the activity for any five years of 10 years that preceded the year in question.
- The activity is a "personal service activity" (also separately defined in the Treasury Regulations) and they materially participated in the activity for any three years preceding the tax year in question.

Active participation. There is a limited exception to the passive loss rules in the case of losses from rental real estate in which the taxpayer or the taxpayer's spouse actively participates. The active participation standard is less stringent than the material participation standard and may be met if the taxpayer or their spouse:

- participates in the making of management decisions, or
- arranges for others to provide for services in a significant and bona fide sense.

The taxpayer or their spouse must own at least a 10% interest of all interests in the activity throughout the year.

Rattiner's Secrets: Many times, I have worked with clients where one spouse is the main breadwinner and the other deals with the family and other at-home interests and responsibilities. In these cases, many clients have the at-home spouse be responsible for all the rental properties they manage. They would keep a log of days worked, hours spent, expenses incurred for that individual to satisfy the active participation requirements discussed above.

Portfolio income

This represents income from interest, dividends, royalties, annuities, and gain or loss from the disposition of property.

Installment sales

Installment sales are usually adopted to allow the seller to spread out the taxable gain from a sale or disposition of property as payments are received per the contract. Since only a portion of the profit is being picked up in each year, a considerable tax saving in any one year may be generated.

What is the definition of an installment sale for tax purposes? It is any sale of certain property in which the seller receives at least one payment after the year of sale. The planner should be aware that securities traded in a secondary market and property held for sale in the course of business, such as inventory, are not accorded the possibility of installment sale tax treatment. Also, if any payments under the sale contract are to be made in a subsequent year, installment sale treatment is automatic or mandatory, meaning that if the seller/taxpayer does not wish to take advantage of the treatment, they must "opt out" by filing a negative election.

The gain must be pro-rated and that portion of the gain must be applied to each payment received by the client under each year of the installment sale contract. The following is the applicable formula:

Gross profit percentage = Profit divided by the total contract price

Once this gross profit percentage is derived, it is then multiplied by the annual payment under the installment contract to determine the amount of reportable (taxable) gain.

Rattiner's Secrets: I am a fan of this type of arrangement because clients can recognize just a piece of each gain per year. Since tax rates are progressive, recognizing a smaller gain may have it taxed at a lesser percentage (tax rate) based on the client's overall income. Losses, however, cannot be used with the installment sale. Losses are recognized in full during year one because all depreciation is recaptured during that first year. For older clients where the asset is sold at a profit, they may like the annual capital gain income stream this provides by receiving payments over a definite time period. In addition, if the seller financed the deal, a second type of income, ordinary income, would be received by the seller on the interest income earned by financing the transaction.

CHAPTER 8

Dispensing Advice on Retirement Planning

So, what does retirement mean today? What will it mean in the future? Will retirement be based on myth or past experiences that we have seen employed by the generation before us? Will we retire once, then again and ultimately again? To sum it up as in previous chapters, "This is not your father's Oldsmobile!" This chapter is going to focus on the strategies that need to be discussed with the client to ensure that the client is maximizing the planning necessary to have a successful retirement (whatever that means!).

Defining Retirement on Your Clients' Terms

Shift in the Definition of Retirement Planning
The Stages of Retirement
Retirement Needs Analysis
Accumulation Stage
Qualified Plans
Personal Retirement Plans
Nonqualified Plans
Conservation Stage
Distribution Stage
Social Security

There is so much discussion within our profession on this subject. Everyone has very definitive opinions. I asked some of the leading experts in our industry about their thoughts on retirement planning. All continue the initial discussion above with some very defining thoughts.

SHIFT IN THE DEFINITION OF RETIREMENT PLANNING

"The biggest fundamental shift we will see is in the concept of retirement. That's going to go away from retirement and toward financial independence. Work would be optional. It will be based on what you'd like to do. In the past, retirement was based on the fact a worker could not work anymore because of that individual's obsolescence. Clients would retire from something with age 65 artificially set when the life expectancy was perhaps close to that age," says Michael Kitces.

He goes on to illustrate his point. "For example, a client retired from the factory because of his obsolescence of simply not being able to do the job any longer. A similar scenario was had with the family farm whereby the parent had enough kids to take over the farm, so the parent didn't have to do it anymore. What do we do with all the people who worked in prior industries? Do we retire them like obsolete equipment?"

"Retirement is an outdated notion. Clients need to have flexibility to keep their options open as many more clients will be working longer," says Wade D. Pfau, PhD, CFA, RICP, Professor of Retirement Income, The American College of Financial Services, King of Prussia, PA.

Bill Carter agrees with Pfau and adds, "Much of the discussion centers around where you are at a particular stage in life. I have clients in their 30s and 40s who specifically have told me that they never plan to retire and then they turn 60ish and they begin feeling burnout and start to think differently. Even so, in today's world, retirement could mean retiring from one venture and entering a new one. Most of my clients who retire want to be involved in giving back something to the community."

Carter goes on to say that people need to "retire to something" and not "from something." He has seen clients experience clinical depression as a result of not thinking it through properly. He sees many retirees travel. Compared with previous years, more of his clients are spending a greater percentage of their money during their lifetime. He adds, "I have seen clients retire for a few years and many of them ultimately come back. The only ones I don't see coming back are golfers!"

"For most clients, retirement is their most expensive goal, but not their only goal," says David M. Blanchett, Ph.D., CFA, CFP®, head of retirement research for Morningstar's Investment Management group. He says, "It's hard telling a 35-year-old that they really need to start contributing and perhaps maxing out their retirement contribution. 'Reshaping' is the way I describe it. Retirement needs have to be considered at the beginning of the journey, not at the end. What happens is that clients initially tend to focus on more immediate goals, such as paying off student loans, buying a house, saving for college, and establishing an emergency fund. Either way, we need to help clients become better savers."

"Historically, Baby Boomers played to traditional retirement, such as retiring by age 65," says Kitces. "Gen Xers followed a similar path even though they would prefer not to do that but deal with it, and Millennials have a totally different view. They say, we'll get meaningful work in our 20s, so work can be flexible in my 30s. Their worldview is that they won't be a generation that slaves away in a bad job(s) till retirement and will make radical view changes," says Kitces.

As part of the Baby Boomer generation myself, I had the conventional framework of retirement at the traditional age as well. The new norm says something otherwise. To quote the great philosopher Yogi Berra, "It ain't over till it's over!" As long as our clients have reason to work, explore, and contribute back to society, the choices they pursue in retirement will allow them to experience a new and exciting direction focused on personal achievement and ultimate satisfaction.

"The human capital of saving for retirement will transpire into a new retirement, which will be comprised of vision and goals one can inspire to afford the retirement life of luxury. Life experiences change during retirement where many people are not as happy during this stage because this is not what they encountered, due to increased social isolation, increased divorce rate, and increased health care costs. Further a new generation will not wait for a particular time, such as age 65, which is an artificial goal, and do things sooner, when they can afford to do so, say at age 50. This is not the world we live in anymore," says Kitces.

"Squaring the curve" as Kitces calls it is where we stay healthy to max out our life span of perhaps age 110. He adds, "You won't need to plan for many mini-retirements and career changes, whereby you may have to go back to school and learn new ways and techniques for doing those future things you have an interest in. You'll plan for meaningful work for a second, third, or fourth career in limited cycles."

It's interesting how different generations view retirement. As you can see from the above, there is no one way of looking at this. Kitces comments, "Generation Z has completely different expectations which have been defined by the crises they have lived through, such as Coronavirus, Great Recession, and 9/11. Their mantra is that life is short and not working for the man for 30 years."

THE STAGES OF RETIREMENT

The three stages of retirement are the accumulation, conservation, and distribution phases. The accumulation phase is how we grow the nest egg. We will go through the different types of plans to see how this is done. The conservation phase is once the funds are in the plan, how do we manage them for great success? Many of these principles have been covered in the investment chapter (Chapter 6). The distribution stage determines what and how we can access or withdraw funds. Determining the inflows that will exist at that time will determine how much money will be needed to withdraw, factoring in required minimum distributions (RMDs) or just a liquidation of some of the plan's assets. Lump sum and different annuity-type options exist here.

Most clients will not have sufficient funds to automatically make them ready for retirement. And if their objectives are pretty strong, then we need to help them figure out what needs to be saved today to accomplish this largest objective.

RETIREMENT NEEDS ANALYSIS

As stated above, with the definition of retirement changing constantly, we need to assist our clients each step of the way to make sure they are being covered currently and are not up for any surprises.

Since life expectancy is increasing dramatically, the numbers will continue to get more difficult. The longer the client waits to begin saving, or taking this process seriously, the tougher it's going to become to achieve what they want during this possibly "undefined" period.

A retirement needs analysis needs to be carried out initially to manage the client's expectations of hitting their marks – whatever they are. This analysis needs to be revisited each year during the monitoring stage of the financial planning process.

Rattiner's Secrets: One of the most effective tools I use when working with clients is the development of a retirement cash flow analysis that shows the client where they will be at retirement and how it will look through retirement. It is set up like this:

Start: Beginning balance
Plus: Additions
Subtract: Withdrawals
Equals: Ending balance

I am a huge believer that when people see things in writing, they get it! They follow along. All of my Fast Track classes have important concepts, highlights and numbers written down, summarized, and flowcharted on my infamous whiteboards. I do the same thing here with clients, usually in print, but also on my whiteboards using different colors to highlight the many cash flow projections, but specifically retirement. Included are rates of return and inflation from the overall investment portfolio projections.

For example, adjusting the numbers annually, if the clients have $500,000 at age 65, expect annual additions of $60,000 from Social Security, retirement plan income, after-tax investment returns, and other income as additions, subtract out $96,000 from fixed expenses, discretionary expenses, taxes, and other expenses as withdrawals, thus leaving an ending balance at age 65 which then becomes the beginning balance at age 66. I do that analysis by year and see where it goes by age 100 (the figure I use as life expectancy unless instructed otherwise). If, for example, the moneys hypothetically last through age 75 and then a "0" balance in red appears, I ask the client what they think they wish to do at that time. I'll then say to the client, "No worries, just call up the children and see which one wants to take care of Mom and Dad at that time and tell me how it works out." They get the message real quick!

Rattiner's Secrets: As an overview to facilitate student and client understanding, one of the examples I use in my Fast Track classes is how to prepare a "retirement needs analysis." This essentially shows how retirement will need to be planned today through end of life. The goal is to figure

(continued)

(*continued*)

out how much needs to be saved today to essentially hit all of their targeted objectives throughout the client's lifetime. I use a three-step process to determine how much they need to fund their existing shortfall in order to have the lifestyle during retirement they wish to have.

I explain it to my students and clients first in this theoretical manner (overview), and then I apply numbers to it to ensure that everyone gets it and can follow along. Now if the client informs me that he cannot do what is necessary to retire on his own terms, I say, "Here are your options." First, you can lower your needs at retirement and perhaps make it easier for yourself by having your existing funds already set to cover that shortfall, or even reduce the amount to make it easier to achieve your retirement objective. Second, you can retire at an older age, thus giving you more time to save toward retirement. Third, you could possibly take a more aggressive position on your investments, but you would have to be really careful with that approach as we would need to work through it and figure out whether that is even a realistic possibility. Fourth, you can reposition an existing asset(s) to provide an income stream, such as purchasing an annuity, to cover the shortfall. The benefit of that approach is if the client lives to age 150, that shortfall is covered the entire time. "That's it," I tell them. It's not rocket science. We have to see how we can make the numbers work to generate the comfort you want and need to hit this retirement planning objective.

Here's the overview:

Step 1: Since today's shortfall will not be the equivalent of today's dollars at retirement, what will today's shortfall need to be the equivalent of at retirement assuming inflation is at 3% (or whatever inflation-only number you wish to use)? When determining this amount, it should be based on what the client wishes to spend during retirement. In other words, expenses that are not relevant for the client should be backed out, such as work-related expenses, daily lunches, work equipment, etc., and replaced with expenses that are likely to occur during retirement, such as vacations, hobbies, etc. – all calculated in today's dollars. The reason for that approach is that we don't know what the numbers will be at retirement, so we have to figure them out today and adjust for when the client will be ready to implement during retirement.

Step 2: Now that we know what the shortfall will be at retirement, to determine the annual amount needed to cover that shortfall while growing at an inflation-adjusted rate of return, fast forward now to the age at retirement. What lump sum do we need in place at retirement that if we then annuitized it over the balance of the client's lifetime, that calculation will provide us with the revised shortfall needed during retirement?

Step 3: Now that we know the amount needed to cover the revised shortfall at retirement, let's work in reverse and determine what we need to begin saving this year. If we continue to save that amount and it earns an investment rate of return of 8% (or whatever investment rate of return you wish to use), what will be the shortfall in today's dollars that will grow into the amount needed at retirement to cover the revised annual shortfall during retirement.

Rattiner's Secrets: Here's a hypothetical scenario with numbers.

Ralph Really is ready to begin planning his retirement. He is age 37 today, wishes to retire at age 65, and plans to expire at age 96 (per his instructions). He wants to spend $100,000 during retirement, but when we figure out what annual income he needs to generate during retirement to offset those needs, in other words looking at the sources of income available to apply against that amount, such as Social Security, a defined benefit plan, real estate rental, annuity, and investment income, that amount totals only $80,000. As a result, his shortfall today is $20,000. Assuming inflation is 4% and he can earn an after-tax rate of return of 9%, the question is, how much does he need to begin saving today to ensure that he has sufficient funds to cover his retirement shortfall?

Here are the calculation steps on my HP12C.

Step 1	Step 2	Step 3
$20,000 CHS PV	$59,974 g beg CHS PMT	$1,002,482FV
28 N	31 N	28 N
4 I	4.8077 I	9 I
FV = $59,974	PV = $1,002,482	PMToa = $8,874

(continued)

(continued)

Conclusion: If the 37-year-old client saves $8,874 per year beginning this year in an account earning 9% per year, by the time the client retires at age 65, he will have amassed $1,002,482 at his disposal, which he can then begin annuitizing and withdrawing $59,974 per year growing at an inflation-adjusted amount of 4.8077%. This will cover the serial payment necessary during retirement.

ACCUMULATION STAGE

Wade Pfau sums up this stage best: "In the past, retirees were more likely to have traditional defined benefit company pensions to manage longevity and market risks. But traditional pensions have virtually disappeared, with many employers having frozen or phased out their pensions. Instead employees and employers now tend to contribute to various defined contribution plans, primarily 401(k)s where the employee accepts longevity and market risk and must make investment decisions."

I have seen many Fortune 500 companies (roughly 80% of them) offer defined benefit plans in the early 1980s to literally just a handful now. With Americans not locked down on one job for their entire career and receiving the gold watch at retirement for their years of service, to now having between 10 and 15 jobs over their career, the landscape has changed. As a result, companies have transferred the risk over to the employees and the investment results, which is why 401(k) plans are most popular today.

Let us discuss the ways our clients can contribute to their retirement account.

Types of retirement plans

If the business owner client could select an appropriate type of retirement plan for the business, you can assist your client with the advantages and disadvantages that could impact funding for retirement.

There are differences among the major types of retirement plans: qualified plans (QP), personal retirement plans (PRP), and nonqualified (NQP) plans. For example, qualified plans have vesting schedules, which means that employer contributions need to be earned over time, while PRP employer contributions are earned immediately. QP are 100% creditor protected while

PRP are not. The rule of thumb for PRP is $1 million based on a court ruling. However, many states have superseded that amount to make it unlimited. QP have 10-year income averaging for those people born in 1936 and before while PRP do not have that. QP may allow for loans while PRP do not. QP are more subject to ERISA than are PRP. Both QP and PRP provide for immediate employer tax deductions. NQP do not and are able to be written off only when the employee recognizes the income. For monies to grow tax-deferred in an NQP, there must be substantial risk of forfeiture, thus subjecting the funds to the claims of company creditors.

Rattiner's Secrets: One of the issues I constantly see with many younger clients is the unwillingness to fund for retirement now. The typical response is, "It's too far away for me to think about now" – they prefer to tackle things that are closer on the timeline first and then worry about retirement. I totally understand that. But if I show a client the results of maxing out with $6,000 for an individual retirement account (IRA) each year for 40 years earning an 8% rate of return (or whatever rate you are comfortable using), and the $1,554,339 FV of those investments alone, I'm sure that will definitely get their attention.

QUALIFIED PLANS

Differences between defined benefit and defined contribution plans

Generally, qualified retirement plans are categorized as either defined contribution or defined benefit plans. A retirement plan that is qualified for income tax purposes means that the plan meets a multitude of technical requirements, as specified in IRC Section 401(a). There are a number of types of qualified retirement plans within each general category.

Defined benefit plans include traditional defined benefit plans and cash balance plans. Defined contribution plans include money purchase, target benefit, and profit sharing. Profit sharing includes 401(k), safe harbor 401(k), age-based profit sharing, stock bonus, ESOP, new comparability, thrift savings, and SIMPLE (Savings Incentive Match Plan for Employees) 401(k) plans.

Sometimes, types of qualified plans are also categorized on the basis of whether they are a pension plan or a profit-sharing type of plan. You should be aware that a profit-sharing type of plan may be used by employers other than to provide a retirement benefit to their employees. For example, profit-sharing plans are often used to incentivize employees to meet employer performance expectations. Conversely, this is not the case with a pension plan, which is used solely to provide for the retirement needs of (former) employees. Defined contribution plans that also are pension plans include money purchase plans and target benefit plans.

Pension plans, both defined benefit and defined contribution, consist of mandatory employer-only contributions whereby the employer promises to pay a benefit at retirement. Employee in-service withdrawals are not permitted, and employer stock is limited to 10% of plan assets.

Profit-sharing plans allow for discretionary contributions for both employers and employees. There are no mandatory funding requirements and no benefit promised at retirement. Employee in-service withdrawals are permitted and there is no limit to the amount of employer stock that can be held in the plan.

Relevant factors and limitations affecting contributions or benefits

Like other restrictions included at IRC Section 401(a), there are limitations on the contributions to and/or benefits that may be paid from a qualified plan. In addition to these limitations on contributions or benefits, the amount of an employee's compensation that may be taken into account when providing for contributions or benefits is "capped" (also known as the "covered compensation limit"). The term "compensation" is separately defined for this purpose – and is not always applied consistently. For example, "elective deferrals" (before-tax contributions) made to a qualified plan count for purposes of the limitation on employee contributions, but they do not count (in other words, are not included) for purposes of the employer tax deduction.

Here are the relevant factors/limitations with respect to contributions made (defined contribution plans) and benefits paid (defined benefit plans) from a qualified plan:

1. **Deduction limit:** Employer contributions to a qualified plan are tax deductible up to 25% of aggregate employer payroll. Thus, it is indeed possible that the employer contribution on behalf of one employee can exceed 25% of their compensation, so long as it is balanced out by another employee's percentage contribution so as not to exceed the overall 25% employer deduction limit.

2. **Defined contribution limit:** The limit on annual additions to an employee's DC plan account is $57,000 (2020) or 100% of compensation, whichever is less.

3. **Defined benefit limit:** The maximum benefit that can be paid from a DB plan is $230,000/year (2020) or the participant's average compensation for the three highest consecutive years. The $230k limit is decreased for early retirement before age 62 and increased for later retirement after age 65.

4. **Annual compensation limit:** A maximum amount of $285,000 (2020) of compensation can be used to calculate employer contributions.

5. **Definition of compensation:** The following items are generally considered as compensation for purposes of applying the contribution and/or benefit limits:

   (a) Wages, salaries, fees for professional services, and other amounts received (without regard to whether or not an amount is paid in cash) for personal services rendered in the course of employment to the extent that the amounts are includible in income, whether earned from sources inside or outside the U.S.

   (b) Elective or salary reduction contributions to a 401(k), or 403(b) or SIMPLE plans or similar arrangement.

   (c) SEP contributions.

   (d) Amounts contributed or deferred under a 457 plan.

   (e) Elective or salary reduction contributions to a cafeteria plan (Section 125).

Multiple plans

Many clients ask me if contributions can be made to multiple plans. Short answer is yes. An employee/participant can be allocated the maximum contribution under a DC plan ($57,000 in 2020) and also be paid the maximum benefit under a DB plan ($230,000 per year in 2020). Nonetheless, the higher administrative cost incurred by the employer in providing multiple plans to employee/participants should be carefully considered. For example, the costs in administering both a Section 401(k) plan and traditional defined benefit plan can be substantial.

Finally, it should be noted that in certain instances, the elective deferrals made by employee/participants are aggregated (or combined) for purposes of those limits. For example, if an under-age-50 employee participates in both a Section 401(k) and 403(b) plan, the client is limited, in the year 2020, to a total elective deferral contribution of $19,500. (The client cannot contribute $19,500 to both plans.)

Defined benefit plan

A defined benefit plan is a qualified retirement plan in which retirement benefits are definitely determinable (rather than defining or specifying the amount of allowable annual contributions to a participant's retirement plan) that defines the maximum benefit that is available at the participant's retirement date. What that means is that we know what can come out of a plan but not necessarily what is going in. Thus, there are no specified contribution limits, other than the amount necessary to meet the "minimum funding standard" under law. This required amount of funding is determined by a licensed actuary, who considers factors and actuarial cost assumptions.

The following identifies any type of defined benefit plan: (1) plan formulas are geared to retirement benefits and not contributions (except cash balance plans); (2) the annual contribution is determined by an actuary; (3) benefits are insured by the Pension Benefit Guaranty Corporation (PBGC); (4) there are special rules for early termination; and (5) forfeitures reduce the company's costs of the plan.

Employees accrue retirement benefits when they are eligible to participate, but they are not vested until a minimum period of time is worked. Participants have the right to receive all or a portion of benefits at the plan-specified "normal retirement age" (NRA), even if they change jobs before retirement, as long as they changed jobs after becoming vested in the plan. There are instances where benefits can be paid before NRA.

It is important to note that the employer contributions to any type of defined benefit plan are mandatory (and not discretionary as in a profit-sharing approach). In addition, the benefit that is due the employee/participant is promised and thus embodies the "pension" type of qualified retirement plan.

There are two other attributes of any defined benefit plan that are important to understand:

- The employer (and not the employee) assumes the risk of all investment performance associated with the "pooled" accounts of all participants (which is why more plans are being transferred to the employee).

- There is a discounting effect associated with all defined benefit plans, thus making the present value amount of the participant's promised benefit greater the less the time period remaining until their retirement date. Therefore, by their very nature, defined benefit plans tend to favor older (rather than younger) participants. Again, as with defined contribution plans, there is no "magic age" at which the participant suddenly becomes "older" for purposes of establishing a defined benefit plan, although it is generally accepted that those employee/participants age 50 or over are benefited more greatly if a defined benefit approach to retirement funding (rather than a defined contribution approach) is implemented.

> **Rattiner's Secrets:** For my business owner clients who are age 50 and above, and who have not done a very good job planning for their retirement because life got in the way, and depending on their company's financial situation, size of the business, and census of employees based on age and years of service, I try to recommend a defined benefit plan. The reason is because DB plans can have the contributions skewed, many times in the client business owner's favor. In other words, it can be actuarially based on age and/or years of service. That means if the client business owner has been at the company longer than other employees and is one of the oldest, and even perhaps if that client wishes to take care of those employees who have helped grow the business to its current success level, more money can be put away on their behalf. Many times, clients think DB plans under ERISA must be designed for equal contributions into the plan, but that is not the case. Your business owner clients could reap the benefit from funding greater contributions per year for a shorter amount of time until retirement, thus trying to maximize their retirement account. As with any pension plan, annual mandatory contributions must be made by the employer, so having a sufficient cash flow is critical.

Cash balance plan

A cash balance (pension) plan is a defined benefit plan with similar features to a defined contribution plan. The distinguishing feature of a cash balance plan is that separate accounts are established for each participant, using a hypothetical account balance. This account balance is credited with hypothetical allocations and hypothetical earnings as defined by a formula in the plan. These hypothetical allocations and earnings are designed to imitate the actual contributions and earnings that would occur in an employee's account under a defined contribution plan.

The amount an employer contributes to the plan is determined actuarially. In addition, employee balances grow based on hypothetical earnings, such as through interest credits. The interest rate varies from year to year and is communicated to the employee at the start of each year. The rate is not tied to actual performance of investments and is determined independently. The minimum rate cannot be more than the lowest standard interest rate, and the maximum rate cannot be less than the highest standard interest rate.

Most cash balance plans permit a lump-sum distribution equal to the hypothetical account balance when an employee leaves the company. However, a cash balance plan must incorporate a formula that a pre-retirement single-sum distribution will always equal or exceed the present value of the participant's normal retirement benefit.

Defined contribution plan

A defined contribution type of retirement plan is one where the employer's contribution is defined as a percentage of an employee's annual compensation, up to a specified "cap" or covered compensation limit, which is $285,000 (2020). The amount available to the employee at retirement is, then, dependent on the amount contributed and the growth of those contributions over time. In other words, there is no retirement benefit promised to the employee by the employer (as in a defined benefit type of plan). The employer contributions (along with employee contributions, if permitted, and forfeitures) are made to an employee's individual account, titled in the name of the employee. This is why defined contribution plans are also known as "individual account balance" plans.

There are two other attributes of any defined contribution plan that are important to understand:

1. The employee (and not the employer) assumes the risk of all investment performance associated with their individual account assets.
2. Because of the compounding effect generated over time by the contributions made by the employer or employee, a defined contribution plan, by its very nature, tends to benefit younger employees more greatly than older employees. While there is no "magic number" with

respect to differentiating a younger from an older employee, it is generally accepted that employees who are younger than age 50 stand to benefit more from a defined contribution type of qualified plan (than a defined benefit type of plan).

Money purchase plan

A money purchase pension plan is a type of defined contribution plan where the employer's contributions are mandatory and are based on the amount of each participant's compensation. For example, the formula for a money purchase pension plan is described as a company that contributes 10% of compensation to each participant each plan year. Failure to make contributions can result in a penalty tax imposed on the employer. Employer contributions are required to be made to a money purchase plan each year even if the company makes no money.

Forfeitures resulting from employee turnover may reduce the company's future contributions or increase benefits for remaining participants. Retirement benefits from the plan are based on the amount in the participant's account at their retirement date, with the account balance then often used to purchase an annuity ("pension") on behalf of the participant.

Target benefit plan

A target benefit plan is a hybrid between a defined benefit plan and a money purchase plan. It is like a defined benefit plan in that the annual contribution is based on the amount needed each year to pay a projected retirement benefit for each participant at retirement. But the plans differ in a large way. Basically, in a defined benefit plan, when the interest rate earned on plan assets is higher or lower than the actuarial assumptions, the employer increases or decreases its future contributions to the plan as needed to match the promised benefit. However, in a target benefit plan, the contributions are allocated to separate accounts for each participant. Therefore, if the rate earned is different than the plan's assumed rate, there is no increase or decrease by the employer for future contributions. Like a money purchase plan, the ultimate retirement benefit payable to the participant either increases or decreases, depending on the interest rate earned.

A target benefit plan and money purchase plan differ in that for a money purchase plan, contributions are allocated as a percentage of compensation regardless of age. In a target benefit plan, age is an important factor in determining the amount of contribution. Indeed, sometimes a target benefit plan is referred to in practice as an "age-weighted money purchase plan." Older employees receive a greater contribution since they have less time to build up assets.

Profit-sharing plan

A profit-sharing plan is a defined contribution plan where the sponsoring employer agrees to make "substantial and recurring," although oftentimes discretionary, contributions to a retirement plan. The difference between a profit-sharing plan and a pension plan is that profit-sharing contributions generally depend on the existence of profits. However, a firm can decide to make or not make contributions regardless of whether it is making or losing money currently.

The actual contribution made to participants is not determined until the company decides on the amount of its contribution for the year. The contribution made to participants is then based on a predetermined formula that provides for an allocation in proportion to the compensation of each participant. The retirement benefit is based on the accumulated amount in a participant's account at retirement. Forfeitures may be reallocated among the remaining participants.

"Clients should invest aggressively in retirement with 50% in stock since stocks have the most upside. Bonds are the least effective way to fund retirement. Annuities, considered a dirty word by some, can provide mortality credits that can exceed returns of bonds. Annuities need to address the question of whether the client will feel comfortable when retiring with less in assets," says Pfau. He goes on by providing an example: "If the client wants to retire on $100,000 a year and have available resources totaling $75,000 per year, repositioning/reducing assets to purchase an annuity providing income of $25,000 per year to cover the shortfall may be a solid way to go."

Section 401(k) retirement plan

A 401(k) plan is a profit-sharing or stock bonus plan that offers participants the option to receive company contributions in cash or contributed to the plan. This salary reduction, also called "cash or deferred arrangement" (CODA), allows for the participant to elect to decrease current compensation or forgo a salary increase in order to contribute these amounts to the plan.

Employee elective deferral amount is $19,500 (2020), with an additional $6,500 (2020) catch-up contributions also permitted for participants aged 50 and over. Employee funds are always immediately 100% vested, the deferral amount is subject to Federal Income Contribution Act (FICA) and Federal Unemployment Tax Act (FUTA), but not subject to income tax, i.e., deferral is made with pre-tax dollars (although the deferral is subject to FICA and FUTA). Deferrals are characterized as employer contributions to ensure that the sum of employee and employer tax-favored contributions does not exceed the 25% payroll limit and the limit on annual additions, and as stated earlier, must meet the employer's requirement of "substantial and recurring" contributions in profit-sharing plans.

Note that the maximum salary deferral to a 401(k) applies to the individual. Salary deferrals made by an individual to any 401(k) plan, 403(b) plan, SEP, or SIMPLE will be treated as one plan even if different employers.

As stated above, employee contributions are always 100% matched while employer contributions have to meet the firm's particular vesting (guarantee) schedule. Employers can use either a three-year cliff whereby 100% of the employer contribution becomes the employee's at that point, or a graded vesting schedule which is earned at 20% per year beginning at the end of year two and continuing through the end of year six.

Hardship withdrawals. These provisions enable employees to access their money from a 401(k) plan under a hardship that is specifically permitted under Treasury Regs, and include:

- medical expenses for participant, spouse, dependent
- purchase of principal residence (not mortgage payments)
- education expenses, i.e., tuition, fees, room and board for next 12 months of postsecondary education
- prevention of eviction from principal residence or foreclosure on the mortgage on principal residence
- any additional events as may be prescribed by the IRS in the future

However, they are still taxed as ordinary income and subject to the 10% premature penalty. They are not considered an eligible rollover distribution, therefore are not subject to the mandatory 20% withholding.

Loans. Loans are allowed if permitted in accordance with plan documents and offered at a reasonable interest rate.

- Available to all employees equally.
- Term of the loan is five years unless for home loans. If loan fails to meet the term requirement, it is a "deemed distribution."
- Repayments must be at least quarterly on a substantially level amortization basis. If payments are not timely, the loan is in default and the entire balance becomes a "deemed distribution."
- Loan is a legally enforceable loan agreement.
- Amount of loan cannot exceed $50,000 or 50% of participant's vested benefit. If vested amount is $10,000 or less, the entire amount is vested. The loan must be adequately secured.

Safe-harbor 401(k) plan. Employers can avoid having to comply with the special nondiscrimination rules at all if the 401(k) plan is established as a "safe-harbor 401(k) plan." In essence, this means that a mandatory minimum employer contribution is required in which the employee must be 100% vested at all times (in other words, no vesting schedule is permitted as would be possible in a regular 401(k) plan). The employer has the choice to select one of two mandatory contribution methods:

- A nonelective contribution of 3% of compensation for all eligible employees (regardless of whether these employees are deferring a portion of their salary into the 401(k) plan or not), and/or
- An employer matching contribution of 100% of the first 3% of non–highly compensated employees (NHCEs) plus a 50% match on the next 2% of NHCEs compensation (a total of 4%) for those NHCEs who are actually deferring salary into the 401(k) plan.

Solo 401(k) plan

A single business owner with no employees, husband only or wife only, or both if each earns income, can set up a favorable tax plan whereby the Section 415 contribution limit can total $57,000 (2020) and $6,500 (2020) catch-up provision. As the employee, you can contribute 100% of compensation up to $19,500 (2020 amount), and as the employer where you are the employee, you can make an additional profit-sharing contribution of 25% of your w-2 employee compensation, up to the $285,000 (2020) compensation limit. For self-employed individuals, the percentage is 20%.

Rattiner's Secrets: For one-person business owner clients, this is my preferred approach. Under 2020 rules you can contribute up to the Section 415 addition limit of $57,000 based on w-2 income of $150,000.

$19,500 @ 100% =	$19,500 employee contribution
$150,000 @ 25% =	$37,500 employer contribution
Total contribution	$57,000
If age 50/older – catch-up	$6,500
Total contribution	$63,500

This represents a contribution of 42% of your income. The stand-out benefit from this approach vs. a SEP is you need to earn $228,000 of w-2 income from your S corporation to max out the $57,000 ($228,000 × 25%); and if you are a sole proprietor with net self-employment income, the limit is 20%, therefore your client would need to earn $285,000 to max out the $57,000 ($285,000 × 20%). Lastly, there is no catch-up provision with a SEP, so your client will still be able to contribute more this way if that person is age 50 or over.

Age-based (profit-sharing) plan

An age-based profit-sharing plan uses age and compensation to allocate contributions to participants. In this way, its concept is similar to a target benefit plan. The plan therefore benefits older employees since they have fewer years to retirement. To satisfy the nondiscrimination requirements, an age-based profit-sharing plan is tested under cross-testing rules.

Under such a plan, each participant's compensation is weighted by an age factor. The employer contribution is then allocated as equivalent to an assumed benefit at the normal retirement age specified in the plan document. Finally, each participant's compensation is age-adjusted by multiplying the participant's actual compensation by a discount factor based on the participant's age and the interest rate elected by the plan sponsor. As a result, the older employees (usually among them the business owner) receive the greatest allocation.

Roth 401(k) contributions. If available from the employer, employees could make similar-size (to traditional 401(k)) contributions to these accounts as a salary deferral (with no AGI limitations), plus catch-up contributions if applicable, without a tax deduction in the current year. The question becomes whether the employee would rather have the tax deferral now or receive the distributions tax free in the future.

Stock bonus plan

A stock bonus plan is a defined contribution plan in which benefit payments are usually made in shares of employer stock. However, the participant can receive cash in lieu of this stock if they elect to do so. In this respect, the stock bonus plan is similar to the traditional profit-sharing plan. The concept of funding a retirement plan with employer stock has also been extended to an employee stock ownership plan (ESOP), as will be discussed shortly.

A stock bonus plan may make sense for a corporation by (1) providing a market for the owner's closely held shares of stock; (2) giving tax deductions while having no effect on cash flows; and (3) protecting company stock from hostile takeovers. It also provides for a major tax advantage for the employee/participant, known as "net unrealized appreciation."

Employee stock ownership plan (ESOP)

An ESOP is a special type of defined contribution plan whose funds are primarily invested in employer stock. An ESOP differs from a stock bonus plan in that the stock bonus plan permits, but does not require, current investment in employer stock. An ESOP must invest primarily in employer stock (in contrast to a stock bonus plan that may invest primarily in employer stock). In addition, an ESOP, but not a stock bonus plan, may use employer credit (including a line of credit) to acquire employer stock.

As just noted, an ESOP has one unique advantage over every other type of qualified plan: it may borrow money in the name of the plan (and backed by the credit of the employer/sponsor) without violating the "prohibited transaction" rules that otherwise apply to qualified plan administration. As such, if the ESOP does borrow money in the plan's name, it is commonly referred to as a "leveraged ESOP" (or, sometimes, "LESOP"). This permits the employer to use the LESOP as a capital-raising device while at the same time creating a market for its stock that may otherwise, perhaps, not exist. Alternatively, the employee/participant also is afforded the "net unrealized appreciation" (NUA) tax advantage as permitted generally for any form of stock bonus plan.

> **Rattiner's Secrets:** ESOPs are excellent strategies for the client business owner who wants to sell their business. It may be easier than listing it with a broker, finding a buyer (locally or nationally), and being uncertain as to the price. Properly planned, the ESOP can provide for a specified price and timetable while giving the owner an official exit strategy and time horizon for relinquishing the business.

New comparability plan

A new comparability plan is either a profit-sharing or money purchase plan where the employee/participants are divided into groups or classes, with each group or class then receiving an employer contribution that is a different percentage of compensation. Such plans work particularly well where there is more than one owner of a business, with each owner of a significantly different age, thus precluding the age-based plan alternative. However, like an age-based plan, the new comparability plan is tested for nondiscrimination on the basis of cross-testing, thus permitting considerable flexibility in design.

A new comparability plan is also often used as a supplement to the traditional 401(k) plan where the employer wishes to make additional contributions to the accounts of highly compensated employees (HCEs) without having to separately comply with the actual deferral percentage (ADP) or actual contribution percentage (ACP) special nondiscrimination tests.

Thrift (or savings) plan

A thrift or savings plan is a defined contribution plan in which employees are directly involved in making contributions. In these plans, employer contributions for the employee are geared to mandatory contributions by the employee. Therefore, employees participate in the plan only if they contribute to the plan, usually, by making after-tax contributions. Employer matching contributions are then made.

"Pure thrift plans," providing for only after-tax employee contributions, have generally been replaced with the Section 401(k) "elective deferral" (before-tax contributions) alternative. However, such plans are often added to the traditional 401(k) plan so as to allow employee/participants to increase their retirement plan contributions beyond the annual elective deferral amounts for a given year.

PERSONAL RETIREMENT PLANS

Traditional IRAs

Individual retirement accounts typically allow salaried workers, self-employed individuals, and others to participate in a retirement plan, whether or not they currently participate in a qualified retirement plan. There are significant advantages for participating in an individual retirement plan, including tax-deferred earnings, possible income tax deductibility of the contributions, and compounding of interest on the earnings.

Many investments are allowable in an IRA. However, collectibles are a prohibited investment in the traditional IRA. Collectibles include art works, rugs, antiques, metals, gems, stamps, coins, and other tangible property. An exception exists for US-minted gold coins, silver coins, and platinum coins (that is, they may be invested in the traditional IRA).

Deductibility

The definition of an "active participant" for purposes of deductibility of traditional IRA contributions is an individual who actively participates in a qualified (employer-sponsored) retirement plan, SEP, SIMPLE plan, or "tax sheltered annuity" (TSA). Notably, participation in any type of Section 457 plan (governmental or nongovernmental) does not make the individual an active participant.

An individual is not an active participant in a defined contribution plan if only earnings are allocated to the individual's account. However, the individual is an active participant if employer contributions and/or forfeitures are made to the participant's defined contribution individual account. For a defined benefit plan, an individual is an active participant if they participate or meet the eligibility requirements at any time during the plan year. Therefore, an individual is an active participant in a defined benefit plan if they are eligible but decline to participate.

Calculation of deductible contribution. In general, individuals who are not active participants can deduct contributions to an IRA regardless of what they earn. However, for an active participant, fully deductible contributions are allowed only if the taxpayer/participant has an AGI below specified limits for the year of contribution. The deduction begins to decrease (phase out) when income rises above a certain amount and is eliminated altogether when it reaches a higher amount. These amounts vary depending on filing status. To determine whether an individual's deduction is subject to the phase-out, the modified AGI and filing status must be calculated (indexed each year).

Early withdrawals – 10% penalty tax. A 10% penalty tax is imposed on withdrawals prior to age 59½ under Code Section 72(t) unless an exception applies. The 10% penalty tax is imposed upon the recipient of the distribution and applies only to the portion of the distribution included in gross income. The portion that represents the cost recovery (i.e., nondeductible contributions) is never subject to the 10% penalty. See the list in the distributions section below.

Excess contribution penalty. If an individual contributes more to an IRA account than is allowed, the excess contribution is subject to a 6% excise tax. The penalty will be charged each year the excess contribution remains in the account. The individual can avoid paying the tax by withdrawing the excess contribution and any earnings before the due date of the federal income tax return. The earnings on the excess contributions are treated as gross income for the taxable year.

Roth 403(b) contributions. Employees could elect to make their salary deferral (again, similar in size to traditional 403(b)) contributions to these accounts (with no AGI limitations), plus catch-up contributions if applicable, without a tax deduction in the current year. This applies to employee contributions only (not to employer contributions). Again, the question becomes whether the employee would rather have the tax deferral now or receive the distributions tax free in the future.

Roth IRAs

Roth IRAs are in several respects similar to traditional (deductible and non-deductible) IRAs. For example, the list of prohibited investments in the Roth IRA is the same as the traditional forms. In addition, loans are not permitted to be made from a Roth IRA, just like any other form of IRA. Finally, a participant must have earned income to contribute to a Roth IRA, as with the traditional forms.

However, Roth IRAs may be distinguished from the traditional IRA since all Roth contributions are made with after-tax dollars (in other words, no deduction is ever permitted for a Roth IRA contribution). The phase-out limits are also much higher for Roth IRA contributions than those applying to active participants in the traditional deductible IRA.

Converting a traditional IRA into a Roth IRA

The analysis of whether to convert a traditional IRA to a Roth IRA (if otherwise qualifying) is not an easy one and requires a thorough tax and accounting work-up. However, as a general rule, if the income tax due on the initial conversion may be paid from assets other than the traditional IRA and the converted assets will remain in the Roth IRA for five years or longer before withdrawal, the conversion is generally advisable. The primary exception to this is if the participant believes they will be in a lower tax bracket at retirement (in other words, if that is the case, keeping the retirement funds in the traditional IRA may be marginally better than converting to a Roth).

Distributions from a Roth IRA: ordering the withdrawals of contributions from a Roth IRA

- From excess contributions: amounts that exceed the annual contribution limits (i.e., exceed annual limit or amounts converted from a traditional IRA that was ineligible). These withdrawals generally are free from federal income tax except for gains (which may be subject to a 10% penalty if individual is under age 59½).
- From annual Roth IRA contributions: the sum of the aggregate annual contributions, for which no deduction was allowed (referred to as the contribution-first recovery rule). These are always recovered without federal income tax liability or penalty.
- From conversion contributions: these distributions are previous taxed amounts (basis) and are not subject to federal income tax. They may be subject to a 10% penalty.
- From conversion contributions made in later taxable years: conversion contributions are considered on a first-in, first-out basis, and for this purpose all conversions that occur within a single taxable year are aggregated. These distributions are not subject to federal income tax. They may be subject to a 10% penalty.

   Note: These first four categories are all returned income tax-free.

- From earnings (gains) on all contributions: earnings on contributions are subject to federal income tax unless they are received as a qualified distribution (see below for what constitutes a qualified withdrawal). Taxable earnings are also subject to a 10% penalty if the individual is under 59½ or an exception does not apply.

Five-year rule

There is a five-year clock that starts on the first day of the first tax year in which any Roth IRA is opened and funded. Note that this applies to the tax year, not necessarily the calendar year. A person can make a contribution up to April 15 for the previous tax year, in which case the clock would start at the beginning of the previous tax year.

Earnings can be withdrawn tax-free and penalty-free after the clock hits five years and a qualifying event (such as turning 59½, disability, etc.) occurs. Remember, contributions can always be withdrawn without penalty or tax; it is only the earnings that are subject to this five-year clock. Additional five-year clocks start running for each traditional IRA that is converted to a Roth IRA. Each clock applies just to that conversion.

There is the special rule for a conversion contribution distributed when a taxpayer is under 59½. A conversion amount being withdrawn before the end of the five-year period starting with the year in which the conversion was made is subject to the 10% premature distribution penalty, unless an exception under section 72(t) applies. This special rule closes the loophole for the converted amount to be withdrawn immediately without penalty.

Thus, to be qualified distributions from a Roth IRA a distribution must be:

- made on or after the date you become age 59½; or made to your beneficiary, or to your estate after you die, or
- made to you after you become disabled within the definition of the IRS code, or
- used to pay qualified first-time homebuyer expenses. A distribution from a Roth IRA is not includible in the owner's gross income if it is a "qualified distribution." The results of this form of distribution are distributions of earnings are tax-free if the participant is at least age 59½, and
- the Roth IRA has been established for five or more years. Contributions are made with after-tax dollars and never taxed.

Simplified employee pension IRAs (SEP IRAs)

SEPs are employer-sponsored plans under which plan contributions are made (by the employer) to the participating employee's IRA. However, tax-deferred contribution levels are generally significantly higher than the maximum contribution limit for traditional IRAs. SEPs are hybrid plans sharing some of the characteristics of traditional IRAs and defined contribution plans.

Here is a summary of these shared characteristics. With IRAs, SEPs are 100% owned by the participant, making them 100% vested immediately, benefits are totally portable, rollovers and transfers are available to IRAs; withdrawals are permitted after age 59½; distributions are taxed at ordinary income rates, there is no forward averaging, and no loans are possible (like any PRP), and they are subject to required minimum distribution.

Here is a summary of these shared characteristics with DC plans. Annual employer-only funded contributions (employer deductions) are limited to 25% of compensation for common-law employees. For owner employees, the limit is 20% of net earnings. Section 415(c), annual additions, are limited to the lesser of 100% compensation or $57,000 (2020), which is the maximum amount that can be allocated to each participant (which is the same as other DC-type plans). The $285,000 compensation cap (2020) that applies to qualified plans also applies to SEPs. Nondiscrimination rules, top-heavy rules, and controlled group/affiliated services group rules apply. Participation in a SEP satisfies "active participant status" for determining deductible IRA contributions, and they may integrate with Social Security. Plans established prior to 1/1/1997 may allow salary deferral contributions. These plans are called SARSEPs and may still be in use in some businesses because they are "grandfathered," but no new plans may be established after 1/1/1997.

Here is a summary of unique SEP characteristics. Essentially, SEPs are required to cover virtually all employees, including part-time workers that earn in excess of a specified annual amount with a certain amount of employment service. Three special eligibility requirements must be met: attaining age 21, worked for the firm in three of the past five years, including the contribution year, and received compensation over $600 (2020). Employees may be excluded if they are a member of a collective bargaining unit or a nonresident alien. Contributions are fully discretionary, giving employers full control and maximum flexibility. As a result, "substantially and recurring" is not required. Lastly, contribution deadline to the SEP is April 15 including extensions; administration costs are very low with no annual filing requirements.

> **Rattiner's Secrets:** SEPs are a good choice for small client business owners because coverage rules are easier to work with than qualified plans, shorter-term employees (who have less than three years) may be excluded from the plan, and there are lower costs and administrative expenses. A SEP could be a poor choice if an employer has many long-term part-time employees because they will have to be covered by the plan.

SIMPLEs

Savings Incentive Match Plans for Employees were established by the Small Business Job Protection Act (SBJPA) in 1996 to replace SARSEPs. The plans come in two types: SIMPLE IRA and SIMPLE 401(k) plan. Since the SIM-PLE 401(k) form is a qualified plan and is more complex to establish and administer, most SIMPLE plans established by small employers (an employer with no more than 100 employees) are set up as an IRA. Here are the common requirements of both forms, followed by the unique provisions of each form.

SIMPLE forms have two conditions that must be met in order to be eligible to establish the plan. The first is the employer must have no more than 100 employees (counting only those employees earning at least $5,000 in compensation from the employer in the previous two years and who are reasonably expected to earn at least $5,000 in compensation this year). If the employer grows beyond the 100-employee limit, the law does, however, allow the employer to sponsor the plan for an additional two-year grace period. The second is that the employer cannot maintain any other qualified plan, 403(b), or SEP at the same time it has a SIMPLE plan in operation.

Contributions. Contributions are 100% vested. The maximum contribution amount that may be contributed for an individual in 2020 is $13,500 ($16,500 as a catch-up provision for those age 50 and older) for a SIMPLE IRA and a SIMPLE 401(k), plus for the SIMPLE 401(k) the annual addition limitations applicable to a defined contribution plan (lesser of $57,000 (2020) or 100% of participant's compensation) are applicable. The employers must satisfy one of the following two contribution formulas:

- The matching contribution of 100% match of the first 3% of employee's compensation (elective match).
- An employer can substitute a 2% nonelective contribution for the matching contribution, but only if eligible employees are notified that a 2% nonelective contribution will be made instead of a matching contribution.

No nondiscrimination testing rules apply, top-heavy rules do not apply.

Taxation issues. These include the employee elective deferrals are excludable for income, employer contributions are deductible, and earnings are tax deferred.

Distributions from a SIMPLE IRA. These are generally the same as IRAs. Distributions are taxed at ordinary income tax rates. Rollovers are permitted from SIMPLE plan to SIMPLE plan and from SIMPLE plan to IRA or SEP if in the SIMPLE plan for two years. If the client discontinues participation after two years, SIMPLE is treated as traditional IRA. Early withdrawals feature a 25% penalty if withdrawal is during the first two years of plan participation, and a 10% penalty after two years of participation. Loans are not permitted and there is limited protection under anti-creditor provisions.

Section 403(b) plans (aka "tax sheltered annuity" or TSA)

A Section 403(b) plan, also known as a "tax sheltered annuity," is a tax-advantaged retirement plan that may be adopted only by certain public or private tax-exempt organizations, specifically those that are covered by IRC Section 501(c) (3). Among the qualifying participants are public school employees, not-for-profit hospital employees, and church employees. You should note that if the tax-exempt organization is not classified as a "501(c) (3)" organization, a private tax-exempt organization may only establish a retirement plan for the benefit of its employees under the provisions of IRC Section 457 (a "457 nongovernmental plan").

Like other tax-advantaged plans, a Section 403(b) plan has its own set of requirements and provisions that must be met before the plan is accorded tax-advantaged status. However, unlike its close cousin in the for-profit world, the Section 401(k) plan, a Section 403(b) plan is technically not a qualified plan but mimics and qualified plan because it does share some of the same features. However, its participants are not afforded certain favorable distribution options, such as the possibility of 10-year lump-sum averaging. Lastly, contrary to popular belief, a 501(c) (3) tax-exempt organization may establish both a Section 403(b) plan and a Section 401(k) plan if it so chooses.

Allowable investments include annuity contracts (fixed or variable), custodial accounts holding mutual funds, and life insurance permitted only if it is incidental to an annuity contract. Incidental is based on the ratio of the life insurance premium to the Section 403(b) contribution. Contribution limits are similar to those of other qualified plans: an annual employee contribution of $19,500 (2020) and Section 415(c) annual additions limit, the lesser of 100% of annual compensation or $57,000 (2020).

A special catch-up contribution exists to certain education, health, and church organizations. First, the employee must have at least 15 years of service with the same 501(c) (3) employer. Second, the catch-up may increase the Section 402(g) limit by $3,000/year for a maximum of five years (lifetime election limit of $15,000) on salary reduction agreements for participants age 50 and over.

Section 457 plans

A Section 457 plan is not really a tax-advantaged plan at all (at least in the same sense as a Section 403(b) plan), but is rather a nonqualified deferred compensation plan by original design. However, the first of the two types of Section 457 – a Section 457 plan for state and/or local government employees (a governmental Section 457 plan) – has, by subsequent legislation, been transformed to look more like a tax-advantaged plan (a retirement plan with its own set of rules) than a nonqualified deferred compensation arrangement.

Plan characteristics. Salary reduction is limited to the lesser of $19,500 (in 2020) or 100% of compensation. Salary reductions must be executed and in place before the month in which the services were performed. Catch-up provisions are also available which are intended to provide an employee who did not make maximum annual deferrals in prior years to make higher contributions in anticipation of retirement, and are available in each of the three years prior to retirement, equal to the lesser of 100% of annual compensation or 200% of the normal limit that had not been used in previous years (for example, $19,500 in 2020 or times two = $39,000). Lastly, the "final three-year" provisions cannot be used if the regular age 50 and over "catch-up provision" is elected. (Note: Only participants in a governmental Section 457 plan are entitled to the regular catch-up, so those participants are the only ones entitled to make this election.)

Nonqualified deferred compensation

Nonqualified deferred compensation (NQDC) is sometimes simply called "executive compensation" since it is almost always afforded only to corporate or business executives. In contrast to a retirement plan that is tax-qualified, a nonqualified plan does not have to comply with the requirements of IRC Section 401(a), including the general nondiscrimination rules. As a result, while not afforded income tax advantages, a nonqualified plan is much more flexible and less costly for the employer to implement than a qualified plan. In addition, nonqualified plans can be structured to achieve other employer business objectives rather than providing for the retirement needs of employees. For example, nonqualified plans (sometimes generally referred to as "deferred compensation" plans) may be used to reward an employee (usually, an executive) for meeting employer sales goals or revenue targets, provide executives with "customized" retirement plans more favorable than that of a qualified plan, circumvent qualified plan nondiscrimination rules, provide retirement benefits in excess of qualified plan limits, and allow executives to defer current compensation.

There are two types of deferred compensation plans. The pure deferred compensation (i.e., a salary reduction plan) allows the employee to give up a specified portion of compensation (e.g., salary, raise, bonus, commissions) and the employer promises to pay a benefit sometime in the future, equal to the amount deferred plus a predetermined rate of interest. A salary (supplemental) continuation plan is where the employee does not give up current compensation for the benefit and the employer makes a commitment to provide the agreed-upon benefit.

NQDC income tax implications. There are two issues here. Constructive receipt doctrine states that an employee is taxed on compensation that they have a right to receive on demand without any risk of forfeiture. In a NQDC plan, if the employee has a choice to receive the compensation but is declined for whatever reason, the IRS will treat the compensation as taxable income to the recipient. Substantial risk of forfeiture exists if the participant's right to the compensation is conditioned upon the future performance of substantial services and would allow the monies to not be currently taxed and grow tax-deferred. The risk of forfeiture must be real and substantial.

CONSERVATION STAGE

In guiding your clients to manage their retirement nest egg, Pfau states the following: "Helping clients understand how risk changes in retirement and provides perhaps less flexibility makes us look at longevity risk to determine how long things will continue to last. Converting Roth-type accounts can help reduce the tax liability in those retirement years. Technology will be difficult to get with anything dynamic. The policy rule is that if market does this, I can do that and vice versa will not be able to be used in planning software. No commercial software will handle a dynamic approach like that."

Once the client has contributed to any type of retirement plan, our objective is to manage that portfolio as we would their after-tax investment portfolio (see Chapter 6). The same principles would be used. The most notable exception is the time horizon. Clients in the early stages of their careers can afford to be a little more aggressive. With clients at or near retirement, care needs to be taken so the clients are comfortable on a distribution model that ties into their risk factor.

DISTRIBUTION STAGE

There are many models that advisors follow in withdrawing funds from client retirement accounts. Certainly, the balances are the key, but there are several distribution "annuity/income-type models" that clients gravitate to in order to receive a level income going forward. "The 4% retirement withdrawal model, providing about 25 times what you wish to spend, will not be as useful a tool with interest rates shooting downwards and since people are living longer. A broader approach anticipating higher valuation will be needed," says Pfau. He states that it will need to be increased to half outside your investment portfolio, thereby providing a lifetime income which would not be as vulnerable to market activity. Pfau believes the client can still get close to 4% by mixing in annuities and/or whole life.

In addition, certain penalties apply to qualified and tax-advantaged plans, notably the 10% penalty for distributions made prior to the participant attaining age 59½ (the "premature distribution penalty") and the 50% penalty for not making required minimum distributions. As a planner, it is important to understand planning options to avoid either or both of these penalties.

Distribution options

In the case of a qualified retirement plan (and depending on plan provisions), there are four basic distribution options that are permitted:

1. A lump-sum distribution.
2. Payment in the form of an annuity or other periodic payment option.
3. A "rollover" of funds from one qualified plan to another, IRA, or another type of tax-advantaged plan.
4. A "direct trustee to trustee" transfer (also known as a "direct rollover").

Premature distributions

This 10% penalty is imposed on most distributions from a qualified plan, 403(b) or IRA, Roth IRA, SEP, and SIMPLE made to a participant before they attain age 59½. However, the following distributions are exceptions (i.e., the 10% penalty does not apply):

- Distributions made on or after the date on which the participant attains age 59½.
- Distributions made to a beneficiary on or after the death of the participant.
- Distributions attributable to the participant's becoming disabled.

- Distributions that are part of a series of substantially equal periodic payments (not less frequently than annually) made for the life (or life expectancy) of the participant or the joint lives of the participant and their designated beneficiary. Distributions under this exception generally cannot be modified for five years unless another exception applied to the distribution when it commenced.
- Distributions for medical expenses in excess of 10% of adjusted gross income.
- Distributions for health insurance premiums made to an unemployed individual after separation from employment if the individual has received unemployment compensation for 12 consecutive weeks under any federal or state unemployment compensation law (IRA only).
- Distributions used to pay qualified higher education expenses (including graduate education expenses) for the individual, the individual's spouse, or any child or grandchild of either (IRA only).
- Distributions made for first-time homebuyers' expenses. There is a lifetime maximum of $10,000. In addition, the distribution must be used within 120 days to buy, build, or rebuild the principal residence of the participant, their spouse, or any child, grandchild, or ancestor of either. A person qualifies as a first-time homebuyer if they had no present ownership interest in a principal residence during the preceding two years (IRA only).
- Distributions made on account of an IRS levy.
- Amounts transferred to an IRA of a spouse or former spouse under a divorce or separation instrument (qualified plan and 403(b) only).
- Age 55 and separation from service (qualified plan and 403(b) only).

Reverse mortgages

"Reverse mortgages can manage sequence risk by taking big distributions from part of the overall portfolio. The 2017 rules now provide for a bigger expense up front," says Pfau. Essentially, a reverse mortgage is a potential source of funding for the client who becomes cash poor but has tremendous equity in the house and wants to stay in their home. It is a loan available to homeowners age 62 and older which an individual who has considerable home equity can tap into it and borrow against the value of the house. It can make cash readily available as an additional or main income stream to help pay for expenses. Funds can be received in a lump-sum, fixed monthly payment of line of credit.

The loan becomes due when the homeowner moves, sells the property, or passes away. The amount of the loan cannot exceed the home's value, and heirs to the property would not be responsible for paying any differential if the loan amount exceeds the home's value. Most of these are federally insured. Advise the client to do their homework when checking these out.

Required minimum distributions (RMDs)

Historically, all qualified retirement plans, and IRAs, SEPs, SIMPLE IRAs, and TSAs are subject to the required minimum distribution rules during the participant's lifetime. The lifetime RMD rules do not apply to Roth IRAs. The SECURE Act changed the age triggering RMDs to 72 (from 70½). Inherited IRAs must still take distributions. The best advice you can offer a client is that if they are in a lower tax bracket this year, it may make sense to convert monies from a traditional account to a Roth to take advantage of the lower tax bracket.

However, the COVID-19 stimulus bill waives the RMD requirements for 401(k) plans and IRAs, including 403(b) plans, SEP IRAs, SIMPLE IRAs (at least for 2020), and represents a repeat of the 2009 RMD waiver during the Great Recession. As a result, we will not include a discussion here.

Inherited IRAs

- The spouse of a deceased shareholder can move the deceased account owner's balance into their own individual tax-deferred account, or continue to own the account as a beneficiary.
- The non-spouse must deplete an inherited IRA within 10 years of the account holder's death under The Secure Act if the owner died after Dec. 31, 2019.

Qualified domestic relations orders (QDROs)

A QDRO creates or recognizes the existence of an alternative payee's (ex-spouse's) right to, or assigns to an alternative payee the right to, receive all or a portion of the benefits payable with respect to the participant under a qualified retirement plan and that complies with stated requirements.

Net unrealized appreciation (NUA)

If a lump-sum distribution includes employer securities, the NUA in the value of the securities will be taxed to the employee at the ordinary tax rate at the time of distribution. The amount of NUA is taxed when the employee sells (on the appreciation over the basis and the securities and then at preferential long-term capital gains tax rates assuming the requisite year-and-a-day holding period is met); and finally, the employee may elect to pay the tax on the amount of NUA at the time that the securities are distributed by including such amount in their income.

SOCIAL SECURITY

Social Security (Old Age, Survivors, and Disability Insurance, OASDI) was never intended to provide full retirement benefits. It was intended to supplement retirement. It replaces approximately 41% of what someone is making at retirement. It's been tougher on clients because years ago many were covered through defined benefit plans which produced an income stream along with Social Security during retirement. Since most of those plans have gone away, the client today is more likely to have a retirement portfolio consisting of a 401(k) plan, IRAs, or some of the other plans where they have made the contributions as mentioned earlier. As part of the financial planning process, the client figures out how to withdraw the income needed coupled with Social Security to get by during their retirement years.

"Our role is in helping people understand what they can do, and what their options are. People get concerned whether their benefits will be there when they are ready to collect. Social Security will never be eliminated," says Kurt Czarnowski, Social Security Expert, of Czarnowski Consulting, Norfolk, MA.

Clients are concerned about which road to take. The Social Security claiming strategies are long gone. The issue became about longevity. "You tell me when you are going to die and I can tell you when to start collecting," says Czarnowski.

The way people have been taking their benefits has changed over time. "Initially we have seen people collecting Social Security more at full retirement age. If you start to collect and change your mind, you have one year to do that. You just have to re-pay the benefits you received," says Czarnowski. He adds that what we see now is that a lot of people who intended to wait to begin collecting benefits have been collecting earlier because of uncertain job status.

The lower wage earner spouse can elect one of these two benefit options. The spouse can draw on their benefit or 50% of the spouse's benefit, whichever is higher. However, if the husband dies first, his wife can receive 100% of the decedent's benefit at the time of collecting.

"For divorced spousal benefits, the client cannot be married, otherwise that person can lose eligibility on a prior spouse's accounts at age 62. The client can find out the 'benefit estimate' of the amount you can collect based on the ex's work history. No personal information can be divulged. You don't need the ex's Social Security number to find out, but it's easier if you have it," says Czarnowski.

> **Rattiner's Secrets:** A story I like to tell is the Black Widow Strategy whereby the client had been married four times, with each one lasting for 10 years, and then she retired. In all seriousness, based on the ages of the ex-spouses, where the first spouse was the youngest and going in sequential order where the fourth was the oldest, she was able to maneuver among the spouses based on their ages in order to receive the highest benefit based at full retirement age.

The basics

Social Security is known as the "old age, survivors, and disability income" program, created by the Social Security Act of 1935. Approximately 95% of all U.S. workers participate (pay a "payroll tax") in the program and receive some form of benefit, typically at their "full retirement age" (FRA) or earlier at the age of 62.

Workers pay into the system by means of a "payroll tax" on a specified amount of wages each year. Above this specified amount (known as the "taxable wage base"), the Social Security payroll tax is not assessed. (Note: This is not the case with the Medicare funding portion of the payroll tax, since an unlimited amount of wages is taxed to fund the Medicare program.)

Employees currently pay a Social Security payroll tax of 6.2% on all wages up to the Social Security taxable wage base for that year. Their employer matches this percentage for a total contribution of 12.4% into the Social Security system. An additional tax of 1.45% is then paid by each employee and employer (2.9% total) to fund the Medicare system, for a combination payroll tax amount of 7.65% for the employee and 7.65% for the employer (or a total of 15.3%). Self-employed individuals pay both the employee and employer portions (a total of 15.3%), although they subsequently receive a deduction for half of this amount (or 7.65%) to reach adjusted gross income (an "above-the-line" deduction) on their personal income tax return (IRS Form 1040).

Eligibility and benefit

There are five types of Social Security benefits: retirement, disability, survivor, family, and Medicare. The types of benefits to which a worker is entitled under the Social Security system depend, generally, on whether they are fully or currently insured. A fully insured worker is one who has participated and paid into the system for at least 40 quarters (effectively 10 years) during their employment career. A currently insured worker is one who has earned six quarters of coverage during the 13 calendar quarters ending with the calendar year of death. In both categories, a quarter of coverage is currently one in which the worker has earned at least $1,410 (2020) of compensation.

Retirement benefits

To receive Social Security retirement benefits, a worker must be fully insured at the date of their "full retirement age" under the system. Historically, the FRA for any worker has been age 65. The date of FRA for any worker under the system depends on their date of birth. As a result, the FRA for some workers may be as great as age 67 (for those people born 1960 and thereafter).

A worker may elect to receive Social Security retirement benefits "early" (at the age of 62), but with a permanently reduced monthly benefit. It started out at 80% but when the FRA was aged, it shifted based on birthday. Again, if the client is born in 1960, of these after, benefits will be 70% of FRA benefit. As a general rule, early retirement will provide the worker with about the same total Social Security benefits over their lifetime, but in smaller amounts to take into account the longer period that the benefits will be distributed. But again, it depends on the client's life expectancy.

Of course, it is also possible that a married couple may be entitled to two sets of retirement benefits under Social Security. This entitles either spouse to receive a benefit based on the greater of their own retirement benefit (that is, based on the worker's employment record) or 50% of the other participant/spouse's retirement benefit.

"Benefits can be had at age 62 with few exceptions. Beyond age 67 the benefits can be delayed and increased (at 2/3% per month) capped at 8% per year till age 70," says Czarnowski. That means a worker who waits to age 70 to max out their benefit will receive 124% of their FRA benefit.

Disability benefits

To qualify for disability benefits payable under the Social Security system, a worker must meet a very strict definition of disability. Specifically, the worker must be so severely impaired, physically or mentally, that they cannot perform any substantial gainful activity. In addition, this impairment must be expected to last at least 12 months from the onset of the disability or to result in the worker's death. Finally, there is a five-month waiting period before the worker may receive benefits once a finding of the requisite disability has been made by the Social Security Administration (SSA).

Survivor benefits

Like retirement and/or disability benefits under the Social Security system, a worker must generally be fully insured before survivor benefits will be paid. As a result, the following survivors are eligible to receive lifetime benefits based on the employment record of the worker:

- A surviving spouse age 60 or over (note: a surviving spouse who elects to receive benefits at age 60 is only entitled to a survivor's benefit equal to 71.5% of the worker's "primary insurance amount"), with this benefit then increasing in percentage amount the longer that the surviving spouse delays receipt of the benefit until their own FRA (when a 100% benefit is payable); a surviving, divorced spouse also qualifies for this benefit if they were married to the worker for at least 10 years prior to the worker's death and the divorced spouse has not remarried prior to age 60.
- A disabled, surviving spouse age 50–59 (again, with the same percentage reductions as just mentioned).
- A surviving spouse under the age of 61 currently taking care of a dependent child under the age of 16 (a 75% benefit is payable).
- A dependent parent age 62 or over (an 82.5% benefit is payable).
- An unmarried child under age 18, age 19 if still in high school, or at any age, if the child becomes disabled before age 22 (a 75% benefit is payable).

A lump-sum death benefit of $255 is also payable to a surviving spouse or dependent child of the Social Security worker.

Finally, it is important to note that (1) the surviving spouse caring for a dependent child benefit, (2) the unmarried child's benefit, and (3) the lump-sum death benefit, all as mentioned above, are also payable as a survivor's benefit if the worker was only currently insured at the time of their death.

"If the spouse has died and the widow is still alive and he or she is greater than or equal to 60, the lowest amount would come in at 71.5% and would go up each month to 100%. Do not forego past age 67 since there is no increase in income past then," says Czarnowski.

Family limitations

An overall "family limitation" applies when Social Security benefits are paid to more than one family member. For example, each qualified child in a family may receive a monthly payment up to one-half of the worker's full retirement benefit amount, but there is a limit to the amount that may be paid to the family as a whole. This total depends on the amount of the worker's benefit and the number of family members who also qualify based on the worker's employment record. The total amount of family benefit varies, but it is generally equal to about 150–180% of the worker's retirement benefit.

How benefits are calculated

All benefit amounts paid under the Social Security system are known as the worker's "primary insurance amount" (PIA). To compute a worker's PIA, it is first necessary to know their average indexed monthly earnings (AIME), which are based on the worker's employment record while covered under the system. Generally, the SSA will compute both the AIME and the PIA for the worker and is now required, under law, to send the worker an annual statement that includes their PIA estimate (assuming no change in earnings prior to their FRA).

Working after retirement

Any worker who has reached their FRA may now earn as much compensation as possible without failing the retirement earnings test and having benefits reduced. A limit on earnings does continue to apply to workers who have not yet attained their FRA when beginning the receipt of retirement benefits. This allowable amount varies by year, but a worker (electing to receive benefits early) is only able to earn a maximum of $18,240 (indexed in 2020) per year between the ages of 62 and 65. Specifically, if a worker earns more than this limit, they will lose $1.00 in Social Security benefits for every $2.00 of earnings above the limit.

In the year a person reaches age 65, benefits are reduced $1 for every $3 earned over a different annual limit ($48,600 indexed in 2020) until the month they reach age 66. There is no reduction in benefits regardless of income level once the recipient reaches age 66.

Taxation of Social Security benefits

If worker/retirees earn substantial income, in addition to the receipt of their Social Security retirement benefits, a portion of those benefits will become income-taxable. Special step-rate thresholds determine the amount on which the worker is taxed. These "base amounts" of a worker/retiree's modified adjusted gross income and the portion of the benefit that is taxable are as follows:

	50% taxable	85% taxable
MFJ	$32,000	$44,000
Single	$25,000	$34,000

If the first specified threshold is exceeded in any taxable year, generally 50% of the amount by which the Social Security benefits exceed the threshold is subject to income tax. Alternatively, if the second threshold is exceeded in any taxable year, generally 85% of the amount by which the benefits exceed the threshold is subject to income tax. However, the includible amount cannot exceed the smaller of (a) 85% of the actual Social Security benefits received in any taxable year or (b) 50% of the benefits, plus 85% of any excess over the second threshold. An example follows shortly.

Finally, the worker/retiree's MAGI is computed in three steps:

1. Begin by including the taxpayer's regular AGI with income derived from any source except Social Security income. (Note: This is also often referred to as "preliminary AGI" when computing the taxation of Social Security benefits.)
2. Add back any tax-exempt interest, such as municipal bond interest, received by the worker/retiree in the current taxable year.

3. Add back 50% of any Social Security benefits received. (Note: This is not the same as the 50% special step-rate threshold described above.)

Retirement planning could be the most intriguing financial planning issue for clients based on the uncertainty of it all. Looking at potential lifespans, expenses now and in the future, and the ability to really contribute and ideally maximize contributions is a challenge unto itself. Leaving you with a strong and practical quote from David Blanchett: "It should be people helping people, or essentially a behavioral alpha. We always picture alpha solely as an investment tool only. We need to help people make better choices with their money. We have to help clients determine what to do. For example, what if lower bond yields are here forever? These have huge implications on what people save in retirement. The destination and complexity of retirement is rapidly changing because of its uncertain path. How do you fund an uncertain lifespan?"

CHAPTER 9

Dispensing Advice on Estate Planning

Estate planning strategies are changing. Gone are the days where the parents wanted to ensure specific amounts for their children or other heirs and would sacrifice themselves to make that happen. Historically, the parents would strap themselves financially in order to leave a sizeable amount, if possible, equally to their children and perhaps other heirs. Today, more clients are concerned about finally having money set aside for that rainy day so they can do the things they always talked about wanting to do but were not comfortable doing during their working years. So, the approach has changed. This chapter focuses on those strategies you may wish to bring up for your clients to gain the closure they need to feel comfortable.

It is important to understand the big picture so we can help determine the exposures that are present, and help plan potential efficient and effective solutions for the client. Estate planning is a process, as we discussed in Chapter 3, for the accumulation, conservation, and distribution of your client's estate. Our role is all about education, especially because there are many fallacies in this arena. Having everyone be on board and go through the process together so that expectations are managed properly from the beginning is a great way to start.

When things go astray, the client may possibly incur significant cost and unforeseen issues, which can make things very messy and financially troublesome to work through. An example of this is acting in a certain manner because that's the way it has always been. That may not work going forward. One of the things Bill Carter says he learned from his dad was, "Things change! I know you are doing well today Bill, but things change!" Carter has stated that he definitely understands that today and not only with himself, but also as he sees it playing out with his clients.

Carter shared the story of a client many years ago who against the firm's advice gave away most of their money to their kids. The client's rationale was that if we need it, the children will give it back to us. There were several children involved. Unfortunately, things turned bad for the parents, with unexpected things happening for which they were not able to support their living standard going forward. When the client approached each of the kids to ask for the money back, they were turned down. Things happen!

> **Rattiner's Secrets:** Talk about things being different today, I have many clients who visit my office stating, "Jeff, my goal is to -$0- out at death! We're not concerned about leaving our money to anyone." Obviously, that's not a realistic assumption, but here's the point. Many clients today feel they did a lot in providing their children with a strong and proper background and support system to move forward and they should be able to take those skill sets and family values to the next level. The clients don't want their kids to become entitled to their money. They don't want the children to have a change of plans and stop working as hard or in trying to advance themselves and take care of their families with the future inheritance in the background. The clients just don't want their children to rely solely on them, because as we said earlier, life happens! The best line I heard from a client was, "Jeff, I want the last check I ever write to bounce!"

Carter believes leaving funds to charity will present a better planning option if the client or family member may need to access funds in the future. He does not see his clients leaving their assets equally to all the children. For many reasons, the client needs to think through what will work out best for the couple who owns those assets. Many times, private discussions involving a single family member or perhaps including other family members or likely heirs will need to be had.

There are a lot of issues to work around in estate planning. There are many interpretations from active planners in the field. I'm not a believer in liquidating a client's assets to get the money out of the estate for the majority of clients. Yes, it does make sense for certain high-net-worth individuals, and in a variety of situations, but specialty attention will be needed for that type of planning.

Working as Part of the Appropriate Estate Planning Team for the Client

Estate Planning Mistakes
Property Titling
Probate
Wills
Powers of Attorney
Trusts
Tax Implications
Gross Estate
Sources for Estate Liquidity
Valuation Issues
Powers of Appointment
Deferral and Minimization of Estate Taxes
Charitable Transfers
Generation-skipping Transfer Tax (GSTT)
Intra-family and Other Business Transfer Techniques
Postmortem Estate Planning Techniques

With the estate and gift tax exclusion at very high amounts – $11,580,000 (2020) indexed each year, and double that for a couple ($23,160,000) – the overwhelming majority of estate tax return filers will not be subject to paying estate tax. In fact, to get a handle on how many people will be affected when it comes to paying estate tax, the last set of numbers I found online through taxpolicycenter.org showed about 4,000 estate tax returns would be filed for people who died in 2018, of which only about 1,900 would be taxable – less than 0.1% of the 2.7 million people expected to die in that year. I'll make the assumption those numbers will remain similar until the estate tax exclusion changes under current tax law on January 1, 2026, and finds its way back to numbers from roughly a decade earlier, 2017, of $5,000,000 indexed, or less than half of the current amount, and that's assuming this amount doesn't change by law earlier. Surviving spouses are generally exempt from these taxes, regardless of the value of the estate or inheritance. A dozen states impose their own estate taxes, and six have inheritance taxes, both of which kick in at lower threshold amounts than the federal estate tax.

The biggest change is the increased exemption, which as of this writing goes back down in 2026, which may throw off strategies for clients. "The increased exemption took the middle class out of the system," says Lawrence Brody, Senior Counsel at Bryan Cave Leighton Paiser, LLP, an international law firm in St. Louis, MO. Brody states that the exemption will go longer since most people won't have to pay estate taxes.

The popular viewpoint from representation of high-net-worth clients is this: "As people get older, there will continue to be trends toward gift giving. Having your client's children benefit from their wealth and receiving family assets before the parents reach age 90 (vs. traditional inheritance). The argument goes as to what kind of benefit will children get if they receive inheritances very late in their lifetimes?" says Daniel Rubin, Partner, Moses & Singer, LLP, New York.

Brody says we need to stay intertwined with the estate, gift transfer tax of the current larger amounts. "The use of irrevocable life insurance trusts (ILITs) no longer works as well as revocable trusts, which are easier to modify or terminate into a better and more modern trust. The intersection of insurance and estate planning can be found by buying life insurance on the lives of the settlor, spouse, and children for the benefit of the grandchildren through a combined trust."

Rattiner's Secrets: The biggest risks imposed upon the client by gifting money early is that since people are living longer today compared with any prior period in history, there is a really good chance the client can run out of money. When I started in this business, we would plan out for clients to have retirement funds through the mid-80s. Today most people plan through age 100 and even longer. If these original retirement needs analysis projections have never been adjusted, then issues of your clients literally running out of money could occur.

Several years ago, I attended my youngest son's college graduation and the master of ceremonies addressing the graduates said that more than 50% of that year's graduates would be living past the age of 100. Pretty amazing! Working off that logic, with people living longer, there may be serious medical issues that arise that are not present in today's world, which could create expensive types of treatments. In other words, unplanned medical expenses or any type of expenses could arise and that could put a damper on finances if that money was given away previously.

Another issue is that gifting does not provide a step-up in basis on the transferred property. The donee (recipient) continues using the adjusted basis of the donor. If assets are in the family for many years, such as a primary residence, or any appreciating asset, chances are that there will have been a significant increase in value. That will probably result in a potential capital gains issue when the donee sells the asset.

And finally, with the number of clients actually paying estate tax, other than annual gifting strategies by both spouses to take advantage of the annual exclusion, Section 529 college funding, helping those children and grandchildren, family members where help is necessary, and things of that nature, for families whose estates are under the threshold there are no estate tax benefits for those clients removing assets from their estate.

When giving away assets, "don't give away cash or low-basis assets," says Brody. "Give away assets likely to appreciate."

ESTATE PLANNING MISTAKES

By definition, since we are not practicing as attorneys but as financial planners, drafting any documentation including contracts and instruments would be considered the "unauthorized practice of law." This should be done by attorneys to assist the client with possible strategies, and that is where we come in. We can help identify those issues and leave to the experts the way to fine-tune what should be done for the client. Part of that strategy is in identifying those weaknesses that are inconsistent with the client's objectives stated in the financial plan (see Chapter 3), which sounds an alarm that the client needs immediate assistance.

Rattiner's Secrets: My biggest concern in the entire estate planning process is the lack of a coordinated game plan. We should take the lead and then work with a coordinated team, including an attorney, a CPA, trust officer, the client's health professional(s), investment and insurance professional (if we do not provide that service), elder care professional, funeral home representative, and others who have a direct impact

(continued)

> (*continued*)
>
> in that client's life (during and afterwards). We should be cc'd on all correspondence and perhaps attend certain meetings, where necessary, to make sure we are all on the same page. My issue is that if we are not all together initially, we will not end up all together representing that client's best interests.

While there could be many possibilities included here, some of the more common ones where we can get involved are the following.

1. **Location of all the client's relevant information** (see below), including separate funeral instructions and other important information that may not be known by the family.
2. **Selection of the wrong executor.** This can be a problem if that individual is not skilled in understanding the particular issues, doesn't understand the financial risk or implications, is not compensated, is lackadaisical, or even has a conflict of interest.
3. **Failure to write or update a valid will.** Wills should be updated every so often to make sure things are in alignment, such as tax law, family changes, or other legal changes. This includes designating the proper heirs, and updating the will for the client's marriage, divorce, or separation. Not having a valid will could make the existing will obsolete and have the client die intestate (subject to state law). In addition, if the client changes their domicile from, let's say, a common law state to a community property state or vice versa, there could be issues that will not have been addressed by the older will.
4. **Lack of liquidity.** If there are no liquid funds available to settle the estate through insurance, self-funding, or cash reserve, and only illiquid assets are available, those assets may need to be sold at a discount to pay the tax.
5. **Leaving everything to or holding assets jointly with the spouse.** The issue here is it puts the assets in the surviving spouse's name, which could increase the assets in that spouse's estate. While naming the spouse could work if the client considers portability (see below) or is under the threshold, there are many safeguards that are not available with this strategy. Setting up a bypass trust could be a better option.

6. **Failure to name contingent beneficiaries.** If the primary beneficiary is deceased and no contingent beneficiaries are named, and the client is concerned about privacy, the assets would be part of the gross and also probate estates.

7. **Inappropriate ownership or beneficiaries of life insurance.** If the client owns the policy in their own name, it would be part of that person's estate, which depending on the size of the estate may or may not matter. Also, if someone is designated as the beneficiary of the policy and is not ready to handle the proceeds, that could become an issue.

8. **Inappropriate titling of property.** This helps ensure that the right people receive the right property at the right time. This could be between non-spouses and others where the property owners don't understand the differences.

9. **Not having a buy-sell agreement for the business owner.** See Chapter 10.

Rattiner's Secrets: I have each of my clients set up a folder for all of their documents and other necessities to help prepare for and be available at their death. I'm sure there are better names you can think of, but I have my clients call it the "Death folder" mainly for the reason that if children or others are looking for the client's information, especially after the fact, it is easier to locate the one folder where everything is located and filed together – wills, trusts, powers of attorney, passwords, key computer information, other legal documents, investment and bank statements, retirement account information, insurance policies, safety deposit box keys, funeral arrangements, and perhaps a zip drive of important and relevant documents including account name, address, account numbers, contact person, account balances, beneficiaries, or other things that may be relevant. Saving all of this information on the cloud would provide a good backup.

PROPERTY TITLING
Community property versus noncommunity property

There are two types of property law systems in the United States: common law (noncommunity property) states and those states that have adopted a community property approach. The basic difference between the two systems is when property rights "vest" (are not subject to restriction or forfeiture) in each spouse.

Common law

In common law states (the majority of states), the spouse does not acquire a vested interest in the property of their (the other) spouse until some point in the future, typically divorce, separation, or death. Such spouse is said to have an "incomplete, unfinished and interrupted interest" in the property of the other spouse which is completed when the one spouse outlives the other. As a result, in a common law state, it is possible for one spouse to title property individually in their own name, and to the exclusion of ownership rights in the other spouse. In contrast, this is not possible in a community property state.

Community property

In community property states (there are nine of them plus Alaska, which has both), each spouse owns an immediate, vested one-half interest in all property acquired during the course of the marriage. Therefore, it is not possible for one spouse to title property in their own name alone (and to the exclusion of the other spouse). All income and assets acquired with that income are deemed one-half owned by each spouse, regardless of who actually earned the income or contributed to the property. If property is acquired in a community property state and then the couple moves to common law, the property is treated as community property.

    Practical example: Brian and Lisa live in Texas, a community property state. Brian acquires some real property in that state and wants to title it in his own name individually. Operationally, he may do so, but legally, Lisa has a vested one-half interest in this same property, restricting Brian from full and complete ownership. Therefore, the titling in Bob's individual name makes no legal difference since Brian and Lisa own the property "in the community."

Rattiner's Secrets: In multiple marriage situations, ensuring the couple enters the marriage with a pre-nuptial agreement could help protect against certain pre-marital assets and other separate property from being considered as community property.

You should note that nine states (Arizona, California, Idaho, Louisiana, Nevada, New Mexico, Texas, Washington, and Wisconsin) are considered community property. Finally, the state of Alaska permits married couples to elect to treat property acquired during the marriage as community property.

Community property is all property that "has been acquired by the efforts of either spouse during their marriage." This includes all property acquired during marriage by either spouse even if the funds to buy the property are earned by only one spouse. However, there is a notable exception to this rule: if property is acquired by one spouse during marriage by gift, devise, bequest, or inheritance, it is considered to be their separate property and the other spouse does not have a vested one-half interest. The same result occurs when property is "brought to" the marriage by one spouse; in other words, if they owned the property before marriage, it is considered to be separate property. The only exception to that is if the property is commingled. Then the property will belong to both spouses.

Community property generally requires the writing of a will to pass the interest, thus making the interest subject to the probate process. However, recently, some community property states (such as Texas) have recognized survivorship rights in community property, if it is so titled. In this event, "community property with right of survivorship" avoids probate.

Finally, there is a major income tax advantage associated with the ownership of community property (as compared with that of common law property). Specifically, at death, the surviving spouse receives a step-up in basis in both halves of the community property interest to its fair market value (FMV) at the date of death. This is not the result in a common law state where property is held in joint tenancy with right of survivorship between the spouses. In this case, only the decedent's half of the total property interest is eligible for the step-up in basis.

Practical example: To emphasize gift and estate basis issues between a married couple, let's work through the following example. If the husband (H) gifts the house to the wife (W), W's basis in the house is $20,000. It's the same whether it is a common law or community property state. However, it works differently for inherited property. If H dies in a common law state, his half of the value is stepped up (thus resulting in a 50% stepped-up basis) and W's basis going forward is $260,000 ($10,000 and $250,000). For a community property state, if H dies, not only is his half stepped up but so is her half, resulting in a 100% step-up in basis to $500,000 ($250,000 and $250,000).

	H	W	Total
Cost	10,000	10,000	20,000
FMV	250,000	250,000	500,000

Quasi-community property

There are five states that follow quasi-community property rules (Arizona, California, Idaho, Washington, and Wisconsin). When a married couple moves to one of the above states from a common law state, the property will be considered quasi-community, which essentially means that it will be treated as community property.

> **Rattiner's Secrets:** Even though there are 10 community property states including Alaska, each state may have its own twist. For example, if the client lives and is domiciled in a common law state and decides to purchase a second home in a community property state, that second state may allow the client to title the property as either common or community based on its rules.

Sole ownership

Sole ownership of property, also known as "fee simple absolute" property, is permitted only in common law states where individuals are married at the time of titling. To dispose of such property at death, the sole owner must either write a will or rely on the state's intestate succession laws to determine the devisees (beneficiaries).

Joint tenancy with right of survivorship (JTWROS)

JTWROS property is concurrent ownership (owned between two or more individuals) in common law states. In JTWROS, each joint tenant has a revocable, 100% ownership in the whole of the property. Thus, they may gift, convey, or devise the entire interest, but if they do any of these, the second (or remaining) joint tenant(s) now owns the property in tenancy-in-common with the donee or devisee. In other words, a notable characteristic of JTWROS property is that the survivorship interest may be severed by one joint tenant without the consent of the other joint tenant.

The major attribute of property owned in JTWROS is that of its "survivorship right." This means that unless the survivorship right is severed during the lifetime of either joint tenant, the property passes at the death of the first joint tenant to the second joint tenant by operation of law and thus avoids the probate process. Essentially, the last one alive wins!

If a married couple are the titled joint tenants on property at the date of the first spouse's death, only 50% of the FMV of that property as of the date of death is included in the first spouse's estate. There is no gift tax when the property is titled in JTWROS, regardless of the respective contributions (or lack thereof) by each spouse. Most property titled in JTWROS is held between spouses, but the form of ownership is also permitted among non-spouses.

Tenancy-by-the-entirety

Tenancy-by-the-entirety (TE) property is permitted only in some common law states. TE is a limited form of JTWROS property that may be held only between spouses; that is, non-spouses cannot hold property in tenancy-by-the-entirety. Many times it is held for liability purposes.

A distinguishing characteristic of TE property, in contrast to property titled in JTWROS, is that severance of the survivorship right may be done only with the consent of the other joint tenant/spouse. Thus, titling of property in TE is not as flexible as the JTWROS form.

However, like JTWROS, there is also only a 50% inclusion of the FMV of the property in the first spouse's estate where property is held in TE at death. There are also no gift tax consequences with TE titling, even in the event of unequal contribution by the spouses.

Tenancy-in-common

Tenancy-in-common (TC) property is a prevalent form of common law titling where property has been inherited by siblings (from their parent's estate) and/or by non-spouses.

TC is the ownership by two or more persons, each of whom owns an undivided, but fractional, interest in the entire property. For example, if there are three tenant-in-common owners, each owner has a $33\frac{1}{3}\%$ interest in the property. To pass such property at death, a will must be written (typically, such a will leaves the TC property to the decedent's spouse or children).

Commensurately, the tenant-in-common owner includes only their fractional interest in their estate for estate tax purposes. Unlike JTWROS or TE, there are no survivorship rights inherent in a TC interest, thus preventing its disposition by operation of law.

Rattiner's Secrets: I have seen many instances where clients own property in a different manner than originally thought. For example, I had a client who was one of four sisters who each owned a four-bungalow property in a resort area. They owned it JTWROS. Three of the sisters were in their 60s and one was in her 40s. The assumption was they would each leave their share of the bungalow to their children, but based on the way the property was titled, that couldn't be done. It needed to be TC. Based on lifespan, the 40-year-old would probably have ended up with the entire property. I had her contact an attorney to change the titling for everyone to reflect what each sister initially thought and wanted to happen.

PROBATE

Defined broadly, probate is the process by which a state or local court validates the will of a deceased individual. As a part of this validation, probate also provides a method to clear the title of any property of the decedent that may be subject to dispute (or "a cloud on the title").

There are both advantages and disadvantages to the probate process. As a result, the decedent needs to weigh these, and if they believe the disadvantages outweigh the advantages, discuss with the client methods of avoiding probate.

Among the advantages of probate is that it provides for clean title of a decedent's property; it implements the objectives of the decedent by enforcement of the local court; it provides for an orderly administration of the decedent's assets; it protects the decedent's creditors by giving them a forum to have their claims heard; and it protects the decedent from an untimely filing of claims by the decedent's lifetime creditors.

Among the disadvantages of probate is that it may prove to be costly; it may prove to be complex and/or complicated for the executor of the decedent's estate; there may be a significant delay in the distribution of the decedent's assets to their heirs (particularly if the validity of the decedent's will is contested); and it is a public process, whereas some wealthy decedents may wish to avoid open knowledge of their assets and affairs.

Ancillary probate

A decedent's last will and testament may typically only dispose of any real property owned by the decedent in their state of residence (technically, "legal domicile") via one probate proceeding. If the decedent's will disposes of real property owned and located in another state, then a second probate proceeding is required. This additional probate proceeding is referred to as "ancillary probate" and should be contrasted to the "original" or "first probate" proceeding that may be followed to pass real property located in the decedent's state of residence, as well as all personal property that is located therein.

WILLS

A last will and testament ("will") is a legal document executed by an individual to specify, among other provisions, how they wish property to be distributed at death. A will is, by its nature, "revocable." This means that the testator may, at any time prior to their death, amend, modify, or totally revoke the provisions of the will. If the testator revokes the will, they are then under no legal requirement to write a new will. But if they do not write a will, they will die "intestate" and the provisions of state intestacy law will then dictate how their property is to be distributed at death.

"A shift to electronic wills compared with the execution of traditional wills is becoming more popular whereby there may not be a need to have two people be witnesses on the documents being signed," says Dan Rubin. He says that in our industry, consolidation of roles with one-stop shopping exists and includes accounting, financial services, estate planning attorneys, and estate planning advisors where they do not draft documents but fill a vital role.

Types of wills

While the most common type of will is a typewritten document, there are several other types, as follows:

- **A holographic will:** This is a will that is written entirely by the testator but is not witnessed by others. Some states do not recognize holographic wills, but in those that do, the signature on such wills must be in the testator's own handwriting and there must be no material omissions in the disposition of the testator's property.

- **A nuncupative will:** This is an oral will spoken by the testator during the days of a last illness, with the words witnessed by the required number of nonbeneficiary witnesses. These witnesses must be readily available to testify in open court with respect to the testator's wishes. Finally, the testator must be legally competent at the time of speaking the words.

- **A joint will (also known as a mutual will):** This is a will (one document) that is written by two individuals, typically spouses. Both testators share the same disposition-of-property objectives. Because of technical legal and tax reasons, the execution of a joint will is usually not a good idea; nevertheless, you will encounter them from time to time.

- **A living will:** This is a legal document executed by an individual directing their physician as to whether to continue (or discontinue) life support measures in the event that the individual is declared "terminal" (expected to die relatively shortly). Most living wills are "statutory," meaning that the state provides the living will form as well as the options with respect to life support.

Modifying or revoking a will

To modify (or amend) a will, a testator must execute what is known as a "will codicil." Such a codicil must also be executed according to "testamentary formality" (witnessed, etc.), but may add to or delete certain provisions from the previously executed will. Like a will, a codicil should only be written by a licensed attorney or the planner may be threatened with unauthorized-practice-of-law allegations.

Avoiding will contests

There are no absolute provisions or measures that may be included in a will to avoid a future will contest by a disgruntled heir or creditor. However, here are some suggestions:

- Do not disinherit any natural heir, particularly an estranged child, without at least recognizing the child in the will. For example, mention the child's name and your relationship to the child. Then include wording that you leave the child a bequest of "one dollar and other valuable consideration." Accordingly, this indicates that you are aware of the child's existence but wish to provide for the child in the method indicated.

- Include an "in terrorem clause" in the will. This clause prohibits an heir from contesting the will at the risk of complete disinheritance.
- Provide for the disposition of your property through a lifetime revocable trust or testamentary trust. This will assist in preventing disgruntled heirs from trying to overturn a will with little dispositive impact, for example, a pour-over will.
- Engage the best estate planning attorney available to draft the will. "Tight drafting" can go a long way in avoiding a potential will contest.

POWERS OF ATTORNEY

A power of attorney is a legal document created by an individual authorizing someone else (known as their agent or power of attorney) to act on the individual's behalf. The individual that grants the power of attorney to another is commonly referred to as "the principal."

The powers granted by a principal can either be "general" (broadly stated) or "limited" (also known as "special"). Most powers of attorney are general and take effect either at the date of the principal's inability to act because of legal incompetence (a "springing power of attorney") or immediately upon execution (a "nonspringing power of attorney"). If the power is "springing," there needs to be a procedure to inform the agent that the principal is now legally incompetent and needs assistance. Typically, an accepted procedure is the concurrence by at least two physicians that the principal is now unable to act.

Historically, powers of attorney have also been classified with respect to their "durability." This means that if the power is written as "durable," the power of the agent to act on behalf of the principal continues in the event of the principal's legal incapacity or incompetency. If this provision is not included, the power is considered as a "nondurable" power and the power of the agent to act terminates when the principal is determined to be incompetent. As a result, nondurable powers of attorney are rarely used anymore, particularly since all 50 states now have provided for the writing of durable powers of attorney by their residents.

TRUSTS

All trusts to be legally effective must have a legally competent grantor, a trustee, and a beneficiary (or beneficiaries). A trust must have a "corpus" or property that is owned by the trust at the time of its execution. If the trust is irrevocable when the grantor transfers property to the trust, a gift is made by the grantor; however, the income from the trust (and gifted property) may still be taxable to the grantor if one of the "grantor trust rules" is triggered.

There are two primary forms of trusts (as based on the powers of the person who created the trust): a revocable and an irrevocable trust. In the revocable trust form, the person who created the trust – also known as the "grantor" – retains the power to revoke the trust during their lifetime. Thus, there is no gift tax liability since there is not a completed gift. Since the grantor also retains a revocable power at their death, under the "grantor trust" transfer tax rules, the entire FMV of the trust property (100%) is included in the gross estate of the decedent/grantor. Alternatively, in the irrevocable trust form, there is a complete gift to the trustee for which, depending on the amount of the gift, gift tax may be due. Moreover, assuming certain prohibited powers are not retained by the grantor, the FMV of the property transferred to the trustee of the irrevocable trust is not included in the grantor's gross estate. The language within the trust typically specifies the length of the trust term.

Simple and complex

A simple trust is one that is required to pay out all its income to the trust beneficiaries at least annually and cannot distribute any trust corpus to charity. Accordingly, such a trust is considered merely a conduit for passing through the income to its beneficiaries. The most common example of a simple trust is the revocable living trust where all income is distributed and reported on the grantor's personal income tax return (IRS form 1040).

Alternatively, a complex trust is any trust that is not a simple trust. This means any irrevocable trust that may accumulate income (within the trust entity) or where a charitable contribution is (or could have been made) from trust principal. An irrevocable complex trust is a separate taxable entity with its own income tax rates.

Revocable and irrevocable

A revocable trust is one that may be rescinded or amended at any time by the grantor. The most common form of revocable trust is a revocable "living" trust (RLT), which is separately funded by transferring the individual title of property to that of the name of the trustee (usually the grantor). RLTs are usually established for one or more of three reasons:

1. To avoid probate of the grantor/decedent's assets at death (including the avoidance of ancillary probate).
2. To provide a mechanism (appoint a successor trustee) to plan for the grantor's possible legal incapacity.
3. To include transfer tax planning measures subsequent to the death of the grantor (for example, the inclusion of marital and nonmarital trusts).

An irrevocable trust is one where the grantor has relinquished all control over the transferred property (in other words, the grantor does not have the power to amend or revoke the trust). When the grantor establishes an irrevocable trust and transfers property to the trustee of the trust, they make a completed gift of the property. Thus, depending on the amount of the property transferred, a taxable gift may be made. In addition, frequently the grantor splits the trust property into life estate and remainder interests. The former (life estate interest) qualifies for the gift tax annual exclusion since it is a present interest; however, the latter (remainder interest) is a future interest that does not qualify for the exclusion.

There are two primary types of trusts used in the estate planning process: the revocable living trust and the testamentary trust. But in some instances, irrevocable trusts (notably, an ILIT) are used extensively in planning. As mentioned, a revocable living trust may be amended or revoked during the grantor's lifetime; however, any form of irrevocable lifetime trust cannot be revoked, altered, or amended in any way. That is a major disadvantage of the irrevocable form of trust, but in some cases this disadvantage may be offset by the estate tax savings that are possible with an irrevocable trust. (You should note that a revocable trust does not afford any estate tax savings to the grantor since the revocable nature of the trust requires inclusion of the assets in the grantor/decedent's gross estate.) Alternatively, a testamentary trust is by its nature irrevocable (the grantor is no longer alive to revoke it) and is effective only at the grantor/decedent's death. Therefore, no estate tax savings in the decedent's gross estate are possible.

An inter-vivos trust is one that is established during the lifetime of the grantor and is also effective during their lifetime. As mentioned, the most common form of inter-vivos trust is a revocable living trust, but an irrevocable trust may also be made effective during the grantor's lifetime.

A testamentary trust is one that is included in the decedent's will and thus is not effective until the grantor/decedent's death. Unlike a revocable living trust, the assets in a testamentary trust do not avoid probate. Thus, the most common reason to establish a testamentary trust is to benefit one or more selected individuals and/or to implement transfer tax planning.

Types and basic provisions (of trusts)

Marital Trust (Type A)

The general power of appointment or "A" trust provides for just what it implies. That is, the surviving spouse is given a general power of appointment by the decedent (or first) spouse to distribute the decedent's property as the surviving spouse determines best. Since the spouse holds a general power, they may also benefit themselves or, perhaps, a new spouse. Many times the A and B trusts are used together to pass the exclusion amount times two.

Bypass Trust (Type B)

This is the nonmarital trust used in marital deduction planning. Since it is usually coupled with a form of marital trust (otherwise referred to as an "A" or "C" trust, as explained below), the nonmarital trust is commonly referred to as a "bypass", "exemption", "family" or "B" trust. Operationally, the "B" trust affords the surviving spouse a lifetime interest in the trust assets, often also including a right-of-invasion of trust corpus on their behalf, limited to an ascertainable standard.

Since it is a nonmarital trust, the bypass or "B" trust does not qualify for the unlimited marital deduction in the grantor's estate. However, the trust assets are also not included in the gross estate of the surviving spouse, thus effectuating favorable transfer tax planning.

The "B" trust may also be used as a qualified disclaimer type trust where the surviving spouse "disclaims" (refuses) property given to them as part of the marital trust. The disclaimed property then becomes part of the nonmarital trust wherein the surviving spouse now has only a lifetime interest in the property, thus precluding its subsequent inclusion among the assets of their gross estate. Where the "B" trust is used to receive disclaimed property, it is sometimes referred to as a "disclaimer" or "D" trust.

Qualified Terminable Interest Property (QTIP) Trust (Type C)

Currently, this is the most popular form of marital trust since it affords the decedent/grantor's estate the unlimited marital deduction while at the same time ensuring that the decedent (not the surviving spouse) retains control over the ultimate disposition of their property. Thus, you will frequently see the QTIP or "C" form of trust coupled with the standard "B" trust in planning for "blended families" (that is, where one or both spouses have children from a previous marriage that they wish to benefit at death). However, as mentioned under the previous paragraph, a decedent may also want to implement a QTIP trust where they are concerned about the possible remarriage of the surviving spouse after their death.

Structurally, the "C" trust is much like the "B" trust. That is, the surviving spouse is given the right to all lifetime income from the trust and, perhaps, a right of principal invasion using the Health, Education, Maintenance and Support (HEMS) standard. Therefore, if the "C" trust is to qualify for the unlimited marital deduction in the estate of the first (or grantor) spouse, the executor of the first spouse's estate must elect to qualify all or part of the trust for the tax deduction. This is done by checking a box on the IRS form 706. But beyond that, since the election is optional (and then may be made in part or in total), certain planning possibilities are possible. In practice, this is referred to as "optimal QTIP planning" and is a very important type of "postmortem" (after-death) planning that may be done by the executor of the first spouse's estate.

> **Rattiner's Secrets:** One of the biggest issues in a society with multiple remarriages (see Chapter 10) is making sure you take care of your kids from your original marriage or others whom you may want to help, and making sure the monies get to those persons, without perhaps ending up in the wrong hands.

"Use dynasty trusts for the long term. Sell assets to those trusts and lend money to them. Private placements work well for wealthy clients and in bull markets variable or equity indexed products usually work best," says Lawrence Brody.

Pour-over trust

A pour-over trust is another name for a revocable living trust created during the grantor's lifetime to hold and manage assets for the benefit of several beneficiaries. Such a trust is usually funded at the grantor's death (when the revocable trust becomes irrevocable) with the use of a "pour-over will."

A pour-over will is usually implemented along with a revocable living trust to pick up any after-acquired property of the grantor (property that is acquired after the drafting of the revocable living trust) or to pass any property that the grantor may have forgotten to transfer to the trust during their lifetime. While the will does operate to "pour over" the after-acquired or forgotten property to the now-irrevocable trust (hence, the name "pour-over trust"), property passing via the will is subject to the probate process.

Spendthrift trust

Some grantors of a trust may be concerned about the future financial well-being of one or more trust beneficiaries, particularly the beneficiary's ability to manage money. As a result, the grantor will include a "spendthrift clause" or provisions in the terms of the trust. Such a clause will protect the monetary interest of the trust beneficiary from their creditors while the yet-to-be-distributed property is still part of the trust corpus. Such a clause also prohibits the beneficiary from assigning their interest to a current or future creditor.

Special needs trust

A common application of the spendthrift concept is that of the special needs trust. When implementing a special needs trust, a spendthrift clause is often included to protect the trust property of a developmentally disabled child from governmental attachment.

Qualified domestic trust (QDOT)

This is a third type of marital trust sometimes established for the benefit of noncitizen surviving spouses.

Sprinkling provision

A sprinkling, also known as a "spray," provision is included in many trusts to allow for the exercise of trustee discretion. Specifically, under the terms of the trust, the trustee is permitted to "sprinkle" or "spray" income among beneficiaries in whatever amount they determine best. Thus, the grantor of the trust is allowing for certain future financial circumstances among beneficiaries that they cannot foresee at the present time.

Trust beneficiaries: income and remainder

An income beneficiary of a trust is one or more individuals who are entitled to the income from the trust property (corpus) for a period of years or for lifetime. A prevalent example of an income beneficiary is the surviving spouse, who must be entitled to all the income (payable at least annually) from either an "A" or "C" type of marital trust. An income beneficiary will almost always have a present right to the trust income, thereby affording the grantor of the trust the annual gift tax exclusion.

A remainder beneficiary of a trust is one or more individuals who are entitled to a distribution of the trust property (corpus) at the expiration of the income beneficiary's interest. For example, in the QTIP or "C" form of marital trust, the children of the grantor are entitled to a distribution of the trust property subsequent to the expiration of the spouse's (usually, their mother's or father's) interest. As such, the children hold a remainder or future interest in the trust property. A remainder beneficiary will always have a future right to the trust property, thereby precluding the trust grantor from taking advantage of the gift tax annual exclusion.

"Wealthy clients sitting on cash should lend cash to the trust in which the trustee uses those monies to buy assets. Other times bank lenders are lending money to trusts to buy insurance in these situations. With low interest rates and asset values, this should be an estate planner's dream scenario. Many clients feel less wealthy and don't want to take advantage of the higher numbers," says Brody.

Estate and gift taxation

This tax treatment depends on whether the trust is revocable or irrevocable in nature.

A revocable trust is not subject to any gift tax at the time established by the grantor, but it is subject to estate taxation so long as the grantor has retained the power to revoke the trust at their death. Further, if the grantor releases or gives up the revocation power within three years of their death, the "three-year rule" will be triggered and the trust property will be included in the grantor/decedent's death at its fair market date-of-death value.

An irrevocable trust is subject to gift tax (if the property value contributed exceeds the allowable gift tax annual exclusion amount), but generally is not subject to estate taxation in the grantor's estate. The notable exception(s) to the excludability of trust property in the estate is where the grantor has retained an income or reversionary interest (of sufficient percentage amount) in the trust. Similarly, if the grantor at their death retains the right to enjoy the trust property, then the value of the trust will be included in the gross estate.

Gifting strategies

Inter-vivos Gifting

An individual may currently gift to a non-spouse (or noncharity) a total of $11,580,000 (2020) in taxable gifts during their lifetime before any federal gift tax is due. (Note that an unlimited deduction is available for lifetime gifts to a spouse and/or qualified charity such that the $11,580,000 limit does not apply.) In addition to this lifetime exemption, an individual may gift a specified amount per year to a non-spouse or noncharity, otherwise known as the "gift tax annual exclusion." This amount is currently indexed to $15,000 per donee. Finally, certain gifts are excludible from federal gift taxation if made directly to an educational institution or medical provider. If all of these gifts are made during an individual's (or donor's) lifetime, they are referred to as inter-vivos gifts.

The major advantage of lifetime gifting is the ability to exclude the future appreciation of the gifted property from the estate of the donor. This is the result in all situations except where the "three-year gifting rule" applies or where any of the retained interest rules apply (to be discussed later under this same topic). Operationally, when a lifetime taxable gift is made, the fair market value at the time of the gift is included in the donor's estate as an "adjusted taxable gift." This is to be contrasted to the estate tax inclusion of the gifted property where the fair market value of the gifted property at the time of the donor's death is included.

There are four requirements that must be met before the donor is considered to have made an inter-vivos (lifetime) gift to another. These are:

1. The donor must be capable of transferring the property (that is, they must be legally competent to make the gift).
2. The individual receiving the gift (known as the donee) must be capable of receiving and possessing the property.
3. There must be delivery to, and acceptance by, the donee or the donee's agent.
4. The donor must not maintain any interest in the gifted property (in other words, they must make a "complete" gift).

Gift-giving techniques and strategies

When designing a gift-giving program, a financial planner should consider having the client do the following:

- Gift assets with higher rates of return as contrasted to assets with lower rates. However, it should be noted here that this is only the case if the donor is not in need of such assets to meet their own future financial goals.
- Gift income-producing property to shift the income tax payable by the donor on the property to the donee, who is presumably in a lower marginal income tax bracket.
- Gift appreciated assets rather than assets that are not likely to appreciate. As mentioned, this removes the future growth from the donor/decedent's estate.
- Sell assets whose current value is less than their basis. If the donor first sells loss assets (and then gifts the resulting cash), they may be afforded a deduction for the loss on their personal income tax return.
- Avoid gifting property that is part of an installment sale. In this manner, the donor will avoid having to "recapture" the entire untaxed proceeds at the time of the gift.

A systematic annual gifting program. This is by far the most heavily used gifting strategy by the average donor. It is a technique that takes advantage of the gift tax annual exclusion amount (to as many donees as possible) on a regular or systematic basis.

Net gifting. This is a strategy used by a donor who has previously used up all of their gift tax lifetime ($11,580,000) exemption but wants to continue making gifts. Therefore, they agree, prior to making the gift, that the donee will assume the gift tax payment obligation (rather than this being the normal responsibility of the donor).

Reverse gift. This is a gift made by the donor to the donee with the expectation that the donor will receive the gifted property back at the donee's death. So why is such a gift made? The answer is to try to obtain the "step-up" in basis that typically occurs with appreciated, inherited property. However, if the donee survives the one-year period, a reverse gift is a valuable gifting strategy that should be considered by most donors.

TAX IMPLICATIONS
Income

The primary income tax reason for making a lifetime gift of property is to transfer the requisite income tax implication to the donee. Whereas the receipt of a gift is not considered to be income to the donee, if the gifted property subsequently generates annual income, the donee (not the donor) is now responsible for the payment of income taxes on this income. Similarly, if the donee subsequently sells the property (and the property is that of a capital asset, such as stock), the donee is now responsible for the payment of any capital gains tax (or the claiming of any capital loss on the property between the date of gifting and the date of sale).

If a lifetime gift is made, the age of the donee matters. For example, if the donee is currently under the age of 19 or a full-time student under the age of 24, the unearned income rules of the Internal Revenue Code apply. These rules are colloquially referred to as the "Kiddie tax" and apply to any income from gifted property.

Gift

The federal gift tax implications of a lifetime gift have been mentioned previously throughout this book. The major implications are as follows:

- The gift tax value of any gift is its fair market value as of the date of the gift to the done.
- Gifts of a present interest are eligible for a gift tax annual exclusion.
- Any consideration received by the donor (for example, gift tax paid by the donee in a net gift) reduces the value of the total gift.
- Certain gifts, such as those made directly to an educational institution or medical provider on behalf of someone else, are not treated as taxable gifts.
- There is an unlimited gift tax deduction for gifts made to a spouse or qualified charity.
- Gifts may be "split" between spouses, thereby doubling the amount of property that may be gifted without gift tax liability to any number of donees.

- Taxable gifts that are made after December 31, 1976 (adjusted taxable gifts), are included in the estate tax computation of the donor/decedent, but at their date-of-gift (not date-of-death) fair market value.

Estate

Lifetime gifts may also be included in the gross estate of the donor/decedent by reason of either the "three-year rule" or the "retained interest rule." Both of these rules are subsequently discussed. However, be aware that if either of these rules applies, there is inclusion of the gifted property in the estate of the donor/decedent at the date-of-death fair market value of the property, potentially a much higher value than that applying to gifts included in the estate tax computation or "adjusted taxable gifts." The most notable of gifted property that is subject to the "three-year rule" is a gift of a life insurance policy within three years of the donor's death where the face value (death proceeds) is included in the donor's gross estate.

Gift taxes paid (not the value of the gift itself, unless the "three-year rule" applies) are included in the gross estate of the donor for any taxable gift made within three years of death. This is known as the "gross-up rule" for federal estate tax and results in tax being paid on tax (a "tax-inclusive" tax result).

Education and medical exclusions

Gifts made by a donor directly to an educational institution or to a medical care provider are excluded from the definition of a total (and therefore taxable) gift. However, gifts made first to the donee, who subsequently pays the educational institution or medical provider, are subject to the normal gift tax rules.

Marital and charitable deductions

Gifts to a U.S. citizen spouse are deductible without limit (an unlimited deduction) so long as not a terminable interest. The most common example of a terminable interest, and thus not qualifying for the unlimited gift tax marital deduction, is a gift of a life estate to the spouse.

Gifts to a qualifying charity are also deductible without limit (an unlimited deduction). Such gifts may also be deductible for income tax purposes, assuming that the donor itemizes deductions. Therefore, there is a double tax benefit to making a lifetime outright gift to charity.

GROSS ESTATE
Inclusions

There are four primary components for inclusion in the gross estate under Section 2033-2038. They are:

1. Property owned by the decedent at their date of death (otherwise known as I.R.C. Section 2033 property).
2. Interests in property where the decedent has retained the right of control or beneficial enjoyment as of date of death (I.R.C. Section 2036-2038 property).
3. Certain property that is gifted within three years of the donor/decedent's death (the "three-year rule").
4. Gift tax paid on any gift made within three years of the donor/decedent's death (the "gross-up rule").

This represents any and all property owned by the decedent either solely or concurrently with someone else (for example, joint tenancy or community property) at the date of their death. Generally, the two major assets that are Section 2033 property are the decedent's equity in their primary residence (or second homes) and their vested account balance in retirement plans.

Section 2036-2038 property commonly includes property that the decedent has gifted to another during their lifetime but retained a right of control or beneficial enjoyment (a "string") at date of death. IRC Section 2036 requires inclusion of property transferred in which the decedent has retained a lifetime income or right-of-enjoyment interest. Section 2037 requires inclusion of transferred property where the decedent has retained a reversionary interest where the value of such interest immediately before the death of the decedent exceeds five (5) percent of the property value. Finally, Section 2038 includes transfers over which the decedent has retained the power to alter, amend, or revoke, and encompasses, notably, property held as part of a revocable living trust at death.

The "three-year rule" is commonly misunderstood to require the inclusion of any property gifted to another within three years of the decedent's death. In fact, most gifts are not included in the gross estate, although the value of taxable gifts ("adjusted taxable gifts") is included in the estate tax computation. The difference between the two entries on the estate tax return is that "adjusted taxable gifts" are included at their date-of-gift value, whereas inclusions in the decedent's gross estate (by virtue of the "three-year rule") are included at their date-of-death value. The most notable gift that is included in the gross estate, if gifted within three years of the decedent's death, is an assignment of a life insurance policy to another. In that event, the face value or death proceeds are included in the gross estate or the same value that would have been included had the decedent not assigned the life insurance policy.

Finally, the "gross-up rule" requires the inclusion of all gift tax paid on property gifted within three years of the decedent's death, regardless of whether the property itself is included in the decedent's gross estate.

Exclusions

The most important of the exclusions from the gross estate, any gifted property over which no "string" is retained, has already been mentioned. However, any property over which the decedent owns an interest that terminates at their death (such as a life estate) is also excluded from the gross estate. If the decedent owns only a life estate in property inherited from someone else (an "inherited" or "straight life estate"), or under HEMS, there is nothing to tax at their death since the remainder interest holder has been specified by someone else.

SOURCES FOR ESTATE LIQUIDITY
Sale of assets

A sale of assets is most frequently between family members and includes intra-family and other business transfer techniques. Assets that have a built-in loss are generally the best to sell since death eliminates the potential estate tax benefit by "stepping down" the income tax basis of the loss property to heirs. Alternatively, low-basis assets (those assets where there is a significant amount of gain) are the least attractive to sell since the estate beneficiary generally receives a "stepped-up" income tax basis (the exception to this benefit being "income in respect of a decedent" assets that pass only at the carried-over adjusted basis). If a sale of assets is made, there are generally two methods for implementing the sale. The first is an outright sale, which, depending on the type of asset sold, will generate either ordinary income or capital gain/loss to the seller. The second is an installment sale. With this method, the gain is spread out for the seller over the life of the note, which can help reduce income tax liability for the seller in each year payment is received. However, losses are picked up all in year one, thus giving the seller the best of both worlds.

Life insurance

Life insurance is the most frequently used method to generate liquidity (cash) to pay estate administration expenses and taxes due. A purchase of a life insurance policy to provide liquidity is an effective "discounted dollar" approach to solve the estate's liquidity problem. However, the purchaser/decedent needs to ensure that their taxable estate problem is not made worse by this purchase, potentially resulting in only more life insurance death proceeds being included in their gross estate. The traditional way of ensuring that no more estate tax liability is incurred is to first establish an ILIT and then have the ILIT purchase the first or additional life insurance policy needed in the name of the trustee.

Loan

As with sales, loans are usually made between family members to provide estate liquidity. If loans are made between family members, they are usually "gift loans." In a gift loan, the lender (usually the parent) has interest income and the borrower (usually the adult child) has interest expense to the extent of imputed interest.

If the loan is made between the decedent and a commercial lender, it is much more likely that a fair interest rate will be charged and that a gift loan will not result. If such a loan is outstanding at the decedent's death, the estate (after payment of the claim by the lender) may take a corresponding deduction for debt owed in determining the adjusted gross estate. In turn, this reduces the decedent's potential estate tax liability.

Regarding gifting assets, first do the numbers and see whether you can afford to make a gift and whether it makes sense. Next, determine the responsibility level of the child. Don't give money to a child who is irresponsible. Money has many emotional ties. If you give money to a child, assuming you can afford to, then you need to let it go. You can't judge what they do with that money.

VALUATION ISSUES

Estate freezes

The term "estate freeze" can be used broadly (for example, in outright lifetime gifting to any donee where the donor removes the future appreciation of the gifted property from their estate) or narrowly (for example, in closely-held business transfers). However, when the term "estate freeze" is used by the financial or estate planning practitioner, it usually refers to several closely-held business transfers addressed by the provisions of IRC Section 2701. These transfers and/or estate planning techniques are the corporate stock recapitalization and the partnership capital freeze.

Typically, in a corporate stock recapitalization, the existing common stock in the corporation is traded for both common stock and preferred stock. The transferor (usually the senior-generation family member business owner) retains the preferred stock, also retaining voting rights with that stock and a right to dividends, and gifts the common stock to the donee (usually the junior-generation family member incoming owner). Thus, any appreciation of the business that occurs after the recapitalization and gifting of common stock is attributed to the common stock (and not the preferred), thereby removing any future appreciation from the transferor's estate (hence the term "estate freeze").

Minority (interest) discounts

A minority interest discount is any interest in a closely-held business that, in terms of voting, is not a controlling interest. In other words, the donor owns (or will transfer to the donee) a less-than-50% interest in the common stock of the corporation.

Minority interests cannot manage the closely-held business or, likely, control the decisions of the controlling shareholders in any way. Thus, outside buyers (in an arm's-length transaction) are unlikely to pay full value for a business interest where they cannot influence the future direction of the business. As a result, in gift tax valuation, the donor is permitted to take a discount (reduce the fair market value of the gifted interest) as a result of the donee assuming a minority interest role.

Marketability discounts

Similarly to the discount that is available for the gifting (or estate inclusion) of a minority interest, a discount from FMV is also permitted for the lack of marketability of a closely-held business interest. This discount is permitted because a closely-held business is much more difficult to sell (it has no ready market) than an equity interest in a publicly traded (listed) corporation. This discount applies to transfers of both an incorporated closely-held business (a C or S corporation) and an unincorporated business (a sole proprietorship or partnership).

Blockage discounts

A blockage discount is a discount that is permitted to the owner of a large block of publicly traded stock. Large quantities of a stock listed on an exchange may result in a temporarily depressed value of the stock if the owner attempts to sell this stock all at one time. Thus, a separate discount is appropriate, with the amount of the discount based on the estimated decrease in the realizable price below the stock's current trading value.

Key person discounts

A key person discount implies the result. That is, if the key person in a business (typically the owner or valued executive) were to suddenly be removed from the business, the FMV of this business would likely decline. Thus, a discount is permitted if the owner or valued executive were to gift their interest (or die still owning the interest).

POWERS OF APPOINTMENT

A power of appointment is a power given to someone (known as the "holder") by someone else (known as the "donor" or "grantor"), allowing the holder to name the future beneficiaries of the donor's property. Such a power is most frequently found in an irrevocable trust (or a revocable trust that becomes irrevocable at the grantor's death), thereby providing for flexibility. Essentially, the donor cannot (or does not wish to) foresee the future circumstances of their intended beneficiaries and thus authorizes the holder to make property disposition decisions on their behalf.

A power of appointment is "general" in nature if the holder can benefit themself, their estate, their lifetime creditors, and/or the creditors of their estate. If any of these circumstances are possible (in other words, there are no restrictions placed on the exercise of the power by the donor), the holder must include the fair market value of the property over which a general power of appointment is held in their gross estate. Generally, the holder must also pay federal gift tax on the exercise, release, or lapse of the power.

Alternatively, a power of appointment is "special" in nature if the benefit cannot benefit them in any way and must exercise the power only on behalf of specified beneficiaries or a class of beneficiaries. The property value subject to a special power is not includible in the holder's estate, nor do they make a gift of the property if the power is exercised, released, or the power lapses.

General and special (limited) powers: 5 and 5 power

If a general power of appointment is granted to the holder, there may be a limitation included that will not result in either estate or gift tax (although this exclusion may be only partially effective). For example, property subject to a general power will be included in the estate of the holder only to the extent that the power "lapses" (remains unexercised) in an amount greater than:

- $5,000, or
- 5% of the property subject to the power at the time of the lapse or the holder's death.

Crummey power

This power is included in an irrevocable trust for the benefit of minors or in an ILIT to convert a future interest gift into a present one. This permits the grantor of the trust to properly claim the gift tax annual exclusion for yearly contributions to the trust.

However, when including a Crummey power in a trust, the beneficiary is also given a general power of appointment by reason of their power to access the grantor's yearly contribution without restriction.

Distributions for an ascertainable standard (HEMS standard)

An exception to the general power of appointment taxability rules is to limit the right of the holder/beneficiary to benefit themselves only to an "ascertainable standard." If the power to invade the corpus of a trust (on the holder's behalf) is limited to such a standard, the inclusion of the trust property subject to the general power will not apply. That means there is no inclusion of the property subject to the power in the holder's estate.

So what is an "ascertainable standard"? As stated before, under Section 2041(b) of the Internal Revenue Code, a general power is limited to an ascertainable standard so long as the power is exercisable only relating to the holder's health, education, maintenance, or support (HEMS).

DEFERRAL AND MINIMIZATION OF ESTATE TAXES
Exclusion of property from the gross estate

IRC Section 2033 essentially states that all property is included in the gross estate unless there is a specific section otherwise that permits exclusion. Notably, following Section 2033, IRC Section 2034-2042 states what is included in the gross estate. Therefore, methods of exclusion focus on shifting or transferring the decedent's interest in property (Section 2033) to someone else irrevocably with no interest retained by the decedent.

Also, like income tax, deductions and credits operate to reduce the gross estate once it is determined what assets are included therein. The two most favorable deductions available to the decedent/taxpayer's estate are:

- the unlimited marital deduction for qualifying property
- the unlimited charitable deduction for property passing to a qualified charity at the decedent's death

Lifetime gifting strategies

Lifetime gifting strategies may be broadly categorized as those gifts that are made outright to one or more donees and those where some form of irrevocable trust is used. In outright gifting, there is usually no question that a present interest is transferred to the donee; thus, the donor is entitled to apply the gift tax annual exclusion before making a taxable gift.

From an estate taxation standpoint, any lifetime gift where the donor/decedent does not retain some form of prohibited interest will remove the future appreciation of the gifted property from the donor's estate. Additionally, as noted before, the federal gift tax is a tax-exclusive type of tax, meaning that not only is the future appreciation of the gifted property generally removed from the donor's estate but so also is the cash used to pay the tax. Accordingly, lifetime gifts provide a double tax benefit.

Among the lifetime gifting strategies that will defer or minimize estate taxes are outright gifting, a systematic annual gifting program, gifts to a spouse or qualified charity, excludible gifts (direct gifting to an education institution or medical provider), gift splitting between spouses to the donee(s), gifts to minors, and gifts made via an irrevocable trust where the donor does not retain a prohibited interest. Finally, remember that any form of revocable gift (including the funding of a revocable living trust) is not a completed gift and thus for federal gift tax purposes, a gift is never made.

Inter-vivos and testamentary charitable gifts

Charitable gifts may be made either "inter-vivos" (during the donor's life-time) or "testamentary" (effective at the time of the donor's death). If the donor is intending to make a charitable gift testamentary, they may wish to consider making this gift inter-vivos instead. Specifically, if the donor makes an inter-vivos charitable gift via the establishment and funding of a charitable remainder or charitable lead trust, the donor can take advantage of not only the unlimited charitable deduction at death (in their estate) but also the income tax deduction for charitable gifts made during lifetime. Thus, two charitable deductions are possible. Alternatively, if the donor waits to establish and fund the charitable trusts testamentary, their estate is generally entitled to only one charitable deduction.

CHARITABLE TRANSFERS
Outright gifts

Most individuals who make a gift to charity do so in the form of an outright or absolute gift during their lifetime. As such, they not only receive an income tax deduction (although it may be limited in the year of contribution) but also remove the taxable value of the property from their taxable estate. Also, a lifetime gift to charity can be made without incurring any federal gift tax since the unlimited gift tax charitable deduction applies.

Charitable remainder trusts (CRTs)

There are two types of privately implemented charitable remainder trusts: a charitable remainder annuity trust (CRAT) and a charitable remainder uni-trust (CRUT). They are very similar in structure to the grantor-retained inter-est types of trusts, except that the remainder interest is now held by a qualified charity. In fact, a condition of either a CRAT or a CRUT is that a qualified charity must be in a remainder interest position and must receive at least 50% of the total value of the trust property.

Unitrusts (CRUTs)

A CRUT is designed to permit payment of a fixed percentage of the trust assets, as revalued annually, to a noncharitable beneficiary (usually the grantor of the trust), with the remainder passing to charity. The amount of the trust percentage to the noncharitable beneficiary must be at least 5% of the current FMV of the trust assets (as revalued annually) and must be paid at least annually to such beneficiary. Thus, like its grantor-retained unitrust cousin (the GRUT), a CRUT may provide an inflation-hedge or variable payment to the noncharitable income beneficiary. Additional contributions of property to a CRUT may be made other than that property originally contributed to the trust. (Note: This is not possible with a CRAT.)

Annuity trusts (CRATs)

The CRAT is structured in the same manner as the CRUT with one major difference: the noncharitable income beneficiary now receives payment of a fixed annual sum of at least 5% of the initial FMV of the trust assets. There is no provision for a fixed percentage or variable payment. Unlike the CRUT, no additional contributions of property are possible with a CRAT; the trust corpus remains equal to the value of the property transferred to the trust in the initial year of funding.

Charitable lead trusts (CLTs)

There are also two types of charitable lead trusts: a charitable lead annuity trust (CLAT) and a charitable lead unitrust (CLUT). But any type of charitable lead trust differs radically from that of a charitable remainder trust. In the CLT, the donor transfers income-producing property to a reversionary trust (in other words, the donor is now in the position of the remainder charity if a CRT was used) and directs that the trust income be transferred to a qualified charity initially for a period of time not to exceed 20 years. Thus, the donor is likely to receive a very large income tax deduction. Moreover, if structured properly, the value of the donor's reversionary interest can equal zero, meaning that a full (100%) deduction of the current value of the FMV of the property to the trust is obtained.

GENERATION-SKIPPING TRANSFER TAX (GSTT)

The federal generation-skipping transfer tax, sometimes referred to as the third type of transfer tax (with the other two being the federal gift and estate tax), is designed to tax transfers from an individual to a "skip person." A skip person is any of the following:

- a related individual (family member) two or more generations below that of the transferor (for example, a grandchild of a grandparent/transferor)
- an unrelated individual who is younger than the transferor by 37½ years or more (note: this is an age-related and not a blood-related rule)
- a trust when all beneficiaries are two or more generations below that of the grantor/transferor

The following persons are excepted from the skip person definition and thus a generation-skipping transfer does not occur:

- the transferor's spouse or former spouse, regardless of their age at the time of the transfer
- a grandchild of the transferor if the transferor's child is deceased at the time of the transfer. (This exception is otherwise known as the "predeceased parent direct skip exception." Effectively in this event, the grandchild moves up one generation so that there is one generation below the transferor involved in the transfer.)

INTRA-FAMILY AND OTHER BUSINESS TRANSFER TECHNIQUES

The following are possible intra-family transfer techniques that involve inter-vivos gifts: outright gift: systematic annual gifting program; gift leaseback; family limited partnership (FLP); limited liability company (LLC); interest-free and/or below-market loans (also known as "intra-family loans").

The following are possible intra-family transfer techniques that involve a sale: installment sale or note; self-canceling installment note (SCIN); private annuity; bargain sale; sale leaseback.

The following are possible intra-family transfer techniques that involve trusts: qualified interest trusts (GRAT, GRUT, and QPRT); ILIT; intentionally defective grantor trust (also known as a "defective trust").

Installment note

The estate tax consequences of the installment sale itself are relatively straightforward. If the seller dies during the installment period, the present value of any future payments, yet to be received by the seller, is includible in their gross estate. However, if the seller survives the installment period (in other words, all obligations arising from the sale are complete), the property sold is excluded from their estate and only any unexpended cash remains. What type of property should be the subject of an installment sale? Likely, the best property to be sold is property that is expected to appreciate rapidly in the future. Thus, growth-type closely-held businesses are very appropriate for sale via the installment payment method. Any depreciable property that may be subject to recapture is not a good candidate for an installment sale since all depreciation must be recaptured (taxable as ordinary income) in the year of the sale.

Self-canceling installment note (SCIN)

A SCIN is an installment note that by its terms cancels or forgives the obligation of the buyer to make any remaining payments to the seller at the seller's death. Thus, unlike the typical installment sale, there are no remaining installment payments to be included in the seller's estate. There are techniques available to the seller to "plan around" even the inclusion of the remaining installment payments in their gross estate, notably by implementing either a SCIN or a single-life private annuity.

Private annuity

A private annuity is the sale of an asset (usually to a junior family member) in exchange for an unsecured promise to pay a lifetime annuity to the annuitant/seller (usually a senior family member). Since the annuity contract must be unsecured, the annuitant/seller needs to be sure that the obligor/purchaser is financially responsible or the annuitant/seller may not receive the income stream from the sale, which likely was a major reason for adopting the technique in the first place. A private annuity commonly provides lifetime-only income to the annuitant; therefore, like a straight life estate, there is no includible value of any annuity payments in the decedent/annuitant's gross estate.

Intentionally defective grantor trust

An intentionally defective grantor trust (also known as a "defective trust") is an irrevocable trust in which the grantor/family member is treated as the owner of the trust for income tax purposes but not for estate tax purposes. As a result, this means that the grantor, under the grantor trust income tax rules, must pay tax on the income from the trust. However, in making these tax payments, the grantor reduces their taxable estate at the same time (thus achieving an estate tax benefit). To ensure that the trust property is not included in the grantor's estate at death, it is critical that the grantor not be named the trustee of the defective trust or be able to control the beneficial enjoyment of the trust property in any way.

An example of when you may want to establish a defective trust is to purchase life insurance. Since the trust is permitted to grow income tax free (remember, the grantor is paying the tax on the trust income), it may therefore support larger premium payments and hence the inclusion of even more life insurance proceeds. Sometimes, then, you will see the defective trust used as an alternative to a funded irrevocable life insurance trust.

Intra-family loan

There are two types of intra-family loans: a below-market interest loan (where some interest is charged to the family member borrower, although not the appropriate amount) and an interest-free loan (where no interest is charged to the family member borrower). As such, both of these loans are really a variation of the lifetime gifting technique to family members.

Bargain sale

A bargain sale is the sale of an asset between family members for less than full consideration. Stated another way, the sale is a part-sale and a part-gift. It is similar to a below-market loan in its gift tax consequences, except that gift tax liability typically occurs on the sale of property instead of on an interest amount that should have been charged on the loan.

For gift tax purposes, the difference between the fair market value of the asset sold and the consideration received by the seller (purchase price paid by the buyer) is treated as a gift. Like the gift tax liability incurred on imputed interest in the below-market loan transaction, if large enough, the "gift part" of the bargain sale may be taxable. As a result, although the property sold (short of any unexpended cash) will not be included in the seller's gross estate at their death, the portion of the property sold that is considered a taxable gift is added back to the seller's taxable estate as an "adjusted taxable gift."

Gift or sale-leaseback

Both the gift and sale-leaseback intra-family transfer techniques involve the same basic concept: the senior family member either gifts or sells property to the junior family member and then leases it back. The advantage of the technique is that if fully depreciated business property is the subject of the leaseback, the senior family member has now substituted a lease payment deduction for the previously used-up depreciation deduction/income tax benefit. Thus, there are important cash flow reasons why a senior family member/parent may wish to enter into a leaseback transaction with a junior family member/adult child who has need of the leased-back property.

Family limited partnership

A family limited partnership is created to transfer assets to junior family members (by the senior family member) at a substantially reduced gift tax cost and valuation. Gifts of family limited partnership interests are advantageous because discounts for lack of marketability and minority interests are permitted to reduce the gift tax value. The senior family member can also retain control of the partnership by retaining a general partnership interest (subsequently, gifting off the limited partnership interest to the junior family members). Finally, the senior family member is afforded limited creditor protection since their general partnership interest can be attached only for business (and not personal) liabilities incurred after creation of the interest.

Limited liability company

The underlying concept of establishing a limited liability company in estate tax planning is the same as that of an FLP, except that the LLC is an incorporated entity. Once the LLC is established, the senior family member/owner takes advantage of the same valuation discounts that are permitted for the transfer of the limited partnership interest to junior family members. However, instead of gifting off limited partnership interests, the senior family member in a LLC arrangement transfers "member interests" that are part of the business entity.

Asset protection

"For asset protection purposes, LLC law is often used. They are set up to protect against unknown threats," says Dan Rubin. Rubin goes on to say,

"In many jurisdictions, there's a trend moving away from the rule against perpetuities into a more perpetual environment since more and more wealth is tied up in trusts governed by the terms of trust agents. Trusts can be set up anywhere. You don't necessarily have to be a resident of that particular state. For example, in Florida you can go 360 years and Wyoming 1,000 years!"

Grantor retained annuity trusts (GRATs) (qualified interest trusts)

In a GRAT, the grantor transfers an asset to the trust and retains the right to be paid a fixed equal payment or annuity for the term of the trust. Thus here, and unlike the GRIT, there is a limitation on the amount of income that may be paid to the grantor. Accordingly, the GRAT is said to be a type of "qualified interest trust," meaning that it "qualifies" for normal estate and gift tax treatment and is an exception to the "zero valuation rule." The GRAT is most effective where a single, appreciating asset (or type of asset, like growth stock) is transferred to the trust by the grantor and the term of the trust is relatively short (say, 10 years or less).

Grantor retained unitrusts (GRUTs)

A GRUT is structured very similarly to a GRAT, except that now the income interest payable to the grantor is in the form of a fixed percentage of the trust assets, as revalued annually. This is known as a "unitrust" payment and provides for a possible inflation hedge to the grantor, which is not possible with the GRAT where a fixed equal payment is used.

Qualified personal residence trusts (QPRTs or house-GRITs)

A QPRT is an exclusion from the Chapter 14 valuation rules. As such, a QPRT is really a form of a statutorily approved GRIT, but includes only a residence as the corpus of the trust. In the QPRT, the grantor transfers a personal residence (either their primary residence or a vacation home, but not both) and retains the right to live in the residence during the trust term. Then, just like the GRAT or the GRUT, if the grantor survives the trust term, the fair market value of the home is excluded from their gross estate.

The primary operating characteristics of (and requirements to establish) a QPRT are as follows:

- The trust may only include one personal residence; therefore, if the grantor wants to transfer both a primary residence and a vacation home to a QPRT, two separate trust documents may be executed.
- The residence cannot be occupied by someone other than the grantor and/or the members of their family (with the IRC definition of "family member").
- The residence cannot be purchased from the trustee of the trust by the grantor or by the grantor's spouse.
- The trust must be irrevocable.
- While the trust may include a small amount of cash to pay for maintenance and upkeep on the residence, the income from the trust (or cash) may not be distributed to anyone but the grantor (and not to a family member).

Finally, the grantor who survives the term of a QPRT does not have to vacate the residence since they can then rent it back from the remainder person/family member. However, the amount of rent paid to the family member by the grantor must be at "fair rental value" and must be part of an arm's-length transaction.

> **Rattiner's Secrets:** Many years ago, I had a husband/wife client who owned a successful long-term business. They had one son who was married to a daughter-in-law (DIL). The parents gave 50% of the business to the son and his wife, where each party now owned 25%. The client put their $3 million primary residence in a QPRT for 20 years. The son alone was the beneficiary. After the 20 years, he received the house and the parents still live there. Fast forward 27 years from the marriage. The son got divorced. The parents stated in no uncertain terms that the DIL was not to continue to participate in the business. Essentially, the son had to buy her out. But since the son had nothing of comparable value to provide his soon-to-be-ex-wife with the appropriate funds, he ended up giving her his parents' former house. Long story short, the DIL now owns the $3 million-plus house from her former in-laws. But I heard she is a good landlord!

POSTMORTEM ESTATE PLANNING TECHNIQUES

The term "postmortem" means after the decedent's death, and the term "postmortem estate planning techniques" refers to techniques or elections that may be carried out by the decedent's executor or administrator to more efficiently distribute the decedent's estate.

Alternate valuation date (AVD)

The general rule is that all property included in the decedent's gross estate is valued at its fair market value as of the decedent's death. However, there is one exception to this rule: an election by the executor to take advantage of the alternate valuation date.

The AVD, six months after date of death, is most properly used when property included in the gross estate declines in value after the decedent's death. Therefore, likely candidates for this valuation method are publicly held securities or a decedent's interest in a closely-held business, both of which may decline significantly during the six-month period subsequent to death.

There are several limitations, however, on the use of the AVD and its election by the estate's personal representative:

- The AVD cannot be used for "wasting assets" or those that automatically decrease with the passage of time. Among these types of assets are annuities, leases, patents, and installment sales.
- The AVD must be applied to all assets included in the decedent's gross estate. In other words, the personal representative cannot "pick and choose" among assets and value some using the general valuation rule and others using the AVD. (Of course, the representative would choose to value the depreciating assets using AVD and the appreciating assets using the general valuation rule if "cherry picking" were allowed.)
- If the AVD election is made, it must result in a reduction to the total value of the decedent's gross estate.
- If the AVD election is made, it must also result in a reduction of the amount of federal estate tax due by the decedent's estate. As a result, if the decedent's estate is nontaxable for any reason (for example, use of the 100% marital deduction strategy), the AVD election cannot be made.

Qualified disclaimer

A disclaimer is an unqualified refusal by a potential beneficiary to accept any benefits of the property bequeathed or devised to them by a decedent. If this potential beneficiary accepts the benefits or income of the property and then disclaims, generally, they make a subsequent gift of this property to the successor beneficiary or "taker in default." However, if the disclaimer is done properly by means of a "qualified disclaimer," the beneficiary who disclaims (the "disclaimant") is considered to never have received the property in the first instance and thus cannot make a subsequent gift.

Here are the requirements that must be met before the beneficiary is considered to have made a tax-qualified disclaimer:

- The disclaimer must be an irrevocable and unqualified refusal by the beneficiary to accept the decedent's property or interest in the property.
- The refusal must be in writing.
- The refusal must be received by the executor of the decedent's estate within nine months after the later of the date on which the transfer creating the interest was made or the day on which the person disclaiming the interest attains the age of 21.
- The beneficiary must not have previously accepted any interest in the benefits from the property (with one exception to be subsequently discussed).
- As a result of the refusal to accept the property or property interest, the property must pass without the disclaimant's attempt to direct the interest to someone else (in other words, the decedent must have named the "taker in default" in their will or trust and not have left it to the disclaimant to make this decision).

Deferral of estate tax (IRC Section 6166)

The postmortem technique, "Section 6166 election," made by the decedent's personal representative allows for the payment of a decedent's estate tax in installments rather than being due all at once (generally, no later than nine months after the decedent's date of death).

To qualify for this favorable tax treatment, the decedent's gross estate must include an interest in a closely-held business exceeding 35% of the value of their adjusted gross estate. In addition, the closely-held business owner/decedent must have been a U.S. citizen or resident as of their date of death.

Corporate stock redemption (IRC Section 303)

In general, under corporate income tax law, whenever a closely-held corporation buys back stock from its shareholders, the proceeds must be treated as dividend (ordinary) income to those shareholders. However, if a decedent's estate qualifies for "redemption treatment" under the provisions of IRC Section 303, the proceeds received from that redemption are treated as capital gain income. Further, since the decedent's interest in the closely-held business normally qualifies for the favorable "step-up in basis" treatment, there may be no gain incurred on the proceeds at all.

These qualifying requirements are the stock that is redeemed must be included in the decedent/shareholder's gross estate; this stock must evidence ownership in a closely-held corporation (in other words, publicly traded stock does not qualify); the value of the stock included in the gross estate must exceed 35% of the decedent's adjusted gross estate (AGE); and only an amount equal to the total of federal and state death taxes, GSTT, administration, and funeral expenses may be redeemed under Code Section 303. The executor of the decedent's estate cannot use redemption treatment to pay debts of the estate.

Special use valuation (IRC Section 2032A)

A third and final liquidity-creating provision to be used by the closely-held business owner, particularly the family farmer, is "special use valuation" under the provisions of IRC Section 2032A. This section was put into the Internal Revenue Code in 1976 to protect the family farmer, whose land was being encroached on by commercial development, from excessive estate taxes. As such, Section 2032A provides significant relief from estate taxes that are not indicative of the real or special use to which the family farm is dedicated.

There are five requirements that must be met before the decedent's estate executor may elect Section 2032A "special use valuation":

1. On the date of the decedent/family farmer's death, the real property (farmland) must be used as a family farm (or, in the words of the section, a "qualified use").

2. The net value of the real and personal property used in the family farming operation must equal at least 50% of the adjusted value of the decedent's gross estate. (Note: The "adjusted value of the decedent's gross estate" is not technically the same as the "adjusted gross

estate" since any debt used in computing the "adjusted value" must be attributable only to the real and/or personal property used in the family farming operation.)

3. The net value of the real property used alone in the family farming operation must be at least 25% of the "adjusted value of the gross estate."

4. The qualifying real property must have been owned by the decedent or a member of their family for a period of at least five (5) out of the prior eight (8) years ending on the date of the decedent's death.

5. The qualifying real and personal property must pass to qualifying heirs. In addition, these heirs must sign a "recapture agreement" stating that the estate taxes saved by the decedent's qualifying for special use valuation will be repaid to ("recaptured by") the federal government if the heirs do not continue the "qualified use" for at least 10 years after the decedent's death. Practically, this means that the farm must continue to be operated as a family farm throughout this period.

There are various practical strategies that can help dissect and understand the client's objectives in this chapter. Before consulting on or providing certain guidance that could be interpreted as gray areas, you may wish to consult an attorney.

CHAPTER 10

Dispensing Advice on Niche Planning

As stated in Chapter 1, many planners today will be finding their niche in which to specialize and help clients. The reality is that there is so much to focus on, we need to do the things we feel comfortable with, where we can add the greatest value. In today's world, every profession has specialists. In the old days, the family doctor was the generalist and even made house calls! Today, whether medicine, law, accounting, our profession, or countless others, we need to know what we do and do it well.

> **Rattiner's Secrets:** In my Fast Track classes and lectures, I always hit this point home. Know what you know and know what you don't know! There is no harm or shame in focusing only in a specific area(s) if you are not equipped to go elsewhere. But there is risk if you do. If an attendee approaches me about something of which I have no knowledge or I don't have the proper skill set, I will say, "I have no clue!" With niche planning, you are making the decision just to work in selected area(s). Also, if you are a generalist who works in all areas, but some of the disciplines necessary may be too steep, like heavy-duty tax issues, or drafting legal documents, you will need to call in the CPA or attorney, respectively. Remember, we are the team leaders where one of our many missions is to bring it all
>
> *(continued)*

(continued)

together. Knowing how the flow works is critical to managing your clients' expectations.

A few more popular niches are presented here to provide an understanding of some of the issues and the talking points to help formulate a game plan that can resonate with the client.

Dispensing Advice on Niche Planning

Education Planning
Divorce
Closely-Held Business Owner (CHBO)

EDUCATION PLANNING
Analyzing the education issues

Student loan debt is the biggest complication when figuring education planning. It affects attitude, discipline, and, yes, discussions as to whether it was worthwhile. Years ago, the cost of college was manageable; it didn't carry the same burden as it does today. Honestly, it is borderline absurd. And if the parents decide for whatever reasons not to help fund their children's college, then the pressure mounting on the children brings it to a different level. As a result, I see many clients start out later in life and not getting the head start they dreamed of. They move to an area they'd dreamed about and purchase their first house, upgrade their car after years of saying they would, and purchase other items or become involved in other activities because the outstanding and larger debt made it more difficult for them to fund their dreams and objectives. Therefore a serious change of plans and direction becomes necessary.

We need to sit down with the client with a list of questions on how they plan to address these issues with their children. Be specific. Start out with what the client wishes to achieve. Have they spoken about college with the children yet? Will the client pay for public or private school? How many years will it take the child to complete? Has the client started funding this objective?

As stated in the financial planning process (Chapter 3), these issues need to be attacked on multiple fronts. One of the biggest issues for clients is funding education. The number of clients with student loan issues is alarming.

The problem is they are not generating the cash flow needed to fund other areas of their financial plan. Part of that is reactive planning by funding the education experience at the time of attending college as compared with planning in advance. Ideally, we would encourage our clients to fund earlier as well as take advantage of the payment options, reductions, or opportunities surrounding them.

"The cost of going to school and incurring less debt needs to be addressed. There's a lot of opportunities out there to help clients take advantage of educational offerings. Consider alternatives to college like trade or prep school. Support internships, apprenticeships, externships," says Adam S. Minsky, Esq., Boston, MA.

This can be a daunting task, especially where things are in a state of flux. The cost of attending school needs to be brought down and students need to incur less debt. Federal loan programs aren't doing the trick and many programs have overlapping issues which need to be reworked.

Many clients are in over their heads and need a way to cut the costs of college repayment. We may need to address clients who already have incurred student debt, or are anticipating it, or are even thinking about alternative routes, such as trade schools, internships, and apprenticeships. Minsky provided a bunch of possibilities for clients to ponder, including federal direct consolidation, refinancing and consolidating through a private lender, postponing repayment, available deferments, economic hardship forbearances, public service loan forgiveness, repayment assistance, income-driven repayment, teacher loan forgiveness, income-contingent repayment options, income-based repayment, and paying attention to new legislation.

Rattiner's Secrets: I know of many families who work out a reimbursement-type arrangement with the parents. The clients will say to the children, "I want you to have some skin in the game! I want you to appreciate the opportunity to go to school." So here's a sampling of what they could propose:

We will reimburse you after the fact based on your grades or other achievements fulfilled from the school.

We will put up 50% of the tuition, with the opportunity of getting reimbursed either each year or after you graduate.

We will reimburse you on an annual basis based on A and B grades.

We will loan you the money to pay for school and we will set up a payment schedule after graduation TBD.

Education needs analysis

The process of computing the educational funding need is a time value of money computation, similar to the retirement needs analysis example in Chapter 8.

- **Step one:** Calculate the cost of the first year of college in today's dollars (this is a future value of a single-sum computation).
- **Step two:** Determine the total lump-sum capital amount required at the beginning of the child's college years using an inflation-adjusted interest rate. Next, determine the monthly contribution required to create this fund. The total is now a future value (FV) that will be funded over 16 years at 8%. This means Bill and Lynn (see below) need to invest $215.00 each month for the next 16 years. (This step is solving for the present value of an annuity due (PVAD).)
- **Step three:** Determine the required monthly savings amount (this is solving for an ordinary annuity payment).

   Practical example: Bill and Lynn Smart want to establish an education fund for their two-year-old daughter, Elizabeth. They want to be able to contribute $10,000 a year in today's dollars for each year Elizabeth is in school. They are optimists and believe she will be able to complete her degree in four years. They assume that education costs will increase at 5% per year and they will be able to earn, on the average, 8% on their invested dollars. Bill and Lynn also would like to have more children. Here are the computational steps (all computations are done using the HP 10 B ii financial function calculator):

- First, inflate $10,000 at 5% for 16 years (assume she starts college at 18). That means they will need $21,829 for Elizabeth's first year of school (+/− $10,000 PV; 5 I/YR; 16 N; solve for FV = $21,829).
- Next, calculate a PVAD for the four years of school using the inflation-adjusted interest rate and the previously calculated number for the first year's payment. This results in a need of $83,745 when Elizabeth is ready to start college. (In BEGIN mode: +/− $21,829 PMT; 2.8571 I/YR; 4 N; solve for PV = $83,745.)
- Finally, determine the monthly contribution required to create this fund. The total is now an FV that will be funded over 16 years at 8%. This means Bill and Lynn need to invest $216.27 each month for the next 16 years ($83,745 FV; 16 times 12 = 192 N; 8 divided by 12 = 0.6667; solve for PMT = $216.27).

Note that this may seem impossible for a young couple with a young child and plans for more. But remember, over time their income will grow and they will be able to increase the monthly funding from what they can afford now, so it isn't a disaster if they can't put the full amount in currently. Further, financial aid is a possibility and there is no reason they cannot contribute to Elizabeth's education while she is in school.

Education savings vehicles

529 Plans (Qualified Tuition Programs (QTPs))

529 plans allow clients to make substantial contributions for paying for college that may be used for any qualified institution, not just those in the state where the plan is funded. The donor rather than the student controls when the money is distributed. It is considered to be an asset of the donor (typically, the parent) for financial aid calculations and the distributions are considered income of the student in the year of distribution for purposes of calculating financial aid.

However, one variation, the qualified tuition prepayment plan (rare these days because of spiraling college inflation), provides that the plan will cover tuition costs, regardless of how much they increase. With these plans, the assets don't count in the parents' assets or the student's income for the financial aid calculation, but the amount distributed directly reduces the amount of aid the student needs.

If the child for whom the 529 private savings plan was funded doesn't use the money, the plan may usually be transferred to another person/family member. If it isn't used for educational purposes, the gain is taxed as ordinary income when it is liquidated and there is a 10% penalty tax on any gain received. Also, if it is established within one state or at a specific school and the student attends school out of state or at a private college or university, the distribution from the plan may be for a lesser amount than if it were used for a state school or the individual school. Many plans allow the funding for schools in any state.

As a sidebar, 529 monies can also be used for private elementary and high school tuition to the tune of up to $10,000 in tuition expenses.

Here is a list of the advantages and disadvantages of the 529 private savings plan.

Advantages:

1. Tax-deferred growth.

2. Gift $75,000 ($15,000 or amount of gift tax annual exclusion for year 2020 × five years) – therefore, a donor can contribute a total of five annual gift tax exclusions on a one-time basis every five years.

3. Can contribute as much as $375,000 per beneficiary in some state plans. This is a state-specific amount (each state may be different), based on the most expensive school in that particular state.

4. Tax-free distribution (contribution and earnings) if used for educational purposes – can include tuition, books, supplies, and room and board (including off-campus housing costs).

5. If child doesn't use it, you can change the beneficiary to another child, usually without tax consequences.

6. Parents can make themselves the beneficiary as well since it can be used to pay for continuing education.

7. No phase-out of income limitations on donors (as with other education savings plans).

8. Some states allow for a tax deduction or tax credit on the state tax return.

9. Usually has an automatic investment option.

> **Rattiner's Secrets:** 529 plans are the superior choice for college funding. I have known clients where the child received a scholarship and, in some cases, didn't attend college, and the parent was able to use that money for their own schooling. You just have to make sure the client finds that out well in advance. I even knew of a client who used 529 funds to study abroad (although there are certain restrictions).

Coverdell Education Savings Account

The Coverdell Education Savings Account has a maximum contribution of $2,000 per beneficiary per year. This amount grows income tax deferred and funds are distributed income tax free if used in payment of qualified education expenses (same qualifying expenses as for Section 529 plans). Money in the account must be used by the time the beneficiary is 30 years of age. However, the beneficiary can be changed to a younger person at that time as an alternative to distribution.

Tax credits/deductions are covered in Chapter 7 on income tax.

The American opportunity tax credit may be able to provide up to $2,500 (in 2020) for qualified tuition and related expenses paid for each eligible student. Thus, this is a per-student credit.

The lifetime learning credit is up to $2,000 (2020) for qualified tuition and related expenses paid for all students in qualified educational institutions. Thus, it is a per-family credit. For each student, you can elect only one of the credits for a given year. There are also phase-outs of income based on taxpayer filing status, above which amount the taxpayer is not eligible to take either credit.

Other possible tax breaks can include tuition and fee deductions and possible cashing in of U.S. savings (EE) bonds.

DIVORCE

My starting quote during my divorce lectures is this: "The person you married is not the same person you are divorcing." I ask my attendees to think about that. The reason is because most people do not enter into a marriage to get divorced. Couples did not anticipate this and as a result can become possibly happy, sad, angry, relieved, bitter, or experience some other emotion. It's definitely a game changer.

Divorce is a "lose-lose" proposition. By its very nature, if the client starts out with 100% and each one tugs at the cash inflows, and now a second residence is needed in addition to other expenses, each party is generally left worse off. The issue is whether each one can try to make the best of this lose-lose situation.

Many of the divorces occurring involve Baby Boomers and others who have been married for a long time, perhaps 20 years or more, once the youngest child leaves the house. The biggest planning issue I hear from divorced individuals is this: I got married when I was 22, 30 years ago. I'm now 52 and have had these grandiose plans for retirement. My problem is I still want to participate in these endeavors and now I have half the money and less time to accumulate what I need to make these objectives happen.

> **Rattiner's Secrets:** Slightly less than half of first marriages fail, 63% of second marriages fail, and 60% of third marriages fail. Roughly 67% of business partnerships fail. Just think of the percentages if you were married to your business partner!

Analyzing the divorce issues

You need to be careful working with divorced clients for many reasons. By definition, each will probably have different interests and issues. If you have worked with the couple together previously and now they tell you they are divorcing, do you represent the husband, the wife, or both? Some planners are comfortable with representing both. I don't agree with that because there is an inherent conflict of interest. If I can't add possible early-on value for both (see Rattiner's Secrets below), I will call it quits with the client. If one spouse views you as representing the "soon-to-be-ex" other spouse more than them, you could find yourself in court. I generally resign or excuse myself from the engagement.

Some planners refer them to another partner or planner in the firm, but I still am not comfortable with that approach. It could cause tension, bitterness, or other problems with the client. You want to be always present with your client.

What about the situation, for example, where the client announces a divorce and you historically worked with the man and not the woman (or vice versa)? If I worked with both husband and wife together initially, I won't do it. I even had the misfortune of hearing about a divorce from a husband/wife client who visited my office some years ago. The male client stated he was getting a divorce. The problem was it was the first that she was hearing of it. Sad, but true.

In my CPA practice, the client announced they were getting divorced after tax season. The wife had misplaced a copy of the tax return and was asking me for a duplicate. I responded to both of them together, informing the husband that the wife was requesting a copy of the return and asking whether he would give me permission to send it to her. He did, but the point is this: if I did that, it could have given the appearance that I was helping one over the other.

The ultimate division of assets or income is certainly an issue.

Rattiner's Secrets: One of the ways we can add value, even for a couple who is divorcing and both of them are clients, is in how we can prepare them to move forward in an effort to accelerate the divorce process, minimize the awkwardness, and perhaps draw fairness to the process. I've had clients visit the office together to purposely tell me. They could be thinking about their individual futures or even looking for help during the process.

I would venture to say no one knows our clients like we do. We probably know more about our clients than most advisors. Their objectives, their finances, what makes them tick. I mentioned earlier that I will not represent either one individually, but here's my pitch to them. "Mr. and Mrs. Smith, as your CPA and CFP® certificant, I probably know you better perhaps than other professionals you work with. Here's what I would like to do for you both. Since I know your needs and your finances and am aware perhaps of other important issues, let me devise a first draft only of your balance sheet and cash flow statement."

The way I work it is like this. I have three columns: total, husband, and wife. Then I go through each of the assets, liabilities, income, and expenses and suggest which items belong in which column, with the ultimate goal of dividing everything equally. It may be prudent to perhaps push some of those items to one or the other so they can try to get close to what they need in order to minimize the lose-lose situation.

For example, one of them may be an at-home spouse caring for a child, perhaps they don't have the capacity to get a high-paying job, they may have health issues or other concerns. In order for the at-home spouse not to have to go back to work after the divorce, perhaps I can suggest some of the income-producing properties to move over to her side of the equation so she can generate money to try to equal out the numbers, with the objective of each one trying to maximize the difficult situation they have been placed in.

I then tell them this is a one-shot deal. After I suggest divisions of all of the items, they will each take their copy to their respective attorney. I am now out of the picture. Even if they wanted me to further comment on any of the items listed on the statements, I will not do so as my job will be done and now it will be left in the hands of the appropriate people, the attorneys. This way it gives the attorneys a legitimate starting point from which to proceed. That's important. The attorneys will then work with each other to derive a final settlement. I have seen couples leave it to their attorneys to divide up property initially, but they unintentionally miss or omit some important items. For example, if one client wants to sell a rental property and is looking for the proceeds, there could be capital gains issues, depreciation recapture issues, like-kind exchange basis carryforwards, or many other items that would complicate the situation if not identified during the process, which at the end of the day would not lend itself to a fair and equitable division of property. Again, we are not attorneys. We don't want to be accused of unauthorized practice of law.

Alimony and child support

The criterion for deducting alimony going forward is that the divorce decree must have been dated before 1/1/19, otherwise it is not deductible. It is supposed to go back to the original law on January 1, 2026. Also, be aware, if the client made changes during 2020 to an existing divorce decree dated before then, it makes the divorce decree fall under the current law whereby there is no longer any alimony deduction or recognition of income.

Pre-2019 Alimony Deductibility Criteria

(a) Payments must be made in cash.
(b) Must end at death of payee.
(c) Can't live together.
(d) Can't be deemed to be alimony.

Child support, Section 71, is never deductible or recognizable as income.

	Deductible	**Income recognition**
Alimony (pre-1/1/19)	yes	yes
Child support	no	no

Property settlements per IRC Section 1041

There is no gain or loss on property settlement transactions pursuant to a divorce. From a purely financial planning perspective, financial planners should not participate in or try to resolve the issues that resulted in a divorce. A two-income family is now two separate entities. Therefore, they may be sharing financial responsibility for dependent children or may be dealing with court-directed financial responsibility. Lifestyles will generally change. Retirement planning is also completely different. Emergency fund planning may need to be adjusted. New legal documents, insurance, health care coverage, and other employee benefit issues must also be considered.

Marriages, cohabitation, and remarriages

"A marriage is a contract you enter into where you can't leave without a penalty because the scope of services going forward has changed," says Daniel Rubin. In order to amend or cancel this contract, you need to go to court to ensure that each party's interest is protected. People not formalizing their living arrangement would want to opt for cohabitation agreements and inter-personal agreements to ensure protection of the property they have owned prior to the living arrangement, since relationships often change.

"Pre-nups must be enforceable for the fewer people getting married or remarried, in order to protect their interests and relationship with each other," says Rubin.

Prenuptial agreement (marital property agreement)

A prenuptial agreement or (prenup) is a legally binding agreement between two future spouses. In estate planning, the agreement is often executed by spouses anticipating a second (or more) marriage, each of whom (or one of whom) has children from a previous marriage. When executing the agreement, each spouse typically waives their right to inherit from the estate of the other spouse. The agreement is also sometimes used to restrict the possibility of a spouse receiving what is perceived to be an unfair property settlement at the time of divorce.

Marital property agreements, while useful, are also fraught with danger. For example, unless the agreement is properly drafted and a full disclosure of each spouse's assets at the time of marriage is made, the agreement will very likely be overturned by a judge if subsequently challenged by either spouse. As such, if a client suggests their preference for implementing such an agreement, as a financial planner you should refer them to a competent attorney. It is then very likely, because of a potential conflict of interest arising, that the attorney will also seek the services of a second attorney to represent one of the spouses. Regardless, as a financial planner, you can really only advise on the feasibility (or nonfeasibility) of the agreement for your client and leave more discussion of the details to the estate planning attorney.

CLOSELY-HELD BUSINESS OWNER (CHBO)
Analyzing the CHBO issues

Probably the biggest issue I see with clients is what to do with the family business. If we decide to keep it in house, do we divide it up equally to all the kids or other family members who have an interest? I don't think giving it equally to all kids a good move. Which kids helped out in the business growing up? Did certain children disdain the business and everything about it? Was it a constant sore point with complaining and money issues that bring back bad memories? Have they ever talked to the client about the business or prospects while growing up?

I have seen many times where certain kids thrive on the business while the others would prefer to sell it and cash out. The problem comes up when the children who would rather sell the business have voting control and just want to sell it, take the proceeds, and move on with life. If the goal is to leave each family member an equal share of the total client assets, that would be a better move since it would allow those heirs to possibly inherit the property they would like.

There are many issues on which we need to be involved with our clients concerning CHBOs, from buy-sell agreements, planning for the disability of the business owner client, managing risks, succession planning, entity formation (Chapter 7), business valuation (Chapter 9), compensation and deferred compensation (Chapter 8), and common business problems. The approach is for us to have frank discussions with all the parties. Even if it is the business owner client who owns the business, bringing possible family members or other possible successors into the picture makes total sense. We're going to discuss the areas I'm asked about most often: buy-sell agreements for life and disability, and compensation planning involving life insurance.

Buy-sell agreements

A buy-sell agreement, sometimes known as a "business continuation agreement," is a contract between the outgoing owner or owners of the business and its new or incoming owners to continue business operation at the outgoing owner's death, disability, or retirement. It is most frequently encountered (and is most advisable) in a small, closely-held business, typically consisting only of family members. It is most often funded with the proceeds or cash value of life insurance and not only can provide for the continuation of the business but also gives much-needed liquidity for the business owner's estate.

There are two types of buy-sell agreements: (1) a cross-purchase agreement, where each business owner purchases a sufficient amount of life insurance on the life of the other owner (then permitting the surviving owner with funds to buy the deceased owner's business interest from their family); and (2) an entity purchase agreement, where the business entity itself buys and owns life insurance policies on each business owner. Each type of agreement has advantages, but because of the number of life insurance policies required, entity purchase agreements are the norm where the business has more than two current or prospective owners.

The primary advantage of the cross-purchase form of buy-sell agreement is that the purchasers receive a step-up in basis of the deceased owner's business interest. Its primary disadvantage is the number of policies that must be used to sometimes fund the agreement. Alternatively, the primary advantage of the entity-purchase form is the ability to generate liquidity for the business. Its primary disadvantage is that if the entity purchaser is a family-owned corporation, the IRS will use the family attribution tax rules to construct a dividend payment to the owner-shareholder.

Typically, both of these types of agreements are funded with the purchase of life insurance policies, with the succeeding owner or corporation named as the respective beneficiary of the policies and the death proceeds then used to buy out the decedent's business interest from their family member/heirs.

Buy-sell agreements – estate planning context

In an estate planning context, the most important part of a buy-sell agreement is the buy-out price of the owner's business interest as agreed to by the parties to the agreement. Typically, if such agreement is entered into by family members, this price may not be representative of the actual fair market value of the interest at the owner's death, disability, or retirement.

Buy-sell agreements are frequently useful in fixing (or "freezing") the value of an owner's interest in a closely-held business at death. Since the IRS is well aware of the possibility of abuse in establishing a proper taxable value for this interest, a number of rules need to be met in drafting such an agreement. Thus, the government has attempted to ensure that a fair price for the interest is derived by implementing "Chapter 14 valuation rules" or, specifically, IRC Section 2703. The basic objective of these rules is to ensure that the interest of a family, closely-held business owner is valued in the same manner (and with the same result) as that value that would be obtained if the seller and buyer were not related (an "arm's-length agreement").

Under the valuation rules of Section 2703, three tests must be met before the government will honor the buy-out price agreed to by the parties. The agreement must:

1. Be a bona-fide business arrangement.
2. Not be a device to transfer property to the decedent's family or the natural objects of the decedent's bounty for less than full and adequate consideration.
3. Include terms that are comparable to similar arrangements entered into by persons in an arm's-length (nonfamily member) transaction.

As a practical matter, the third of these requirements is very difficult to satisfy where the respective parties to the agreement are family members. Thus, as a financial planner, if you have a client who is considering a business continuation agreement, it is probably best to engage the services of both an experienced estate planning attorney (to draft the agreement) and a qualified appraiser (to value the decedent's interest). Generally, in order to establish a fair price for the owner's business interest, a logical and realistic formula to determine its fair market value at some future point in time (for example, at the owner's death) should be included in the agreement. It is much more likely that the IRS will respect such a "flexible" value rather than one that is "fixed" under the terms of the buy-sell agreement.

> **Rattiner's Secrets:** A common formula to figure out the number of policies needed in a cross-purchase buy-sell agreement can be calculated by "using the formula $n \times (n-1)$, where n is the number of owners, to determine the number of life insurance policies needed. For example, if there are three owners of XYZ S corporation, the calculation would be $n(n-1) = 3(2) = 6$. As a result, six life insurance policies must be purchased if a cross-purchase agreement is adopted. Alternatively, if, instead, an entity-purchase agreement was used (with ABC corporation as the owner), only three life insurance policies would be needed (one for each owner). ABC corporation would then use the proceeds to buy out the business interest of the deceased owner from their family.

Buy-sell disability income insurance funding

A disability income (DI) insurance policy may also be used to fund a buy-sell agreement. As noted, one of the triggering events to make effective the agreement is if the first or original owner becomes disabled. As a result, sometimes a disability insurance policy is used in conjunction with a cash value life insurance policy to fund the agreement. However, unlike the possible step-up in basis at the owner's death (thereby resulting in no capital gains tax to be paid by the succeeding owner), this is not the case with disability funding. Specifically, where a disability policy is used and the triggering event of disability occurs, there is no step-up in basis of the owner's interest (rather, the original owner uses their own adjusted basis), meaning that there is potentially a significant capital gains tax consequence.

Practical example: Bob is one of several owners of Bob and Dave's Paints, an S corporation. Bob enters into a disability buy-out agreement with the policy owned by the corporation. He is in the 33% marginal income tax bracket. Bob's basis in the S corporation stock is $100,000; however, the terms of the buy-out agreement specify that he will be paid $500,000 in the event of disability as a triggering event. As a result, if Bob becomes disabled and is bought out by the corporation (an entity purchase type of agreement), he now has a capital gain of $400,000 ($500,000 amount realized less $100,000 basis). Bob must pay tax on this gain at a rate of 15%, the capital gain rate that applies to taxpayers in a 25% or higher marginal income tax bracket. This results in total tax for Bob of $60,000 ($400,000 × 0.15) as a result of the buy-out.

Key-employee life insurance

Key-employee life insurance is life insurance applied for, owned by, and payable to the business on the life of key employees, typically management employees or corporate executives. Premiums paid for the policy are not deductible, but death benefits received by the employer/business are income tax free. However, on receipt of the proceeds, some businesses, such as a regular C corporation, may be subject to corporate alternative minimum tax (AMT). The most prudent method of managing the impact of this tax is simply to purchase more life insurance on the life of the key employee to cover the anticipated income tax liability of the employer.

Split-dollar life insurance

Split-dollar life insurance is a method of paying premiums on the insurance; it is not a separate type of policy. Split-dollar insurance is most often secured in business for key employees, but it can be done whenever one party has money (typically, the employer) and the other has a need for additional insurance (the employee).

There are two basic methods of setting up split-dollar plans. One is to have both parties apply for the policy as co-owners. The one party that needs the insurance (the employee) owns the death benefit and the other party (the employer) pays the bulk of the premium and owns the cash value. This is known as the "endorsement method" of split-dollar coverage. The other method has the insured (the employee) apply for the policy and when the policy is issued, they assign its cash value, or an amount equal to the premiums paid by the other party, whichever is greater, to the other party (the employer). This is known as the "collateral assignment method" of split-dollar coverage. When the collateral assignment method is adopted, the insured always will pay the portion of the premium that supports the death benefit. When the insured dies, the other party recovers its investment and the beneficiary of the insured receives the death benefit, less any amount owed to the other party, income tax free. However, unless the insured assigned their right to the death benefit, the proceeds will be included in their estate.

Strategies for closely-held business owners

Stock in a closely-held corporation may also be a very good asset to gift; however, care should be taken to ensure that excessive gifting does not occur. If too much closely-held stock is gifted, it could preclude availability of one or more very important liquidity elections for the closely-held business owner. Specifically, three liquidity elections for closely-held business owners are possible, all of which are based on a certain percentage of the owner's adjusted gross estate (AGE), consisting of a minimum percentage of closely-held stock. These elections are:

1. The (IRC) Section 6166 election for the installment payment of estate taxes.
2. The Section 2032(A) special use valuation election.
3. The Section 303 stock redemption election.

As you can see from all 10 chapters in this book, there are many disciplines in which we can work effectively with our clients. Everything we covered is pretty heavy-duty information from the standpoint that discussions need to be well thought out, shared, magnified perhaps, and certainly unified in their approach. Our clients are expecting that at the very least.

In closing, let me bring to the forefront a summary of key concepts shared in this book that resonates with many of our peers who truly get it.

Mark Milic has a great quote to share: "Having a long-term relationship with a client means that you go through life together. You go through up markets and down markets, you look like a hero at times and less so during others, and you might stumble along the way. But in the end, good relationships take hard work and are always worth it."

Tying to what I said earlier in the preface, Bill Carter, quoted in 1973, said, "This is the greatest profession and we can really make a difference in people's lives by improving client lives and achieving personal satisfaction. Life gets better every year and so does this profession."

I have mentioned throughout this book, as well as in others, that the key to our success is in managing our clients' expectations. Everybody needs to be on the same page. If we start out with our clients from the same starting point (Point A), discuss the relevant issues and work through them together as part of the financial planning process (roadmap), then we will all end up in the same place (Point B). Listening first, adapting to their needs second, and then dissecting through all of these issues to find possible exposures that could truly have an impact on our clients third, is where we begin. Taking the process forward by deriving and implementing appropriate recommendations to help our clients take it to the next level will surely breed successful results.

I'll leave you with this appropriate quote from Ron Carson: "The opportunity has never been greater in our profession than now. With every relationship in play, we have the capability of helping people accomplish their objectives and do well economically."

What a blessing!

Index

339